THE ENGLISH EXPERIENCE IN F

The English Experience in France c. 1450-1558
War, diplomacy and cultural exchange

Edited by
DAVID GRUMMITT
History of Parliament, London

LONDON AND NEW YORK

First published 2002 by Ashgate Publishing

Reissued 2018 by Routledge
2 Park Square, Milton Park, Abingdon, Oxon OX14 4RN
711 Third Avenue, New York, NY 10017, USA

Routledge is an imprint of the Taylor & Francis Group, an informa business

Copyright © David Grummitt 2002

The editor hereby asserts his moral right under the Copyright, Designs and Patents Act, 1988, to be identified as the editor of this work.

All rights reserved. No part of this book may be reprinted or reproduced or utilised in any form or by any electronic, mechanical, or other means, now known or hereafter invented, including photocopying and recording, or in any information storage or retrieval system, without permission in writing from the publishers.

Notice:
Product or corporate names may be trademarks or registered trademarks, and are used only for identification and explanation without intent to infringe.

Publisher's Note
The publisher has gone to great lengths to ensure the quality of this reprint but points out that some imperfections in the original copies may be apparent.

Disclaimer
The publisher has made every effort to trace copyright holders and welcomes correspondence from those they have been unable to contact.

A Library of Congress record exists under LC control number: 2002016497

ISBN 13: 978-1-138-74292-5 (hbk)
ISBN 13: 978-1-138-74289-5 (pbk)
ISBN 13: 978-1-315-18200-1 (ebk)

Contents

List of Contributors vii
Abbreviations ix

1 Introduction:
  war, diplomacy and cultural exchange 1450-1558
  David Grummitt 1

PART I: ENGLAND'S FRENCH POSSESSIONS

2 The Loss of Lancastrian Normandy:
  an administrative nightmare?
  Anne Curry 24

3 'One of the mooste pryncipall treasours belongyng
  to his Realme of Englande':
  Calais and the Crown, c. 1450-1558
  David Grummitt 46

PART II: WAR, DIPLOMACY AND DYNASTY

4 The Practice of English Diplomacy in France
  1461-71
  Edward Meek 63

5 The Myth of 1485:
  did France really put Henry Tudor on the throne?
  Michael K. Jones 85

6 'To Traffic with War'?
  Henry VII and the French campaign of 1492
  John M. Currin 106

PART III: FRIENDSHIP AND CULTURAL EXCHANGE IN THE RENAISSANCE

7	'Une haquenée . . . pour le porter bientost et plus doucement en enfer ou en paradis': the French and Mary Tudor's marriage to Louis XII in 1514 *Charles Giry-Deloison*	132
8	Sir Nicholas Carew's Journey through France in 1529 *Robert J. Knecht*	160
9	Courtesy and Conflict: the experience of English diplomatic personnel at the court of Francis I *Luke MacMahon*	182
10	The Private Face of Anglo-French Relations in the Sixteenth Century: the Lisles and their French friends *David Potter*	200
Index		*223*

List of Contributors

David Grummitt is a Research Fellow at the University of Oxford and has published a number of articles on Calais under English rule.

Anne Curry is Professor of History at the University of Reading and has published numerous books and articles on the Hundred Years War.

Edward Meek has recently completed a PhD at the University of Cambridge on the diplomacy of Edward IV.

Michael K. Jones is a freelance historian who is writing a book on the Battle of Bosworth and is co-author of *The King's Mother*, a biography of Lady Margaret Beaufort.

John M. Currin is Adjunct Professor, Arizona Center for Medieval and Renaissance Studies, Arizona State University and has written extensively on the diplomacy of Henry VII.

Charles Giry-Deloison is Maîtres de Conférences, Histoire Moderne at the Université d'Artois. He has written widely on Anglo-French diplomacy in the fifteenth and sixteenth centuries.

Robert J. Knecht is Emeritius Professor of History at the University of Birmingham and author of biographies of Francis I, Catherine de Medici and Cardinal Richelieu.

Luke MacMahon has recently completed a PhD on English diplomacy during the reign of Henry VIII.

David Potter is Senior Lecturer at the University of Kent. He is author of *A History of France 1460-1560* and numerous articles on Anglo-French relations.

Abbreviations

ADN	Archives Departementales du Nord, Lille
AN	Archives Nationale, Paris
BL	British Library, London
BNF	Bibliothèque Nationale de France, Paris
CAF	*Catalogue des actes de Francois Ier* (10 vols., Paris, 1887-1908)
CPR	*Calendar of Patent Rolls Preserved in the Public Record Office 1399-1509* (17 vols., London, 1903-16)
CSP Milan	Cal
CSP Spanish	*Calendar of State Papers Spanish*, ed. P. de Gayangos, G. Mattingley, M. A. S. Hume and R. Tyler (15 vols. in 20, London, 1862-1954)
CSP Venetian	*Calendar of State Papers Venetian*, ed. R. Brown, C. Bentinck and H. Brown (9 vols., London, 1864-98)
EHR	*English Historical Review*
Feodera	*Foedera, Conventiones, Litterae, et Cujuscumque Generis Acta Publica . . . etc.*, ed. T. Rymer (20 vols., London, 1727-35)
Lisle Letters	*The Lisle Letters*, ed. Muriel St. Clare Byrne (6 vols., Chicago and London, 1981)
LP	*Letters and Papers, Foreign and Domestic, of the Reign of Henry VIII, 1509-1547*, ed. J. Brewer, J. Gairdner and R. H. Brodie (21 vols. and addenda, London, 1862-1932)
NMS	*Nottingham Medieval Studies*
PRO	Public Record Office, Kew
RP	*Rotuli Parliamentorum, 1278-1504*, ed. J. Strachey *et al*, (6 vols., London, 1767-1832)

Scarisbrick	J. J. Scarisbrick, *Henry VIII* (first published 1969, 2nd edn. New Haven, CT, 1997)
SR	*Statutes of the Realm*, ed. A. Luders et al. (11 vols., London, 1810-28
State Papers, Henry VIII	*State Papers Published under the Authority of his Majesty's Commission, King Henry VIII* (11 vols., London, 1830-52)

1 Introduction: war, diplomacy and cultural exchange, 1450-1558

DAVID GRUMMITT

The nine essays presented in this volume represent some of the latest research on the relationship between England and France in the century after the end of the Hundred Years War.[1] They fall into three main categories: the administration and importance of the English possessions in France; the practice of war and diplomacy; the personal experiences of Englishmen in France and the friendships they developed there. All explore one or more of the three themes of this volume – war, diplomacy and cultural exchange. The purpose of this introduction, then, is to outline the main events and historiographical trends in these three areas and to provide the background to the arguments presented in the essays themselves.

War

The Hundred Years War ended in ignominious defeat for the English.[2] The second phase of the wars had begun in 1415 with Henry V's expedition to Normandy, ending in the decisive victory at Agincourt. The following year a naval victory secured the beachhead at Harfleur and in August 1417 Henry

---

[1] These papers arose from a conference held at the Public Record Office, Kew, in November 1999. The editor and contributors would like to thank the Keeper of the Public Records and the staff of the PRO for their hospitality and kindness in hosting the conference. Eight of the nine papers were read at the conference: John Currin was unable to deliver his paper on the day but it is included here; Cliff Davies's paper, 'The Boulogne War 1543-1546: the end of an era?' was read but it was not possible to include it in this volume.
[2] For the end of the Hundred Years War see Ralph A. Griffiths, *The Reign of King Henry VI* (2nd edn. Stroud, 1998), pp. 482-522; B. P. Wolffe, *Henry VI* (2nd edn., New Haven, 2001), pp. 184-212.

set about the conquest of Normandy; by January 1419 Rouen had fallen and Henry V's name had become synonymous with English military glory in France. In May 1420 the treaty of Troyes, accepted by Philip, Duke of Burgundy and Queen Isabeau of France in the name of her incapacitated husband, Charles VI, vested the crown of France in Henry V and his heirs. Nevertheless, by 1450 the treaty of Troyes had become something of a poisoned chalice for the Lancastrian government of Henry VI. Succeeding to the throne in 1422 at only nine months of age, Henry VI had proved himself by the late 1440s to be an inadequate successor to his father. Whilst historians argue about the exact nature of the king's role in the government of his two realms of England and France, it is clear that much of the blame for defeat in 1449-53 must lay with Henry.[3] Even if his involvement in domestic politics was erratic, Henry showed some appetite for intervening in foreign affairs and by the end of 1446 was committed to the surrender of Maine and Anjou in order to buy peace with France. However, the idea of a totally pacifist king, resigned to peace at any price, seems at odds with the decision taken soon after to support his close friend, Gilles de Bretagne's, son of Duke Jean IV and Jeanne of Navarre, claim to the dukedom of Brittany. In March 1449 the town of Fougères in Brittany fell to an assault in the name of Henry VI; if this break of the terms of the truce negotiated at Tours in 1444 (and extended in 1448) was not enough, the accusations of French perfidy which arose from the town's surrender to Charles VII of France the following November provided the immediate backdrop for the French reconquest of Normandy. Between May 1449, when the castle at Pont de l'Arche was taken by the French and Bretons, and 12 August 1450, when Cherbourg surrendered, the Norman conquests of Henry V were lost in one of the most spectacular military campaigns of the fifteenth century. After Normandy, Charles and his armies turned their attention to Gascony. On 23 October 1452 Bordeaux fell and on 17 July the following year an English army, led by that great hero of the wars with France, John Talbot, Earl of Shrewsbury, was defeated at Chastillon. The death of Talbot and Henry's ensuing collapse into madness sounded the death-knell of Lancastrian kingship.

---

[3] For the recent argument that the king played no role in the government of the realms of England and France and in policy generally see John Watts, *Henry VI and the Politics of Kingship* (Cambridge, 1996).

Introduction 3

While Chastillon is generally acknowledged as the end of the Hundred Years War, it did not mark the end of English military activity in France or English claims to the French throne, a claim that would periodically be reasserted through war. English armies fought in France in 1475, 1489, 1492, 1512-3, 1522-3, 1544-6, 1549-51 and 1557-8. On four occasions, in 1475, 1492, 1513 and 1544, kings of England led expeditions to France in person. Outside of these periods of formal war Englishmen frequently experienced France and the French in a hostile context. In the immediate aftermath of the expulsion from Normandy and Gascony this often meant acts of piracy in the Narrow Seas. English pirates along the south coast and their French counterparts regularly took hostages and attacked those who sought to trade with the enemy. Ending up a hostage in Harfleur or some other French port remained an occupational hazard for English merchants well into the 1470s.[4] Moreover, acts of violence remained commonplace on the frontiers of Calais, the last remaining English possession. Englishmen from Calais and elsewhere were also involved in border warfare around the Calais Pale and in Picardy and Artois and in the Duke of Burgundy's service. In 1461, for example, a large French force intervened to force the lifting of the siege of the Lancastrian garrison at Hammes castle and in 1480 soldiers from Calais raided the port of Dunkirk, then a haven for pirates.[5] Service against France, albeit under a foreign prince, offered the chance to win the honour and excitement only available through war. The Yorkshire knight, Sir Thomas Everingham, for example, served with the Burgundians at the Battle of Nancy in 1477 and with the Archduke Maximilian at Guinegate in 1479.[6]

The opportunities that war offered for honour and personal advantage largely explain Edward IV's decision to invade France in the summer of 1475. J. R. Lander doubted if this was a serious attempt to assert Edward's claim to the French crown, but it seems clear that by at least 1472 the king was determined to emulate the achievements of Henry V. This is apparent in his interest in the order of the Garter and in the scale of the

---

[4] See, for example, C 76/147, m. 20.
[5] For the French intervention at Hammes see *CSP Milan*, i. 89. For the raid on Dunkirk, PRO, E 101/198/13, fo. 9v.
[6] E. L. Meek, 'The Career of Sir Thomas Everingham, "Knight of the North" in the Service of Maximilian, Duke of Austria 1477-1481', *Historical Research*, 74 (2001), 238-48.

preparations to ensure that his army was well-equipped and prepared.[7] In the event the campaign of 1475 did not live up to expectations. Edward joined his army in Calais on 4 July but it was not until ten days later that he was joined by his ally, Charles, Duke of Burgundy. Charles, much to English chagrin, failed to bring his army with him, it still being employed in the siege of Neuss. Francis, Duke of Brittany, also failed to take the field and by 14 August Edward was forced to begin negotiations with Louis XI. This resulted in the treaty of Picquigny, leaving Edward with a French pension of £10,000 a year (and similar lucrative sweeteners for many of the English nobility), a trade agreement and promises of dynastic union.[8]

War, as Edward III and Henry V knew, also united the English political classes against a common enemy. The need to bring harmony to a discordant polity was also a factor in Edward IV's desire to invade France so soon after the events of 1469-71.[9] This same motivation also had a role in Henry VII's aggressive policy towards France up to 1492. As Michael Jones has shown in this volume, Henry did not need to feel indebted to Charles VIII for the victory at Bosworth and war against France offered a good means of healing the rifts in the political nation only partly assuaged by his marriage to Elizabeth of York. It is now clear that Henry was no pacifist, a picture confirmed by John Currin's essay. In war in Brittany, France and Scotland he attempted to live up to the martial reputation of his predecessors and underline his royal authority through success in war.[10] By the last decade or so of Henry's reign the need to assert royal authority through successful war was lessened owing to his final victory over the pretender, Perkin Warbeck, and the king's own desire for financial security.[11]

---

[7] J. R. Lander, 'The Hundred Years War and Edward IV's Campaign in France', *Tudor Men and Institutions: studies in English government and law*, ed. A. J. Slavin (Baton Rouge, 1952), pp. 70-100.

[8] For the conclusion of the 1475 campaign see Charles Ross, *Edward IV* (2nd edn. New Haven, 1997), pp. 231-4.

[9] See the chancellor's address to the parliament of 1472: *Literae Cantuarienses*, ed. J. B. Sheppard (3 vols., London, 1889), iii. 274-8; Lander, 'Hundred Years War', pp. 81-5.

[10] Ian Arthurson, 'The King's Voyage into Scotland: the war that never was' in *England in the Fifteenth Century*, ed. D. T. Williams (Woodbridge, 1987), pp. 1-22 ; John M. Currin, '"The King's Army into the Parties of Bretaigne": Henry VII and the Breton Wars, 1489-1491', *War in History* 7 (2000), 379-412.

[11] For Henry's foreign and financial policies in the last decade of the reign see S. B. Chrimes, *Henry VII* (London, 1972), pp. 282-97; David Grummitt, 'Henry VII, Chamber Finance and the "New Monarchy": some new evidence', *Historical Research* 72 (1999), 229-43.

If the desire to emulate Henry V was an important factor in Henry VII's dealings with France in the early part of his reign, it was the dominant concern of his son, Henry VIII, in most of his dealings with France.[12] Henry VIII often made explicit his claim to the kingdom of France; even when making war on the Emperor Charles V in concert with Francis I, Henry argued that he was bound to defend France 'which is our true inheritance and for which our brother and ally the French King, payeth us yearly a great pension and tribute' (the pension negotiated in 1475 and renegotiated at various times under Henry VIII).[13] More frequently this claim to the kingdom of France was a *casus belli*. As is well known, Henry VIII's French wars were fought principally for the king's personal glory. It was Henry who provided the impetus for war, often against the wishes of his counsellors. He was 'not unmindful that it was his duty to seek fame by military skill' and as early as December 1509 the Venetian ambassador reported that the new king was 'eager' for war with France.[14] This desire to win personal honour and, crucially, the belief that the kingdom of France belonged to him by right, led Henry to lead invasion armies in 1513 and 1544. In 1513 the campaign ended inconclusively with the capture of Therouanne by the English (although later handed over to the Emperor Maximilian) and Tournai by the Imperial army (but presented to Henry to hold until its return to France by treaty in 1518). Henry's honour, however, was satisfied by the ignominious French flight at the so-called Battle of the Spurs before the gates of Theruoanne.[15] In 1544 hopes of a march on Paris were thwarted by the actions of Emperor Charles V. The English captured Boulogne, a town they held at great cost against repeated French assaults

---

[12] S. J. Gunn. 'The French Wars of Henry VIII' in *The Origins of War in Early Modern Europe*, ed. Jeremy Black (Edinburgh, 1987), pp. 28-51; Clifford S. L. Davies, 'Henry VIII and Henry V: the Wars in France' in *The End of the Middle Ages?*, ed. John L. Watts (Gloucester, 1998), pp. 236-32.
[13] For the pension see Charles Giry-Deloison, 'Henry VIII pensionnaire de François Ier' in *François Ier. Deux princes de la renaissance (1515-1547)*, ed. Charles Giry-Deloison (Arras, 1997), pp. 121-43.
[14] Susan Doran, *England and Europe in the Sixteenth Century* (Basingstoke, 1999), pp. 13-6.
[15] The events of 1513 are described in Charles Cruickshank, *Henry VIII and the Invasion of France* (2nd edn. Stroud, 1990).

but which, by 1546, represented, along with Calais, a greater block of French territory under English rule than anytime since 1453.[16]

Henry VIII's campaign in 1544 was unsuccessful in its original grandiose aims not because of the failure of the English armies but because of the withdrawal of support for the English cause by their erstwhile Imperial allies. In August, on the day Henry took Boulogne, Charles V made a separate peace with Francis at Crépy.[17] The emperor had more pressing concerns in Germany against the forces of the Schmalkaldic League. The English, under the Duke of Norfolk, were lucky to escape with their forces intact from the siege of Montreuil. The dependence of English military adventures in France upon the support of the Habsburgs, or earlier the Valois Dukes of Burgundy, was a reality of the English experience of war in France. Despite the genuine desire of Edward IV, Henry VII and Henry VIII to recreate the glories of the Hundred Years War, after 1450 England could only successfully wage war on France with the help of its allies in the Low Countries, Spain and Germany. From 1475 English military objectives in France were consistently hampered by the fact that their allies' main interests were elsewhere; to them the English recreating the Lancastrian dual monarchy was at best a pointless distraction and at worse a direct threat to their own interests in France. Thus in 1475 Charles the Bold was more concerned with his conquest of Lorraine than in Edward's campaign in north-west France;[18] in 1492 the campaign around Boulogne was just one part of a wider campaign for Maximilian I, King of the Romans, that centred upon the Franche-Comté. Similarly, in 1512 Henry VIII's attempt to reconquer Gascony with the aid of King Ferdinand of Aragon failed because the latter was more interested in adding Navarre to his realm than helping Henry add Gascony to his.[19]

The principal reason for England's reliance on foreign allies was logistical. England's resources compared unfavourably to those of France and the Empire. In the early sixteenth century England's population of two and a half millions was dwarfed by the sixteen millions of France; Henry VIII's annual revenues stood at some £110,000 in the early 1520s,

---

[16] For the 1544 campaign, described in very unfavourable terms, see Scarisbrick, pp. 424-57.
[17] Ibid., p. 448.
[18] R. Vaughan, *Charles the Bold: the last Valois duke of Burgundy* (London, 1973), pp. 329-58.
[19] Scarisbrick, pp. 29-31.

compared with the £350,000 enjoyed by Francis I and the £500,000 or so of Charles V.[20] Moreover, by the end of the fifteenth century armies had grown in size to that extent that the kind of forces necessary to wage successful war on a European scale could not be recruited solely from England. The army with which Henry V had conquered Normandy was just over 10,000 strong; that which Edward IV led in 1475 probably numbered about 12,000; in 1492 Henry VII invaded with as many as 14,000. But by 1513 Henry VIII's army was over 30,000 strong and in 1544 contained over 44,000 with 37,000 Englishmen.[21] Furthermore, these armies, particularly those of Henry VIII, relied almost exclusively on the Low Countries to provide them with food, munitions, carts and other forms of transport. When the political support of the Habsburgs was withdrawn, Henry VIII's military adventures in France simply ground to a halt.

Nevertheless, despite these strategic limitations, many Englishmen continued to have their experience of France defined by war. The many thousands of Englishmen who crossed the channel in English armies between 1450 and 1558 must have vastly outnumbered those who experienced France in more peaceful ways, as scholars, diplomats, merchants and travellers. As Edward Meek and Luke MacMahon demonstrate below, soldiers, men like John, Lord Wenlock and Sir John Wallop, continued to serve as ambassadors in a period marked by the professionalisation of diplomatic contacts. Wallop, even though a resident ambassador at the court of Francis I in the early 1540s, typified the English military aristocracy who were as much at home on the battlefield and in the camp as at the princely courts of Renaissance Europe. As Lieutenant of Guînes in the mid 1540s his feats of arms were recorded by the privy council on more than one occasion: in June 1545 they wrote to him and Lord Grey de Wilton 'wyth thankes for theyre

---

[20] David Potter, 'Foreign Policy' in *The Reign of Henry VIII: politics, policy and piety*, ed. Diarmaid MacCulloch (Basingstoke, 1995), pp. 112-4. All three princes could, of course, expect to roughly double these figures through extraordinary taxation but all faced the same problem that their incomes were not sufficient to sustain prolonged military action.
[21] Anne Curry, 'English Armies in the Fifteenth Century' in *Arms, Armies and Fortifications in the Hundred Years War*, ed. Anne Curry and Michael Hughes (Woodbridge, 1994), pp. 44-5; Lander, 'Hundred Years War', pp. 93-5; C. S. L. Davies, 'The English People and War in the Early Sixteenth Century' in *Britain and the Netherlands*, vi. *War and Society*, eds. A. C. Duke and C. A. Tamse (The Hague, 1977), pp. 1-18.

8   *The English Experience in France*

lusty courages in the defense of theyre peces'.²² Lord Grey's experience of France in the 1550s demonstrates the continuities between the mid fifteenth and mid sixteenth centuries; it differed little from that of many of his Lancastrian predecessors a hundred years previously. Serving in the defence of Calais for long periods between 1531 and 1558, he was captured after a week long siege at the castle of Guînes in January 1558 and passed into French captivity. The payment of his ransom of 24,000 crowns impoverished the family, forcing the sale of the castle and estate of Wilton, the ancient seat of the family and title of the barony.²³

War with France continued to exert a popular appeal. It has been argued that the declining ratio of men at arms to archers in English armies in the last years of the Hundred Years War reflected the withdrawal of support by the aristocracy from the wars in France. Thus, Lander, noting that the ratio of men at arms to archers in 1475 was 1:10 compared with the 1:3 that prevailed at Agincourt, has asserted that 'the aristocracy and gentry were no longer enthusiastic for foreign war' by the second half of the fifteenth century.²⁴ But this is to misunderstand the nature of the sources from which these numbers are calculated: the terms men at arms and archers were, by the middle of the fifteenth century, merely convenient accounting terms for the central government and bore little resemblance to the realities of English armies.²⁵ War with France continued to offer a great appeal to many members of the English aristocracy in the late fifteenth century. The treaty of Picquigny was greeted with disdain by the king's brother, the Duke of Gloucester, and other members of the English nobility; from 1477 service under Margaret of Burgundy or Maximilian, Archduke of Austria, provided an outlet for the energies of the English military classes.²⁶ Henry VIII's 1513 campaign proceeded amidst general enthusiasm and expectation and, despite a speech in parliament credited to Thomas Cromwell calling into question the financial sense of invading France, the campaigns of 1522 and

---

²² *APC 1542-1547*, p. 198.
²³ For Grey de Wilton see *A Commentary of the Services and Charges of Lord Grey de Wilton, K. G..*, . . ., ed. Sir Philip de Malpas Grey Egerton, Camden Society, 1ˢᵗ series 40 (1847-8).
²⁴ Lander, 'Hundred Years War', p. 100.
²⁵ This point is discussed at length in my forthcoming book on the Calais garrison.
²⁶ David Grummitt, 'William, Lord Hastings and the Politics of Yorkist England', *The Ricardian* 12 (2001), 262-74; Michael K. Jones, '1477 – the Expedition that Never Was: chivalric expectation in late Yorkist England', ibid., 274-92.

1523 were similarly welcomed. Only with the excessive taxation of those years and Wolsey's attempt to levy the Amicable Grant was the general support for war with France called into question.[27] By the 1540s government propagandists like Richard Morison were whipping up support for renewed war with the old enemy using the new, nationalistic language of the Henrician supremacy.[28] Even in 1557-8, when England was involved in war largely to meet the demands of Mary I's husband, Philip II of Spain, the political classes on the whole greeted war enthusiastically. Despite some grumbling from ordinary people reported by the Venetian ambassador, it was seen on the whole as an opportunity to unite a divided nation and win honour and advancement.[29]

Diplomacy

The English were engaged in open war with the French for less than fifteen years between 1450 and 1558. The end of the Hundred Years War marked a period of extended truces and, after the treaty of Etaples in 1492, an age of more formal peace treaties delineating intermittent periods of war. The conduct of diplomacy, as well as war and trade, shaped the experience of the English in France. To what extent though did English diplomatic relations with France represent a coherent policy in the century or so after 1450? It used to be thought that the Tudors, and Henry VII in particular, eschewed wars of conquest and sought to build a 'modern' foreign policy vis-à-vis France. This was based upon protecting England's commercial interests whilst retaining a 'balance of power' in continental Europe.[30] More recently, however, historians have stressed the importance of honour and the personal ambitions of princes and their servants in determining the rhythms of

---

[27] George Bernard, *War, Taxation and Rebellion in Early Tudor England: Henry VIII, Wolsey and the Amicable Grant of 1525* (Brighton, 1986), pp. 3-7.
[28] Richard Morison, *Exhortation to Styrre all Englyshmen to the Defence of theyr Countrye* (1539).
[29] C. S. L. Davies, 'England and the French War, 1557-9', *The Mid-Tudor Polity*, eds. J. Loach and R. Tittler (Basingstoke, 1980), pp. 159-85; David Loades, *The Reign of Mary I: politics, government and religion in England 1553-1558* (London, 1991), pp. 308-9.
[30] See the most recent exponent of this view W. B. Wernham, *Before the Armada: the emergence of the English nation, 1485-1558* (London, 1966).

relations between England and France.[31] Whilst many of the essays in this volume do indeed stress this new orthodoxy, it is nevertheless important to appreciate as well the forces that constrained English kings in their diplomacy with France.

In the latter half of the fifteenth century the most important factor affecting the kings and princes of western Europe was 'the future power of the French monarchy'.[32] The French crown was looking to expand its power at the expense of both the dukes of Burgundy and Brittany, vassals yet with the resources and standing of independent princes, and members of the French nobility, such as the dukes of Anjou and Orleans, who sought greater political independence from the French crown. England, in partnership with Burgundy and Brittany, and to a lesser extent members of the French nobility, sought to limit the king of France's ambitions. Thus as Cliff Davies has argued, before 1471 Anglo-French diplomacy existed largely as part of this balancing act. In 1456 the Duke of Alençon lent his support to the Duke of York's plans to mount a reconquest of Normandy; similarly, the Duke of Burgundy lent his support to the Yorkists in 1460-1 solely because Charles VII had lent his tacit support to the Lancastrians.[33]

In his relations with France Edward IV was constrained by the need to balance the growing power of the French crown, as well as other factors. As Edward Meek shows below, before 1471 the conduct of Anglo-French diplomacy was at times removed from the king's control and controlled instead by the Earl of Warwick and his Calais-based servants. From the mid 1470s the fact that the ambitions of Charles the Bold, Duke of Burgundy lay further east, aiming to become a force in the Empire, further constrained Edward's dealings with France. Charles's Imperial designs eventually led to his death at the Battle of Nancy in 1477 and Edward rejected calls, principally from his brother Richard, Duke of Gloucester, to intervene on behalf of his sister Margaret, Duchess of Burgundy, to protect her dominions. Margaret made further attempts to get Edward to intervene in Burgundian affairs in 1480. The death of Charles's daughter, Mary, in 1482 further curtailed Edward's independence: the estates of Flanders rejected the plan for her husband, Maximilian, Archduke of Austria, to exercise a

---

[31] The latest literature on this subject is summarised in Susan Doran, *England and Europe in the Sixteenth Century* (Basingstoke, 1999), pp. 13-30.

[32] C. S. L. Davies, 'The Wars of the Roses in European Context' in *The Wars of the Roses*, ed. A. J. Pollard (Basingstoke, 1995), p. 162.

[33] Ibid., pp. 167-8.

regency for her infant son, Philip. The estates and Louis XI then concluded the treaty of Arras, forcing it upon Maximilian and thus isolating Edward.[34] Edward and Louis both died the following year and ushered in a period when diplomacy was no longer controlled by the agendas of either the English or French kings. The French king, Charles VIII, was a minor and the government in the hands of his sister, Anne of Beaujeau. Richard III's own domestic situation and the support for Henry Tudor given by Duke Francis of Brittany forced the English king to back the government of the duke's treasurer, Pierre Landais, when Francis fell ill, and to be drawn inadvertently into conflict with France. Landais himself was seeking Richard's support against the Bretons' enemies in France.[35] As far as the French were concerned Richard's defeat by Henry Tudor, alongside the fall of Landais, was a happy coincidence; as Michael Jones demonstrates, it was certainly not the product of French diplomacy or military assistance.

Henry VII's diplomacy was perhaps more the product of the royal will than most late medieval kings. Nevertheless, it would be wrong to argue that he 'cared more for policy than glory'.[36] As John Currin shows, Henry VII was as motivated by war and honour as any of his contemporaries. This sense of honour was an important factor in shaping the diplomacy of the early years of his reign. Before 1492 Henry's support for Breton independence was as much a result of the personal debt he owed to Duke Francis for his support whilst an exile, as to any wish to limit the power of the French crown and preserve a European 'balance of power'.[37] Henry's desire to remain at peace with Charles VIII after 1492 was a reciprocal one. The treaty of Etaples, which ended the 1492 war, should be linked with the treaty of Senlis the following May between Charles, Maximilian and Archduke Philip. In 1494 Charles set out to assert his rights in the Italian peninsula. Anglo-French relations, therefore, benefited from a strategic shift

---

[34] Ibid., pp. 174-5. For the chivalric pressure of Edward to act to defend Margaret in 1477 see Jones, '1477 – the Expedition that Never Was', 282-5.
[35] C. S. L. Davies, 'Richard III, Brittany and Henry Tudor, 1483-1485', *NMS* 37 (1993), 110-26.
[36] *Letters and Papers illustrative of the Reigns of Richard III and Henry VII*, ed. James Gairdner (2 vols., London, 1861-1863), i. xxvii.
[37] David Potter, 'Anglo-French Relations 1500: the aftermath of the Hundred Years War', *Journal of Franco British Studies* 28 (1999/2000), 41-66 at 45-9; Charles Giry-Deloison, 'Henry VII et la Bretagne: aspects politiques et diplomatiques' in *Bretagne terre d'Europe*, ed. J. Kehervé (Brest, 1992), pp. 227-39; J. M. Currin, 'Henry VII and the Treaty of Redon (1489): Plantagenet ambitions and early Tudor foreign policy', *History* 81 (1996), 343-58.

in French policy towards Italy. Although Henry signed the treaty of Rome of July 1496 committing himself to the anti-French League of Venice, he was both unwilling and unable to commit himself to action against France without Spanish support.[38] In May 1497 England signed a commercial treaty with France and, underpinned by regular payments of the pension granted at Picquigny and the sums promised by the French at Etaples in reimbursement for Henry's expenses for the defence of Brittany, owed by Duchess Anne, Anglo-French relations passed into a period of détente which would last throughout Henry VII's last decade.[39] Henry sought by a series of trade treaties and marital alliances to keep England on good terms with France, Spain, Scotland and the Empire. In 1496 the French proposed a marriage between Mary Tudor and Charles-Orland, the dauphin, and an alliance between Prince Arthur and the daughter of the duke of Bourbon. In 1505 there was even a talk of a match between Henry and Mary of Angoulême, Louis XII's niece.[40] The success of these policies is shown by the fact that in 1508, when all the other major European powers committed themselves to the anti-Venetian League of Cambrai, Henry was able to remain aloof but suffered no consequent loss of honour or influence.[41]

Henry VIII, as we have seen, was unwilling to follow his father's pacific policy towards France. He was, however, constrained because his chosen policy – war – was thwarted by the unhelpfulness of his allies, Maximilian and Ferdinand of Aragon, and by its cost and practical limitations. Moreover, in January 1515 Louis XI was succeeded by Francis I, equally as bellicose as Henry and determined to secure the return of Tournai. Thus, in his initial dealings with Francis, Henry was forced to

---

[38] The Holy League of Venice had been formed in March 1495 by the treaty of Venice and reconstituted to include Henry in next year. The English ratified the treaty in September 1496: J. C. Lünig, *Codex italiae diplomaticus* (4 vols., Frankfurt and Leipzeig, 1723-35), i. cols. 111-8; *Foedera*, xii. 638-42. I am grateful to John Currin for discussing this with me.

[39] Potter, 'Anglo-French Relations', pp. 52-4; John M. Currin, 'Persuasions to Peace: the Luxembourg-Marigny-Gaugin embassy and the state of Anglo-French relations, 1489-90', *EHR* 114 (1998), 886-904. Polydore Vergil made the link between Charles's Italian ambitions and peace with England. In 1497 he wrote 'Nam Carolus rebus Italicis inplicitus apprime cupiebat, cum Anglo in amicitia perpetua esse' ('For Charles, committed to his Italian projects, was above all anxious to remain for ever at peace with England'): *The Anglica Historia of Polydore Vergil, A.D. 1485-1537*, ed. Denys Hay, Camden Society, New Series, 74 (London, 1950), pp. 94-5.

[40] Chrimes, *Henry VII*, pp. 288-9.

[41] Wernham, *Before the Armada*, p. 60; Potter, 'Anglo-French Relations', p. 54.

temper his aggression and adopt a policy that sought to maintain his honour through peace and diplomacy. In this the English were helped by two factors: first, Francis's own desire for peace with England in order to free resources for the war with Spain; and, second, an initiative by Pope Leo X for a crusade against the Turks. This resulted in October 1518 in the treaty of London, which included a universal peace between Christian princes, and a specifically Anglo-French agreement restoring Tournai in return for a cash payment and a marriage treaty between Princess Mary and the Dauphin. Henry was thus able to win honour through diplomacy, posing as the architect of a general European peace. Moreover, as Susan Doran notes, 'at a more personal level he upstaged Francis; the French king might have proved himself the master of war, but war was now outlawed under the auspices of the English king'.[42] The most conspicuous show of this new policy of winning honour through peace was at the Field of the Cloth of Gold, just outside Guînes, in 1520. The two princes bid to outshine each other by, in Glenn Richardson's words, 'magnificent ritualistic displays of royal friendship'.[43]

War remained, however, Henry's preferred option and the years 1522-3 saw a return to conflict between England and France. In 1525 the defeat and capture of Francis by the Spanairds at Pavia gave Henry an opportunity to exploit France's political crisis but the taxpayer's revolt against the Amicable Grant showed again the constraints on royal policy. Between 1525 and 1543 Henry entered into a series of diplomatic treaties with Francis which Charles Giry-Deloison has called 'une alliance contre nature'.[44] The principal treaties and events which marked this sixteenth century *entente cordiale* were: the treaty of the More (30 August 1525), a series of five separate agreements which formally ended the war begun in 1522; the treaty of Hampton Court (8 August 1526), by which both Henry and Francis agreed not to conclude a separate agreement with Charles V; a treaty of Perpetual Peace and the anti-Imperial treaty of Westminster (30 April 1527) which committed England and France to war with Charles V;

---

[42] Peter Gwyn, *The King's Cardinal: the rise and fall of Thomas Wolsey* (London, 1990), pp. 144-51; Doran, *England and Europe*, pp. 18-9.
[43] Robert J. Knecht, 'The Field of the Cloth of Gold; in *François Ier et Henry VIII*, ed. Giry-Deloison, pp. 38-51; Glenn Richardson, 'Good Friends and Brothers? Francis I and Henry VIII', *History Today* (1994), 20-6.
[44] Charles Giry-Deloison, "Une alliance contre nature?' La paix Franco-Anglaise de 1525-1544' in *François Ier et Henry VIII*, ed. Giry-Deloison, pp. 53-62.

and a new treaty of alliance signed at London on 23 June, followed by the meeting of Henry and Francis in Calais in October 1532.[45] This period did indeed see a reversal of traditional policy towards France. English claims to the French crown were conveniently forgotten: indeed, the 1527 treaty of Perpetual Peace explicitly renounced the treaty of Troyes of 1420, by which Charles VI had devolved the French crown upon Henry V and his heirs. Moreover, in 1527 Henry also remitted payment of the French pension and promised to aid Francis financially in his wars in Italy.[46]

Nevertheless, the significance of this period of intense diplomacy in shaping Anglo-French relations should not be overestimated. Although, as Robert Knecht, Luke MacMahon and David Potter show, the experiences of some Englishmen in France were shaped by this new era of peace and cooperation, the policy was not one of choice for Henry. First, his grand designs to partition France with the emperor following Pavia had been curtailed by lack of support at home, showing again the practical limitations of war as policy in early modern Europe. Second, from 1527 Henry was constrained by his need to find allies in his quest for a divorce from Catherine of Aragon. The capture of the Pope Clement VII by Imperial forces in May of that year meant that Henry needed an alliance with Francis in order to pressurise Charles V to allow the Pope to grant the annulment. Charles, of course, could not countenance the public repudiation of his aunt. In 1529 Clement signed the treaty of Barcelona with Charles, thus ending all hopes of a settlement of the divorce through Rome.[47] Furthermore, Francis's relationship with Henry was by no means exclusive. Both princes were wary of their erstwhile foes and had their own agendas to follow. In August 1529, for instance, Francis and Charles signed the treaty of Cambrai, agreeing peace between them and isolating Henry in flagrant disregard of the 1526 treaty of Hampton Court. In June 1538 Francis and Charles signed a ten year truce, engineered by the Pope, at Nice.[48] This threatened a catholic alliance against the heretical English. Henry, however, remained ready to exploit any Franco-Imperial split. Thus, in June 1542, with Catherine of

---

[45] For these treaties and this period of diplomacy see Scarisbrick, pp. 135-47, 305-9; Charles Giry-Deloison, 'A Diplomatic Revolution? Anglo-French relations and the treaties of 1527' in *Henry VIII: a European court in England*, ed. David Starkey (London, 1991), pp. 73-83.
[46] Giry-Deloison, 'Une alliance contre nature?', pp. 56-9.
[47] Doran, *England and Europe*, pp. 23, 83-5.
[48] Scarisbirk, pp. 361-2.

Aragon long dead and the emperor's strategic goals again turning to northwest Europe, Henry and Charles concluded a trade agreement and a secret treaty of amity not to negotiate with any other party, obviously aimed towards France. In May the following year this new relationship was confirmed in the secret treaty of Mutual Aid. In July both declared war on Francis.[49] Henry VIII's diplomatic relations with France had come full circle.

The treaty of Campe in June 1546, which brought that war to an end and agreed to the English retention of Boulogne for eight years until the arrears of the French pension had been paid, was perhaps the last time in the period under review that any kind of diplomatic initiative rested with the English.[50] Henry VIII died in January 1547; Francis I died on the following 31 March. Between 1547 and the end of 1558 England was ruled, first, by a minor, Edward VI, and then two women, Mary I and Elizabeth I. France, on the other hand, was ruled by Henry II, an ambitious and energetic adult ruler whose aims towards England were bellicose.[51] Thus, from 1547 until after the fall of Calais in January 1558, England's diplomacy towards France was largely reactive and constrained by the limitations of her monarchs. In the first two years of Edward VI's reign, under the direction of the duke of Somerset, the focus of English diplomatic and military efforts was Scotland. Henry II recognised this too and sent 6,000 French soldiers to Scotland in June 1548; he then assumed the title 'Protector of the Scots' and carried the young Mary, Queen of Scots, off to France to marry the Dauphin. In 1549, following the rebellions in England and the collapse of Somerset's regime, Henry finally mounted an unsuccessful attack on Boulogne.[52] Nevertheless, with French pressure mounting through attacks in France, Scotland and, in 1549 in Ulster, the new regime of John Dudley, Earl of Warwick, later duke of Northumberland, was forced to sue for peace. The treaty of Boulogne of 24 March 1550 relinquished English control of that town, in return for a generous financial settlement, and effectively abandoned the English position

---

[49] *LP* xvii. 440; Potter, Foreign Policy', pp. 121-3.
[50] For the Campe negotiations see Scarisbrick, pp. 463-4.
[51] Frederic Baumgartner, *Henry II, King of France 1547-1559* (1996).
[52] For the English shift in emphasis to Scotland see M. L. Bush, *The Government Policy of Protector Somerset* (London, 1975), pp. 7-13; Jennifer Loach, *Edward VI* (New Haven and London, 1999), pp. 52-4. For French aims in Scotland see Elizabeth Bonner, 'The Recovery of St. Andrews Castle in 1547: French naval policy and diplomacy in the British Isles', *EHR* 111 (1996), 578-98.

in Scotland. In June the following year Henry II was created a knight of the Garter and the entertainment of the French ambassadors revived memories of the *entente* of the late 1520s. However, in 1550-1 the choice of peace was one forced upon the English. Northumberland's government, whilst at peace with France, constantly needed to maintain its defences on the northern borders lest the French attack through Scotland. The political weakness caused by prolonged war on two fronts and the minority of Edward VI ensured that the diplomatic initiative had passed from England to France.[53]

The accession of Mary I in August 1553 led to new constraints on the formation of English policy towards France. Principal amongst these was Mary's gender. Mary was expected to marry and the choice of Philip of Spain was an obvious one, given the constant support she had received from her uncle, Charles V. Nevertheless, to Henry II it seemed to threaten an anti-French Anglo-Habsburg alliance. Mary was forced to give guarantees that the Anglo-French peace would continue. England, however, saw itself dragged slowly into the Habsburg-Valois struggle. In 1555 Mary had succeeded in bringing the two parties together at the Gravelines conference but she lacked the force of Henry VIII and failed to bring about a universal peace such as that achieved by Henry at London in 1518. Indeed, when a truce was finally agreed at Vaucelles in February 1556 it was done without consulting the English. This truce lasted only as long as it took the two sides to replenish their resources for war and in September Philip resumed hostilities in Italy. Naturally Philip expected his wife to aid him, despite the terms of their marriage treaty, arriving in England in March 1557 to that end. Mary and her councillors tried desperately to keep England out of the war at first, but the invasion of the rebel, Thomas Stafford, at Scarborough Castle in April forced England into war. Although there is little evidence that Henry II supported the scheme, it provided a welcome *casus belli* for Philip. Although it was defined as one of national defence against French aggression (no mention was made of ancient claims to the French crown), in reality the war was forced upon England because of the unique circumstances of a queen regnant. The war ended disastrously in the loss of Calais. Mary did not live to see the cessation of hostilities negotiated at Cateau-Cambrésis in

---

[53] Loach, *Edward VI*, pp. 107-8.

April 1559 and her diplomacy with France bears the stigma of having been determined as much in Madrid as in Westminster.[54]

It is clear that in their diplomatic relations with France the rulers of England had clear agendas. At times these were, to use a deliberate anachronism, to preserve the balance of power in north-western Europe and to prevent France gaining a complete dominance of the region. At other times, as recent historians have stressed, it was to win and maintain kingly honour. Nevertheless, it is also evident that in their diplomacy, as in war, the English operated under certain constraints. Diplomacy depended on the personality and ability of the prince: thus for different reasons, Henry VI, Edward VI and Mary were never masters of their relationship with France. Events, such as the sudden death of a rival or friendly prince, could alter the diplomatic scene overnight. In the sixteenth century, as the least powerful of the three major powers, English rulers often found themselves simply trying to avoid being ignored by their Valois and Habsburg counterparts.

Cultural Exchange

How did the English perceive France and the French? Equally, how were the English perceived by the French? Given the traditional antagonism between the two and the fact that for many the experience of meeting was marked by violence, were French and English cultures mutually exclusive? How did the relationship between the two peoples and cultures change over time and how did factors such as chivalry and religion foster and strengthen bonds between them?

The xenophobia of the English in the late middle ages was well known. The Venetian description of England written in 1500 noted this as being an essential characteristic of the English. 'Whenever they see a handsome foreigner', he observed, 'they say that "he looks like an Englishman" . . . and when they partake of any delicacy with a foreigner,

---

[54] Loades, *Mary Tudor*, pp. 189-91, 304-8. The view that Marian diplomacy was merely a pawn in a wider European game finds its most forceful expression in work of E. Harris Harbison. He wrote that the rival French and Spanish ambassadors 'made of England a battleground where Habsburg and Valois fought for European hegemony': *Rival Ambassadors at the Court of Queen Mary* (Princeton, 1940), p. 331.

they ask him, "whether such a thing is made in *their* country?"'[55] The English, unsurprisingly, reserved their most hardened prejudices for the French. In 1512 the king's printer, Richard Pynson (ironically himself a Frenchman by birth), printed two justifications for Henry VIII's war with Louis XI. For a more refined audience James Whytston's *De Justicia et sanctitate belli per Julium pontificem secundam in scismaticos* offered a scholarly argument portraying Louis as a schismatic usurper. For a wider audience, *The Gardyners passetaunce Touchyng the outrage of Fraunce* presented similar arguments but drew upon popular dislike of the French. Using familiar imagery of the English rose and French lily, it contrasted the sweet smell of the former with the stench of the latter.[56] Around the same time, Edward Hall's *Chronicle* characterised the French as 'cowards, braggarts and dishonest traders'.[57] Nor were such sentiments merely the attempts of royal propagandists to whip up support for Henry's wars. In 1533 the Londoners who lined the route of Anne Boleyn's coronation procession poured equal scorn on the queen and Jean de Dinteville, the French ambassador, calling him 'whoreson knave' and 'French dog'.[58] At times, dislike of the French spilled into open violence. Usually attacks on foreigners in London had an economic motive, as with the Evil May Day attacks in 1517, but in December 1536 a servant of the French ambassador was murdered near Bridewell Palace for no apparent reason other than his nationality.[59]

French dislike of the English was similarly evident. The author of the Venetian report noted in 1500 how the English 'have a very high reputation in arms; and from the great fear the French entertain of them, one must believe it to be justly acquired'.[60] Certainly, it was widely reported in England that French mothers frightened their children with tales of John Talbot, Earl of Shrewsbury, one of the leading English captains of the

---

[55] *A Relation or Rather a True Account of the Island of England*, ed. Charlotte Augusta Sneyd, Camden Society, 37 (1847), pp. 20-1, 23-4.
[56] *The Gardyners Passetaunce (c. 1512)*, ed. Franklin B. Williams (London, 1985), p. 27;
[57] Glenn Richardson, 'Anglo-French Political and Cultural Relations during the Reign of Henry VIII' (University of London, PhD thesis, 1995), pp. 23-4.
[58] *LP*, vi. 585. It is interesting to speculate whether Anne's identification with the French court and French fashions added to her unpopularity.
[59] *LP*, xi. 1334. Apparently the victim was pursued by his assailants to cries of 'Down with the French dogs'. For the Evil May Day riots see Martin Holmes, 'Evil May-Day, 1517: the story of a riot', *History Today* 15 (1965), 642-50.
[60] *Italian Relation*, p. 23.

Hundred Years War.⁶¹ As Charles Giry-Deloison shows below, the dislike of the English was particularly marked in those areas of northern France that experienced the ravages of English armies. Moreover, the evident disdain towards the English exhibited by the university of Paris in 1515 was reminiscent of English attitudes towards the French.

Nevertheless, the two peoples did have things in common. This was especially marked amongst the political elites. First, they frequently shared a common language (French), although the numbers of Englishmen who could speak French was certainly in decline by the early sixteenth century. As Luke MacMahon's examples show, for Englishmen at the court of Francis I their lack of understanding of French could often cause confusion and ill feeling. A second common experience and set of beliefs that bound the political elites of the two nations was the concept of chivalry. Some of the most important chivalric texts of the late fifteenth and early sixteenth century were French in origin and French remained the language of aristocratic, chivalric culture, even if the model of courtly and chivalric behaviour was that of the Valois dukes of Burgundy.⁶² In practice, however, French displays of chivalry sometimes failed to live up to English expectations. The French royal chivalric order of St. Michael was considered to be a poor imitation of the English order of the Garter. In June 1527, at a meeting of the order of St. Michael, Sir Anthony Browne was surprised at the knights' attire: 'sum having on their collars of the Order, and sum none, but a sochen of Seint Mighell, being none otherwise apparailled that they go daily'.⁶³ Perhaps Henry hoped to introduce some English discipline when he was elected to the order later that year. Nevertheless, as Glenn Richardson has argued, a common chivalric outlook was instrumental in personal relationship between Henry VIII and Francis I. This found its expression not only in the exchange of gifts, ambassadors and chivalric honours but also in such set-piece displays of chivalric culture as the Field of the Cloth of Gold in 1520. The Field of the Cloth of Gold allowed rivalries and antagonism to be displayed and controlled within a shared chivalric culture. On the first day of the jousts, for example, Henry's

---

⁶¹ A. J. Pollard, *John Talbot and the War in France, 1427-1453* (London, 1983), pp. 1-2.
⁶² Colin Richmond, 'The Visual Culture of Fifteenth-Century England' in Pollard (ed.), *Wars of the Roses*, pp. 186-209; Gordon Kipling, *The Triumph of Honour: Burgundian origins of the Elizabethan renaissance* (The Hague, 1977).
⁶³ *State Papers, Henry VIII*, vii. 8.

horse-bard was decorated with 'waves' or 'waterworks'; according to Hall, this signified English mastery of the channel.[64] But even so carefully stage-managed an event as the Field of the Cloth of Gold could not control all tensions: Lord Leonard Grey and another unnamed nobleman, for example, were imprisoned by an enraged Henry for declaring 'If I had a drop of French blood in my body I would cut myself open to get rid of it'.[65]

The close contact between the English and French courts in the 1520s and 1530s has recently been identified as an important period in English cultural history. Due to the influx of French fashions, ideas of courtly behaviour and tastes, and French artists and artisans England became 'a cultural colony of France'.[66] From the mid 1520s Henry VIII increasingly looked to French merchants to supply his court with drapery, jewels, and other ornaments.[67] The Burgundian and Italian fashions and artistic styles, which had characterised English tastes in the fifteenth century, were now displaced by French. This trend should not, however, be overestimated. There is little evidence, for example, that English courtiers with experience of France chose to build their English country homes in the French style. Cowdray House, owned successively by Sir William Fitzwilliam and Sir Anthony Browne, both ambassadors and soldiers with first-hand experience of France, shows no such influences, although Sir Richard Weston's (treasurer of Calais from 1526) Sutton Place does.[68] As Glenn Richardson notes, the predominance of French fashions at the Henrician court from the late 1520s may be explained by the nature of the king's diplomacy: 'many of the avenues through which ideas and objects might once have come were closed . . . Strained relations with the Emperor and the Pope curtailed the flow of gifts, ideas and personal exchanges'.

---

[64] Joycelyne G. Russell, *The Field of Cloth of Gold: men and manners in 1520* (London, 1969), pp. 128-9.
[65] *CSP Venetian, 1520-1526*, 108.
[66] Starkey (ed.), *European Court*, pp. 12-3. The quotation is from Eric Ives, 'Anne Boleyn and the *Entente Évangélique*' in *François Ier et Henry VIII*, ed. Giry-Deloison, p. 102.
[67] Richardson, 'Anglo-French Political and Cultural Relations', pp. 243-4.
[68] Maurice Howard, *The Early Tudor Country House: architecture and politics, 1490-1550* (London, 1967), pp. 78, 96, 111-2, 129-30. Sutton Place has some of the characteristics of the chateau of Bury, built in 1511 for Florimond Robertet, secretary to Louis XII and Francis I. Cowdray, of course, was decorated with murals of the 1544 Boulogne campaign; one example of how their experience in France affected some Englishmen's domestic scenario.

Moreover, those French artists and craftsmen who did visit the English court adapted their skills to meet the demands of the English market.[69]

The extended period of peace between England and France from the late 1520s also allowed Englishmen to travel and study more widely in France. English travellers in France were aided by French dictionaries and grammars published in England, notably John Palsgrave's *L'Esclaircissement de la langue françoyse* (1530), although, interestingly, a corresponding French interest in the English language was not apparent until the 1570s.[70] The poet and antiquarian, John Leland, took advantage of the diplomatic situation to study at the university of Paris in the late 1520s. His poem *The Union of the Lily and the Rose*, written in the 1540s, recalled a golden age of friendship between the two peoples.[71] The most prominent English poet to visit France during this period was Henry Howard, Earl of Surrey. In 1532 Surrey visited France in the train of the king and Anne Boleyn. Later, accompanied by Henry Fitzroy, duke of Richmond, he visited Paris and Foutainebleau palace. Here, according to his recent biographer, Surrey learnt 'new shapes of beauty and the Renaissance sense of form', which he incorporated into his own poetry and, perhaps, into the architecture of his new house in Norwich, Mount Surrey.[72] In his next visit to France, however, Surrey returned in a more familiar guise: as the king's Lieutenant of Boulogne in 1545-6 he defended the town against French attack and employed the new language of honour learnt in France to express his military achievements and those of his servants.[73] Another English visitor to France was Andrew Boorde, the traveller and physician, who visited the university of Montpellier on his return from a trip to the Middle East in 1542. Boorde noted that the French 'dayly . . . make new toyes and fashions; Al nacions of me example do take'. Although he described France as 'a rych countre & a plesaunt' one, Boorde could find little positive to say about the French themselves and also reiterated the English claim to the French crown

---

[69] Richardson, 'Anglo-French Political and Cultural Relations', p. 270.

[70] Potter, 'Anglo-French Relations', 63-4.

[71] J. P. Carley, 'Leland in Paris: the evidence of his poetry', *Studies in Philology* 83 (1986), 1-50. A similarly positive view of Anglo-French relations had, of course, been expressed in 1490 by Robert Gaugin in his *Le passé temps d'oysiveté*: Gaugin, *Epistole et orationes*, ed. Thusane, ii. 366-423. I am grateful to John Currin for reminding me of this.

[72] W. A. Sessions, *Henry Howard, the Poet Earl of Surrey: a life* (Oxford, 1999), pp. 85-107, 143-9.

[73] Ibid., pp. 299-318.

in his description of the country.[74] Few Englishmen, it seems, cultivated the kind of real friendships, described below by David Potter, that Lord Lisle, deputy of Calais between 1533 and 1540, enjoyed with French families.

An increasingly important factor in cultivating contacts between England and France in the early sixteenth century was religion. Although reform followed very different paths in England and France, the Reformation was essentially an international movement which cut across traditional political allegiances and encouraged both evangelicals and conservatives to seek allies across national boundaries.[75] Although there were domestic, Lollard influences on early reformers and a much more influential flow of books and ideas from the Low Countries transported by the mercantile community, evangelicals' ideas also came from France. As Eric Ives has argued, Anne Boleyn, 'wholly French – in style, in elegance, in sympathy, and in culture', encouraged reformers at the English court. Anne's books and ideas on religious reform were exclusively French and, given the Henrician court's Francophone atmosphere in the early 1530s, this may have made reform more palatable to the political elite of Henrician England.[76] Religion also provided the means for increasing numbers of Frenchmen and women to be welcomed in England. From 1540, but particularly after 1547 when Henry II stepped up the persecution of Protestants in France, large numbers of French refugees settled in London and the south east of England. As co-religionists, they received a warmer reception in England than previous French visitors.[77]

*   *   *

Anglo-French rivalry, developed during the Hundred Years War, continued unabated throughout the period 1450-1558. At different times this was variously expressed through violence (both official war and unofficial actions such as piracy and border-raiding), diplomacy and chivalric competition between princes and aristocrats. Although on a personal level,

---

[74] Andrew Boorde, *The Fyrst Boke of the Introduction of Knowledge*, ed. F. J. Furnivall, Early English Text Society, Extra Series 10 (1870), pp. 190-1, 194, 206-9.

[75] R. J. Knecht, 'The Early Reformation in England and France: a comparison', *History* 57 (1972), 1-16.

[76] Ives, 'Anne Boleyn', pp. 83-102.

[77] Andrew Pettegree, *Foreign Protestant Communities in Sixteenth Century London* (Oxford, 1986).

Introduction 23

whether at court, in the universities or even in their own private houses, increasing numbers of the French and English discovered friendships and common interests and aspirations, there remained a sense of an underlying hostility between the two nations. By the end of our period, however, there were signs that this emnity was beginning to be laid to rest. The long period of peace in Henry VIII's reign had fostered greater cultural links. Moreover, in the later sixteenth century it was religion, rather than dynastic or chivalric issues, that decided the nature of England's relations with other European states.[78] In the new order it was Spain rather than France that emerged as the principal enemy of England and Englishness, defined by the early seventeenth century by its Calvinist sense of national identity. It was not until after 1689 that France emerged again as England's main rival in Europe. However, the caricatures of the French and France which dominated English popular imagination throughout the eighteenth and nineteenth centuries were echoes of a more distant antipathy between the two nations.[79]

---

[78] Doran, *England and Europe*, pp. 95-101.
[79] Linda Colley, *Britons: forging the nations 1707-1837* (London, 1994), pp. 33-5, 251-2.

2 The Loss of Lancastrian Normandy: an administrative nightmare?
ANNE CURRY

The Hundred Years War was arguably the last major war which the English lost. In July 1449 the French king, Charles VII, began his major onslaught on the duchy of Normandy which the English had held since Henry's V's campaigns of thirty years previous. Slightly over a year later, on 19 August 1450, John Gresham wrote to John Paston: 'Today is Cherbourg gone and we have now not a foot of land left in Normandy'.[1] Gascony, a possession of the English crown since the mid twelfth century, was soon to follow, and although there was a brief hope of its recovery in 1453, the English fate was sealed by the defeat of the Earl of Shrewsbury at Castillon on 17 July of that year. In the interim, Calais had been deemed vulnerable: Gresham's letter had added 'and men are [afraid] that Calais will soon be besieged'. There were several abortive attempts to send armies to France, with plans in January 1452 for the king even to lead an expedition in person. On the other side of the Channel in Normandy the French remained in readiness for a possible English *revanche*. But shortly after the battle of Castillon – in response, it has been suggested, to hearing news of the defeat – Henry VI succumbed to his first bout of debilitating madness. Minds were now concentrated on how the government might be conducted in his 'absence'. Richard, Duke of York, was appointed protector; the terms and conditions which he subsequently negotiated reveal continuing concern for the defence of Calais.[2] In the face of such pressures at home and abroad, no further attempt was made to recover the lost provinces of Normandy and Gascony. With their loss, any claim the English kings had to the crown of France by virtue of the treaty of Troyes

---

[1] *Paston Letters and Papers of the Fifteenth Century*, ed. N. Davis (2 vols., Oxford, 1971-6), ii. 42. Cherbourg had fallen on 12 August.
[2] *RP*, v. 254-7.

of 1420, or consequent upon the hereditary right of the descendants of Edward III, was rendered a dead letter, if it was not already so well before Charles VII invaded the duchy of Normandy in July 1449.

We could expend much time and effort trying to explain this English defeat in the Hundred Years War. I could even pose one of the questions my students like least – was the war lost even before it was begun? Was there ever any real chance of an English king becoming King of France, either in the early years of the claim under Edward III, or after the acceptance of Henry V as heir and regent by a legitimate French monarch in 1420? And once the claim had been advanced by a series of English kings to the constant – and, in the case of Crécy, Poitiers and Agincourt, considerable – humiliation of the French, was there any real chance of the latter being prepared to let the English have even 'a foot of land' within their kingdom? In short, the claim to the French throne may have served English rulers well as a bargaining counter, and, in particular, as a way of pressurising the French into making territorial concessions at times of English military success. But it was such an insult that once the French were in what we might call 'the driving seat of war', as they were in 1449, it was only a matter of time before they sought to remove the enemy from their soil, even from lands such as Gascony where the English king's rights were long established by virtue of feudal and not dynastic right. But I do not intend to provide here a wide-ranging analysis of why the English lost the Hundred Years War nor why they did relatively little to recover their lost lands in the 1450s and beyond. That last comment may, of course, seem rather dismissive of fellow contributors in this volume interested in the campaigns of Edward IV, Henry VII and VIII, but I make it on the grounds of the relative lack of effort after 1450 compared with the previous century or so.

What I do intend to do here is to ask another difficult question. Why is British Library Additional Manuscript 11,509 not in the Public Record Office? This may seem much more restricted in scope than why the English lost the Hundred Years War and why they did little to redeem the situation in the 1450s. But, as I hope will be revealed, the answer to my question will explain much about the last few years of Lancastrian Normandy, and thus contribute something to the broader perspective of English defeat and defeatism. British Library Additional Manuscript 11,509 is the account book of the receiver-general of France and Normandy from Michaelmas 1448 to Michaelmas 1449. It was purchased by the British Museum from the bookseller, Thomas Rodd, in 1838. The resulting entry in the *Catalogue of*

Additions tells us that it is 'imperfect at the beginning and end'.[3] Although the book now has a modern foliation in arabic numerals appropriate to its surviving 142 leaves, its current first folio was, according to the original mid fifteenth century numbering in roman numerals, originally fo. 215. Thus the first 214 folios are absent, a considerable loss given that both sides of the missing pages would have been written on, as can be seen by what survives of the rest of the book. The whole of the income side of the account is lost, as well as the first part of the expenditure section. The original foliation ends on what is now fo. 106 recto but which was once fo. 320 recto. There are no gaps in the extant text down to that point. The final 36 folios of the book, however, bear no original foliation, so it is difficult to be certain that they constitute a continuous and complete run, although it seems likely from their contents that they do. There are clearly some pages missing at the end of the book, but exactly how many is impossible to ascertain. It is feasible, of course, that the account book was never completed, and that its current end point was as far as it was ever compiled.

What is most fascinating about this account book is that, although it relates to a period of *English* control of Normandy from Michaelmas 1448 to Michaelmas 1449, it was written up in part, and audited in its entirety, by the officials of Charles VII in the wake of the latter's conquest of the duchy. Thus the book offers a unique insight into the transition from one regime to another. This was misinterpreted by Vallet de Viriville in a brief note on the manuscript published in the *Bibliothèque de l'École des Chartes* in 1846 where he claimed that the expenditures in the account were incurred under French as well as under English administration.[4] Although the account was partly a product of the French regime in its compilation and auditing, *all* of the expenditures recorded in it were incurred under English rule. Thus the book casts important light upon the last throes of English-held Normandy, and may therefore assist us in assessing why and how Henry VI lost this part of his continental dominions.

But first we must address the question of why the book is in the British Library and not the Public Record Office, nor indeed in an archive

---

[3] *Catalogue of Additions 1836-40* (London, 1843), p. 16. For Rodd (1796-1849), see *Dictionary of National Biography*, xlix. 78.

[4] 'Ainsi comme on a pu le remarquer, le document produit par le comptable embrasse à la fois les dépenses faites sous l'administration anglaise et sous l'auctorité nouvellement rétablie du roi de France': *Bibliothèque de l'École des Chartes*, 2nd series, 3 (1846), 135.

repository in France. This explanation will, I hope, permit a brief overview of how the duchy was administered in the period of English occupation. There are seven other surviving account books for Lancastrian Normandy. Four are to be found in the Public Record Office, and three in the Bibliothèque Nationale de France in Paris. The reason for the different locations is basically chronological, as the following outline will reveal.

Accounts from the reign of Henry V are in the Public Record Office because of the distinctive fashion in which Normandy was ruled by the English during his reign. From the fall of Harfleur in 1415 to the treaty of Troyes in May 1420, this was a result of conquest. From the sealing of the treaty to Henry's death in 1422, Normandy remained in his hands as a special personal enclave. Distinct phases are revealed in the surviving documents. Harfleur was Henry's sole holding from September 1415 to August 1417. In January 1416 a treasurer of the town was appointed, Thomas Barneby, who was accountable to the exchequer in England in a manner which emulated the administration of Calais. His account book, covering the period from 22 January 1416 to 21 January 1420, is to be found at Public Record Office E 36/79. There is also classified at E 101/48/7 the book of Barneby's controller, Simon Flete, which covers from 31 December 1415 to 21 January 1420. In addition there is a copy of the enrolled account of Barneby at E 101/48/8, and some further loose particulars of account at E 101/695/37. Together, these accounting materials show efforts to maintain the garrison of Harfleur as far as possible out of local revenues. They also reveal the early stages of English control and settlement. All of these documents concerning Harfleur follow the practices of the English exchequer, and show many similarities with the contemporary and past administration of Calais.

A separate exchequer was maintained at Harfleur until early January 1420 when it was closed and the town and garrison placed under the authority of the *chambre des comptes* at Caen. The latter had been established by Henry soon after his second invasion of the duchy in 1417.[5]

---

[5] For a fuller discussion, see A. Curry, 'L'administration financière de la Normandie anglaise: continuité ou changement?, *La France des principautés. Les chambres des comptes xive et xve siècles*, ed. P. Contamine and O. Mattéoni (Comité pour l'histoire économique et financière de la France, Paris, 1996), pp. 83-103, with a selection of relevant texts in 'La chambre des comptes de Nomandie sous l'occupation anglaise 1417-1450', *Les Chambres de Comptes en France aux xive et xve siècles*, ed. P. Contamine and O. Mattéoni (Comité pour l'histoire économique et financière de la France, Paris, 1998), pp. 91-125.

The first surviving documents date from November of that year but it is likely that the *chambre* at Caen was set up soon after the fall of the town on 4 September 1417. Although it was staffed in part by English officials, its practices right from the start followed those of the principal French royal *chambre des comptes* at Paris and not those of the English exchequer. Henry had 'gone French', so to speak. Before his invasion, Normandy, as part of the French royal domain, had been administered by the *chambre* at Paris, although the duchy already had had its own receiver-general. Whether, by establishing a French-style *chambre* at Caen, Henry was intent upon stressing his claim to the French throne or upon creating a separate duchy of Normandy is not entirely clear, and is certainly an issue which cannot be addressed here. No account book is known to survive for Sir John Tiptoft as treasurer-general of the duchy, a post to which he was appointed on 1 November 1417. Nor is there one for the receiver-general, John Golafre, appointed on 20 May 1418. But two account books survive for William Allington, who was appointed treasurer-general on 1 May 1419, and under whom there does not seem to have been a receiver-general. Allington's surviving books cover the first and fourth years of his office, but the latter is incomplete as Henry V died part way through the accounting year. They are now to be found in the Public Record Office at E 101/187/14 and E 101/188/7 respectively. Intriguingly, Allington's commission of appointment of May 1419 obliged him to submit his accounts to the English exchequer for audit, but Henry subsequently changed his mind on this in the summer of 1420, perhaps as a result of the treaty of Troyes. Allington's first account book was thus audited at the Caen *chambre des comptes* in October 1420, and there is evidence to suggest that the missing second account book was also audited in Caen. Allington's fourth account book, however, was definitely audited in the English exchequer, and probably the third too, for both were enrolled in the Foreign Accounts of 1426-7.[6] By this stage, Allington's first account had also been returned to the English exchequer, although many of the subsidiary documents for his period of office, as for Tiptoft's and Golafre's, were retained at Caen.

We could conclude, therefore, that Lancastrian Normandy after Henry V's invasion of 1417 was in a transitional state in terms of financial

---

[6] PRO, E 364/61, rot. 2.

administration. There was a *chambre des comptes* within the duchy which operated according to French practices, but which was generally intended to be under English control and subject to overall and final scrutiny by the English exchequer. This was appropriate in the circumstances of conquest, and also by the terms of the treaty of Troyes where Normandy had been left outside French royal control until such time as Henry should inherit the throne from his mad father-in-law. But by the terms of the same treaty, once there was a single holder of the double monarchy in the person of the infant Henry VI, the duchy had to be reunited with the French crown. Thus in July 1424 the *chambre des comptes* at Caen was suppressed and Normandy placed once more under the authority of the *chambre des comptes* at Paris as it had been in the period before the English invasion. The documents subsidiary to the account books which were held at Caen and which dated back to 1417 were taken to Paris and housed within the principal *chambre* archive there. It is not surprising, therefore, that surviving account books for the duchy in the 1420s should be the product of French officials under the control of the *chambre* at Paris, and hence preserved within the latter's archive. Thus we have the account book of Pierre Surreau as receiver-general of Normandy for the period from 16 November 1423 to 15 January 1425 at BNF manuscrit français 4485, and his account book from 1 October 1428 to 30 September 1429 at manuscrit français 4488. There is also his *journal de la dépense* for the year from 16 January 1425 at manuscrit français 4491.[7]

When the English lost Paris in May 1436, a new *chambre* had to be established by them within the duchy of Normandy. This was placed not at Caen but at Rouen, where we have evidence of its existence from October 1436. Only one account book is known to survive for the last period of English control of the duchy from 1436 to 1450, and that is now British Library Additional Manuscript 11,509, the receiver-general's account for the year 1448-9. Its location is unique. We should not be surprised that this book is not in the Public Record Office for it sprang from an entirely French-based system of financial administration. Even after the loss of Paris,

---

[7] See also BNF, manuscrit français 32,510, an extract from the first account of Benoit Colenot, *trésorier des guerres*, 25 May 1425 to 88 Feb. 1426, and manuscrit français 4484, the account of Andry Esparnon as *trésorier des guerres*, 20 Feb. 1427 to 30 Sept. 1428, both of which are useful in showing English expenditure in northern France outside Normandy.

30 *The English Experience in France*

the English continued to rule the duchy of Normandy and its environs according to French practices and institutions as legitimate kings of France. The *chambre* at Rouen established in 1436 thus operated in exactly the same way as that at Paris. Some of its officials, at least in the early days, were those who had chosen English allegiance and hence exile from the French capital in 1436. The officials which this account book reveals as serving are all French, with Thomas Basin, Bishop of Lisieux, as president of the *chambre* at Rouen. The name of the receiver-general is not given in the account itself, but was probably Pierre Baille.[8] As had been the case for almost the whole of the English occupation, the treasurer-general was an Englishman, Osbern Mundford, but he did not present his accounts to the English exchequer, despite Henri Jassemin's claims to the contrary.[9] In no way at all did the Rouen *chambre* fall under the scrutiny of the English exchequer.

One might speculate, of course, that this account book for 1448-9 produced in Rouen is now in England simply because at the loss of the duchy in 1450 the English brought back home with them the archives of the Rouen *chambre*. But that was not what happened to it. As was noted earlier, the account book was partly written and audited under the *French* administration of Charles VII after his conquest of the duchy. The English did not bring back their documents at the loss of Normandy, but left them all behind in Rouen, and, after the surrender of the Norman capital on 29 October 1449, in the subsequent but short-lived English base at Caen. Charles VII kept the Rouen *chambre* open until 1451 but then placed the

---

[8] Baille had already occupied the post from at least Jan. 1436 to Nov. 1444, being replaced then by Remon Monsault (BL, Add. Ch. 1506), but it would seem that Baille had resumed the office at some point, and certainly by 5 Nov. 1448: BNF, manuscrit français 26078/6029. Since the appointment of Pierre Surreau on 28 Jan. 1423 (AN, Collection Lenoir 21, p. 237), the receiver-general had always been a Frenchman, although Englishmen had usually occupied the office of treasurer-general and controller of the receipt. In 1448-9, the treasurer-general of Normandy was Osbern Mundford, who had held the office since Sept. 1448 in succession to John Stanlowe. The name of the controller of the receipt at this point is not known, but in Oct. 1446 it was Anthoine Huet: BNF, Collection Clairambault 10/463. The president of the *chambre des comptes* at Rouen was at the date of the account Thomas Basin, Bishop of Lisieux: BL, Add. MS 11,509, fo. 27. The account book also mentions two of the officials of the chambre, Thomas Louraille, *conseiller et maître* (fos. 60, 61v) and Jean Cousin, *clerc et auditeur* (fo. 66v).

[9] H. Jassemin, *La Chambre des comptes de Paris au xve siècle* (Paris, 1923), p. LXVI.

duchy once more under the control of the Paris *chambre*.[10] Papers were thus transferred to Paris, although the exact date of this is unclear. The date of audit of the receiver-general's account of 1448-9 is not known. Based on other evidence of the time lapse between the end of an account and its audit, I am tempted to suggest that the 1448-9 account was audited in Rouen before the *chambre* was closed in 1451.[11] It is not impossible, however, that the auditing occurred in Paris after that date. Whatever the case, at some point after 1451 the archives of all three *chambres* used by the English over the course of their occupation from 1417 to 1450 – Caen, Paris and Rouen – were reunited and placed within the general and massive archive of the *chambre des comptes* of Paris. Over the next four centuries, this archive suffered many vicissitudes: a fire in 1737; frequent *dépouillement*, as the French term it, by antiquarians interested in noble titles; and deliberate destruction at the decision of the *Bureau de Tirage* during the Revolution when such noble titles were no longer a matter of respectable interest.[12] It is remarkable how much does survive, but it has been much dispersed, as is revealed by the fact that it is now to be found in and the USA. Materials thus found themselves in the hands of private individuals, and in the saleroom. The account book for 1448-9 came into the hands of Thomas Rodd from whom the British Museum purchased it in 1838. Ironically, therefore, manuscripts concerning the financial administration of Normandy during the English occupation found their way to England, albeit four centuries later. The British Library houses many stray documents arising out of the administration of the duchy from at least 1419 to 1450. These all derive from the archives of the *chambre des comptes* of Paris and were purchased in the nineteenth century. Documents from at least fourteen different archive repositories in England, France, Canada now at Additional Charters

---

[10] P. Le Cacheux and M.J. Le Cacheux, *Archives départmentales de la Seine-Inférieure. Répertoire numérique de la série B; Chambre des Comptes de Normandie* (Rouen, 1934), pp. 12-13.

[11] Allington's account for 1 May 1419-30 Apr. 1420 was audited on 31 Oct. 1420, six months after its end date: PRO, E 101/187/14, fo. 1. In royal lands in Cheshire, auditing usually occurred between Jan. and Apr. following the Michaelmas of the end of the account, a gap of three to seven months: A. Curry, 'The Demesne of the County Palatine of Chester in the early Fifteenth Century' (unpublished MA thesis, University of Manchester, 1977), p. 80.

[12] M. Nortier, 'Le sort des archives dispersées de la chambre des comptes', *Bibliothèque de l'École des Chartes*, 123 (1965), 460-536.

1,060-1,246, for instance, were purchased from Thomas Rodd in 1836, and several other runs within the same collection derived from the collection of the French antiquarian, the Baron de Joursanvault, part of whose archive is also housed in the Archives départmentales du Loiret at Orleans.

It is only by the accident of history, therefore, that such materials from the *chambre des comptes* found their way to England. Internal evidence in Additional Manuscript 11,509 shows that this account of the receiver-general for the financial year Michaelmas 1448 to Michaelmas 1449 was not finally drawn up or audited until after the effective end of English rule. The contents of the account concern a whole year of English rule but within it, the term *le roy notre seigneur* refers sometimes to Henry VI and sometimes to Charles VII, and there are references to *le temps des anglois*. The point at which the regime changes can be precisely identified in the account. Folio 16v ends halfway through an entry. This entry is continued on the next folio but in a new hand. On the verso of folio 17 we have the first indication of the new order. The entry here concerns Pierre Poitevin, previously resident at Pont-Audemer. The King of England had ordered payment of 120 *livres tournois* by letters of 19 August 1449, which were in turn expedited by the treasurer-general on the 20th of the month, for what was due to Poitevin for a *certaine fortification* which he had constructed at *Moustreville* (Montivilliers) at royal order for the benefit and security of the town. Payment was made to Poitevin because of the fact that at the taking of Pont-Audemer 'by our lord the king' (in other words, Charles VII), he had been taken prisoner, had lost his goods and been put to ransom. (Pont-Audemer had fallen on or around 12 August so it is interesting to note how quickly recompense had been given. Indeed, this seems to be one of several examples of late attempts by the English to keep their Norman supporters sweet, a point which will be returned to later.) The payment of 120 *livres tournois* was being awarded to him on such grounds. Thus we have the irony of Charles VII's officials writing up an entry which recorded compensation granted by the previous government for damage which the incoming, and now controlling, French regime had caused. One suspects, of course, that many of the officials in Charles VII's *chambre* at Rouen were the self-same men who had served the English. In fact, we know that this was true in at least one case (Thomas Louraille), and it might be possible to prove it for others if we were able to identify the officials in both regimes.

For the French to complete the writing up of the account and then to go on to its auditing required them to have access to documentary materials subsidiary to the account, materials produced and filed during the English period of control. Amongst the latter would have been indentures, warrants, *quittances* (receipts) and other documents issued during the year in relation to payments made. The survival of such material confirms what we knew already, that the English gave up Rouen without much of a fight, and hence without real damage or dislocation to their archives. Indeed, they seem even to have offered as part of their negotiations for its surrender that they would hand over the archives of the *chambre des comptes* intact.[13] There is little to suggest that the French were not able to verify the entries in the account book. This can be shown by the extensive marginal annotation entered by the French auditors in the same hand throughout the surviving book, showing how they were able to draw on documents to validate the entries. Thus some entries for the payment of troops have against them *per mandatum expeditum* (or *verificatum*) *cum rotulo monstrariorum et quittencia hic redditis*. This reveals access to the justificatory texts: the order to pay, the roll of muster, and the *quittance*. In other words, the treasurer-general had authorised payment, and there was proof that the troops had served and that the leader of the retinue had received the pay due. The entries also refer to other documentation such as the commissions to take musters. In some sections, for instance in that concerning the payment of officials (fos. 15-16), reference is also made to consultation of the previous account, in other words, that of the preceding year, Michaelmas 1447 to Michaelmas 1448. This is referred to in the text and also in the margin, the latter sometimes with *vidimus* or *sic continetur in compoto precedente*. The payment to Thomas Hoo as chancellor in November 1448 for his journey to England is justified by royal letters sent to the treasurer-general as well as by *quittance* of Hoo himself. There are also marginal annotations which cross-reference the text, sometimes referring to pages now missing, as, for instance, when a payment was made directly out of local revenues and then allowed to the accountant (as on fos. 56-57).

---

[13] A. Pottier, 'Reduction de la ville de Rouen en 1449', *Revue rétrospective Normande* (1842), 11. I am grateful to Dr Michael K. Jones for this reference. He has further suggested that French interest in acquiring the archives might have been to seek proof in them of the Duke of Somerset's connivance in the capture of Fougères.

These marginal notes leave me in somewhat of a dilemma, provoking my own administrative nightmare. There is no doubt that much less of this justificatory documentation now survives for 1448-9 compared with other years of the occupation. This observation is based upon my study of the archive as a whole, divided as it is between many repositories.[14] It led me initially to speculate that the military administration of the duchy was already in disarray before the invasion of Charles VII. But the marginal annotations of the account book for 1448-9 suggest otherwise. The fact that so much justificatory documentation could be produced when the account was compiled and audited would imply that the English administration before the surrender of Rouen was functioning adequately, and that the English had indeed handed over their *chambre* archive intact. It is a pity that we do not have the part of the account dealing with the regular garrisons. If it had survived with its marginal annotations, then we would have been on even firmer ground in this assertion. Here we experience a further problem for there are very few surviving documents for the regular garrisons for the financial year 1448-9. The musters and *quittances* which survive are almost all for additional companies put into garrisons. What should we make of the lack of both the account folios and the justificatory documentation for the regular garrisons. Does it mean that the system of regular garrisons was in disarray, perhaps in the face of lack of revenues? Or that the relevant part of the account as well as its supporting material was at some point separated from the remainder of the account and its material? This could have happened, perhaps, when the French audited the account, or when they transferred the archive of the Rouen *chambre* to Paris. But it is equally possible that the loss of the first part of the account and its supporting material occurred in later centuries as the *chambre des comptes* archive was pillaged and dispersed.

For the surviving part of the receiver-general's account, however, there are many cases where surviving documents can be linked to entries. To cite only one example, on fos. 16v-17r of the account, a payment is noted to Sir Henry Norbury for a company which was ordered to have its *retrait et*

---

[14] From what I can see, too, the justificatory material for the period in question is divided between the various archive repositories with no obvious pattern discernible. See also A. Curry, 'English Armies in the Fifteenth Century' in *Arms, Armies and Fortifications in the Hundred Years War*, ed. A. Curry and M. Hughes (Woodbridge, 1994), p. 49.

logis at Domfront.[15] The relevant *quittance* for the period from 21 October 1448 to 19 January 1449 is to be found at BNF manuscrit français 26078/6071. Thus overall we can suggest that the financial administration of Normandy was still to a considerable degree operating according to proper accounting practices in 1448-9. Nonetheless, some entries in this account book do betray difficulties, both in finding enough money and in administering it in proper fashion. This is increasingly obvious in those entries which post-date Charles VII's invasion of the duchy in July 1449. Let us take, for instance, the entry concerning a company of 20 archers under Thomas Kathersby (or Akathersby) ordered to be held as an additional garrison at Pont-Audemer.[16] A series of payments are noted from 21 October 1448 onwards, all properly referenced down to and including that for which he is noted as giving *quittance* on 20 July 1449. A final payment was made to him on 18 August 1449. This was after Pont-Audemer had fallen to the French and the Duke of Somerset had ordered Kathersby's company to Gisors. For this final payment, the text tells us, the Duke did not take musters or ask for *quittance*s. In times of emergency the niceties of satisfying the accountants obviously took a lower priority. The entry continues by telling us that this final payment of 18 August and many others had been paid by the Duke himself, and that he was later given restitution by the receiver-general by virtue of royal letters dated 11 September, despite the lack of proper justificatory documentation. This indicates how the financial administration of the duchy was beginning to falter as the French advanced. In some ways we could argue that administration had been placed on an emergency footing, with Somerset taking it upon himself to make payments where necessary. Even so, there was still some attempt to keep everything above board through the issue of royal letters, albeit retrospectively.

A similar conclusion can be drawn concerning the payment of the salary of the Duke of Somerset, who as the French scribe puts it – this is in the section written up after the taking of Rouen – 'lequel ou temps des anglois estoit lieutenant et gouverneur de France et de Normandie' with the

---

[15] These were essentially mobile field companies ordered to have their base in a particular place, in addition to the regular garrison.
[16] Fo. 5v. There is a similar entry for a company at Château-Gaillard, and a reference suggests that a similar situation had arisen at Touques, where the full reference would no doubt have been on an earlier, and now lost, page.

hasty insertion by the scribe at the end of the phrase of 'pour les anglois'.[17] The Duke was due to receive 30,000 *livres tournois*. (The exchange rate for the pound sterling, as expressed in another entry in this account book, is 9 *livres tournois*, which makes the salary worth £3,333 6*s* 8*d* per annum.) *Quittances* for the payments for the first three quarters had been given on 24 January, 4 April and 1 July. For the fourth quarter there was simply 'ung feuillete de papier montant xii m livres tournois signe en la fin du signe manuel de mondit seigneur le duc rendu sur la dernier partie de sa retenue cy devant cy servant pour l'autre quartier'. No date is given to this piece of paper, but it survives today in BNF manuscrit français 26078/6092. Was Somerset acting fairly hastily in ensuring he collected his last instalment from the coffers as Rouen fell? Whatever the case, the piece of paper was seen and accepted by the later French auditors, who were reassured by sight of the other three *quittances*, and by consultation of the previous year's account that Somerset had indeed been entitled to a full 30,000 *livres tournois*.

Others may not have fared so well. We know that soon after Somerset had arrived in the duchy he had ordered that for the quarter June to September 1448, soldiers should receive only two out of every three months wages due.[18] This was a money-saving tactic which had previously been used in the payment of officials and troops in the wake of the raising of the siege of Orleans in 1429. Although, as we have noted, the regular garrison section of the account for 1448-9 is missing, a reference in the surviving folios suggests that for some garrisons at least this policy of part payment was repeated for the autumn quarter (September-December) of 1448. Indeed, it may have continued into 1449 when we find, in stray survivals of *quittances* and orders to pay, Somerset making ad hoc payments to captains of additional companies to help them support their troops 'en attendant que plus ample paiement leur puisse estre fait'.[19] A further case of money saving can be cited. Matthew Gough was entitled to an annual pension of £200 sterling (it is here that the conversion rate is clearly stated as this sum is said

---

[17] Fo. 38.

[18] The policy of part payment is reflected in surviving *quittances* and orders for payment. See, for instance, AN, K 68/29/11, quittance dated 4 Nov. 1448 for service of the garrison of Alençon in quarter from Jun. to Sept. 1448.

[19] See BNF, Collection Clairambault 163/70, for such a payment to Matthew Gough in July 1449; and BL, Add. Ch 12,394, Bodleian Library, MS Ch. For. 492 for other examples.

to be equivalent to 1,800 *livres tournois*), but Somerset orders that in the quarter following Easter 1449 Gough should only be paid 600 *livres tournois*, 'enrestraignant ladit pension a xiiC livres tournois par an'.[20] Although the income side of the account is missing we can be fairly certain that there were already difficulties in finding enough cash. This was particularly true when it came to assignments made out of tax revenues from local sources. After petitioning the king directly, the inhabitants of Harfleur had been allowed in March 1446 8,000 *livres tournois* from the revenues of the *quatrièmes* and of the *grenier du sel* in the *vicomté* of Montivilliers as recompense for their expenditure on the fortifications of the town. A further 1,600 *livres tournois* had been allowed by royal letters of 9 November 1449 but this could not be taken from the revenues of the *vicomté* 'attendu la petite value et les grandes charges estans sur iceulx'. Only by the good offices of the Earl of Shrewsbury, captain of Harfleur, was it possible for the mayor and *conseillers* of the town to have a further set of royal letters allowing them an immediate payment from central funds of 400 *livres tournois*.[21]

What, then, can the account as a whole tell us about the state of Lancastrian Normandy on the eve and in the early months of the French conquest? When the French took over the writing of the account after the fall of Rouen, over 200 folios had already been drawn up but most of these are now missing. It is a particular pity that the receipts section does not survive as it would have helped us gain a firmer impression of the financial position of the English on the eve of the reconquest. We can use some entries on the expense side of the account which refer to an *aide* of 188,000 *livres tournois*, but how much of this had been collected is not clear. An assembly was held in Rouen in May-June 1449 of deputies from the *bailliages* of Rouen, Caux, Evreux and Gisors, 'to advise on payment of troops and other important matters concerning the seigneurie of the King of England',[22] but we must remember that in the last two of these *bailliages*, relatively little land actually remained in English control by this point. We can also see that often payments were to be made at source by the local receivers of the tax, rather than the money passing through the central treasury. There are many

---

[20] Fos. 40v-41.
[21] Fos. 52v.
[22] Fo. 62v.

references to the transportation of money.[23] The account is also incomplete at its end, terminating within the section on *menues messagers* and other small expenses. Thus no final balance is struck which might have given us a firmer picture of the financial position in this crucial year of 1448-9.

The manuscript begins halfway through an entry of expenditure. The first complete entry relates to the payment of a company of 25 mounted men-at-arms and 75 archers under Sir Francois de Surienne for the first quarter (September-December) of 1448. These troops were supplementary to his regular garrison of Verneuil. Other entries near the beginning of the surviving folios are also for additional garrisons. Thus, as noted earlier, another major section which is missing is that covering the regular garrisons and personal retinues.[24] This is unfortunate for we would dearly like to know exactly how many troops there were in the defence of Normandy at this crucial stage. The account does at least give us some idea of how garrisons were being boosted in sise through additional companies. Nine such companies are noted, some being moved from one location to another during the period of the account. Locations mentioned are Verneuil, Domfront, Torigny, Bricquebec, Argentan, Sées, Château-Gaillard, and Rouen. The total payments for this purpose were 7,885.3.4 *livres tournois*. Such additional companies were usually recruited from men who had no existing company or garrison.[25] This was a policy which, although it had earlier precedents, had begun in earnest in 1445 as a way of rounding up surplus troops during the truce, thereby helping to solve disciplinary problems as such ex-soldiers had taken to living off the land.[26]

On fo. 12r we have the first sub-heading – 'other payments made by the said receiver general to several men at arms and archers and otherwise for the journey (*voyage*) made in the company of the Earl of Shrewsbury to Pont-Audemer and elsewhere in the month of June 1449, thus, and in the manner as is said, in this chapter'. The earl had been commanded to go with a large company to Pont-Audemer and to other locations at his discretion in

---

[23] See, for instance, fo. 74 concerning the journeys of Mundford.

[24] See the later cross reference on fo. 39v mentioning for the Earl of Shrewsbury 'le nombre des gens de sa retenue pour sa conduite'.

[25] As noted on fo. 17.

[26] A. Curry, 'Les "gens vivans sur le pais" pendant l'occupation anglaise de la Normandie (1417-1450)' in *La guerre, la violence et les gens au moyen age. 1. Guerre et violence*, ed. P. Contamine and O. Guyotjeannin (Comité des travaux historiques et scientifiques, Paris, 1996), pp. 209-21.

order to put into execution several matters to which he had been charged by the Duke of Somerset. The receiver-general had given Shrewsbury an advance of 1,240 *livres tournois* by virtue of royal letters of 1 June 1449. The whole entry is deleted, with a marginal entry which is difficult to read but which seems to imply that the payment had been dealt with earlier in the account. There are a few other entries for this *voyage* to Pont-Audemer, such as payments to William Hirling (master of the ordnance, although not so named here)[27] for the reimbursement of carters and labourers. But this show of force had been too little, too late. The French advance had continued and escalated into total, and official, war.

On fo. 14r the account moves to another section of payments made to miscellaneous persons, for instance to the Bishop of Avranches for his services as a member of the *grant conseil* in France, mentioning specifically his involvement in the *reformation générale* ordered by Somerset in the summer of 1448. Other members of the *conseil* in Normandy were also paid their salaries in this section, as were officials such as the *maître des requêtes*. From fo. 20 onwards other payments made by the receiver-general in gifts and compensation are recorded. These included 1,550 *livres tournois* paid to Somerset as part of compensation against his loss of the county of Maine, out of the 10,000 *livres tournois* ordered to him for each year of his life out of the *quatrièmes* of the bailliages of Caen and Cotentin, surely a considerable drain on these local revenues. He had not received full payment of what he was due on 30 September 1448, so this was now remedied by allocating 1,000 *livres tournois* from the profits of the sales of forfeitures in the *Echiquier* of Normandy and from other profits of *reformation générale*, and 550 *livres tournois* owed by the receiver of the *quatrièmes* at Alençon for the year ending at Michaelmas 1448. This was only one of several siseable payments of compensation being met out of Norman revenues at this stage. John, Lord Beaumont was also receiving compensation for the loss of lands in Maine out of sums which were to be levied from the king's subjects in lieu of the *appatis* which were accustomed to be paid in wartime (fo. 21v). Later sections show compensatory payments to the Duke of Buckingham concerning Bellême. We are also reminded of a further drain on Norman resources by the fact that Somerset was also due to payment of

---

[27] Hirling was controller of the ordnance and artillery in Normandy from 1443 to 1445 (BL, Add. Ch. 12, 237; BNF, pièce originale 1550 Hunch 2), taking up office as master of the ordnance from at least Jan. 1446: BL, Add. Ch. 148.

6,000 *livres tournois* to be used for maintenance of men-at-arms and archers who had been in Maine serving the King of England until the county had been delivered to 'our king' (i.e. to the French) so that they would be kept in good order and discipline until fuller provision could be made. This payment had been agreed at Somerset's arrival in Normandy by the deputies of the Three Estates of the *bailliages* of Caen and Cotentin out of their vote of 90,000 *livres tournois* (May 1448). A pension was also paid to Shrewsbury in addition to his wages as marshal but, interestingly, payments to him end on 1 August 1449 (fo. 39v). This is a marked contrast with Somerset who, as we saw, was able to gain access to funds right up to his departure from Rouen. Payments to Lord Fauconberg also end on 30 June 1449, although he did not sign a *quittance* for the last instalment until 20 August (fo. 40r).

There is also a striking number of payments being made to Norman knights who supported the English. Sir Jean de Saane's lands in the Pays de Caux had been ruined and lost, so he was given money to compensate for this and to reward his services as councillor, 'iusques a ce que le dit roy d'Angleterre leust autrement pourveu ailleurs ou dit pays de Normandie de semblable somme'. This was by virtue of royal letters of 11 December 1448 and gave rise to a *quittance* dated 17 July 1449 (fo. 22v). Sir Raoul de Gal was also recompensed for losses in war and to help him effect the marriage of one of his daughters who had been promised and betrothed to 'a young gentleman of the English nation' (fos. 23r-23v, letters dated 16 December 1448, with *quittance* of 10 March 1449). In the folios which follow, there are several payments to religious houses which had petitioned the King of England for compensation for war damage. Further rewards and payments to local people follow. The inhabitants of Alençon, for instance, by letters of 19 August 1449, were given a reduction of 200 *livres tournois* from their contribution to the second instalment of the last *aide* because they had defended the town at their own expense. A similar gesture is made to Rouen, where the *quittance* is dated 5 September. There were also payments made to men of lower status. Colin du Pont, *labourer*, of the parish of Saint-Aubin-de-Scie (near Offranville), had been captured by the French nine times, and had paid them everything he had. Now he and his wife could hardly live. They had the extra expense of a young daughter about to marry as well as of a son recently ordained and about to celebrate his first mass. Du Pont was given 20 *livres tournois* (fos. 36r-v, *quittance* dated 18 June

1449).[28] We might suggest that every effort was being made to keep the local population sweet as crisis loomed. Compassion had its price, but charitable activity in war was not missing: Laurens a Trebr' 'dit Jehsus mercy', native of England, had served in the wars and had lost his sight, forcing him to live by begging. The king had already made an award to him but he claimed that he had not received it all so he was granted a special payment 'for as long as it pleased the Duke of Somerset' (fo. 36v).

Defensive measures are also much in evidence. Moneys were paid to the city of Rouen for digging ditches in early September 1449 (fo. 54r), and a *crue* (an additional detachment of mobile troops) had been ordered there in the previous month. We can also see the frequent comings and goings to and from England, especially the visit of Thomas Hoo, the chancellor of Normandy, to England in November 1448. The intricate negotiations with Brittany are evidenced by the presence of Malo King of Arms awaiting the reply of Somerset in April 1449 to letters of his own duke 'touchans plusieurs grans maters et besongnes' (fo. 35r). In these respects, the section from fo. 55r onwards, 'voyages, legacions, grosses messageries', is important, but earlier in the account too we see gifts to those Frenchmen involved in protracted and, as it turned out, hopeless, diplomatic negotiations at Rouen in June (fo. 45v).

For those who returned to England in the wake of the fall of Normandy in 1449-50 there was, of course, more than an administrative nightmare. They suffered considerable loss of income as well as of face. Even if the account of 1448-9 is able to show us that the financial system of Lancastrian Normandy was still operating reasonably effectively to the end of the financial year at Michaelmas 1449, there is much to suggest that thenceforward it was in a state of collapse. Very few documents survive for the period after the loss of Rouen. Somerset's credence presented to parliament in May of that year had reported the financial difficulties of the duchy in general and the need for money to be sent from England.[29] In October 1449, before the fall of Rouen, it was reported in the duchy that there was little money in Norman coffers, certainly not enough to pay garrison wages, whilst there was a desperate need to send detachments into the field (where, incidentally, there was a further complication because troops customarily received pay in the field on a fortnightly basis rather

---

[28] For other payments of compensation to Frenchmen, see fos. 41, 47-7v.
[29] *RP*, v. 147-8.

than, when in garrison, quarterly in arrears – the latter allowing some breathing space to the administration, the former not). Lack of pay had led to recent desertions and to soldiers living in disorderly fashion on the country, scarcely the sort of behaviour a government wanted when trying to defend its lands from an invader. Also by this point the situation was too perilous to call a meeting of the Estates so all that could be done was to make an unauthorised levy on the inhabitants of the *vicomté* of Caen, again not a wise move when the English desperately needed to retain Norman sympathies and support.[30] The Berry herald tells the story that when Charles VII took Sainte-Catherine de Rouen in mid October, he told the English troops therein to depart without taking anything from the surrounding country. They replied that they had neither money nor lodging, so he gave them 100 *francs* and even allowed them to stay in Sainte-Catherine for an extra night.[31]

After being driven out of Rouen in November 1449, Somerset established his base at Caen, but what he had there can only have been a skeleton administration at most. It is highly unlikely that he was able to set up a real *chambre* there. Indeed it is not clear how much of the financial administration survived the fall of Rouen. The treasurer-general, Osbern Mundford, had been captured at Pont-Audemer on 12 August 1449 along with Fulk Eyton and other gentlemen, and by 22 August was a prisoner of the French in the castle of Châteaudon.[32] Mundford was still a prisoner in March 1450 when Andrew Trollope surrendered Mundford's garrison of Falaise, but the composition for its surrender involved Mundford's own release from French captivity.[33] Even if Somerset had some financial officials still in his company, it is interesting to note that, in a discharge given to Thomas Pellevé, *Vicomte* of Caen, on 12 May 1450, it was reported

---

[30] BNF, manuscript français 26079/6169. Note also the concern of the mayor and townspeople of Mantes at the attempts of Mundford to collect money and produce in the vicinity of Mantes in July 1449: Mantes-la-Jolie, Bibliothèque Muncipale, Archives Communales, Serie BB (Déliberations de la ville), 5 fo. 24v.

[31] *Les Chroniques du roi Charles VII par Gilles le Bouvier dit le Héraut Berry,* ed. H. Courteault and L. Cellier (Société de l'Histoire de France, Paris, 1979), p. 319.

[32] See AN, Collection Lenoir 16, 319-25, for various reports and messages on the French capture of Pont-Audemer. See also Mundford's deposition concerning the taking of Pont-Audemer in *Chronique de Mathieu d'Escouchy,* ed. G. du Fresne de Beaucourt (3 vols., Société de l'Histoire de France, Paris, 1863-4), iii. 354-8.

[33] Robert Blondel, 'De Reductione Normanniae' in *Narratives of the Expulsion of the English from Normandy,* ed. J. Stevenson (Rolls Series, London, 1863), pp. 156-7.

that the duke had examined Pellevé's account himself 'au deffault des gens des comptes nont point encore institutees en Normandie depuis la rebellion naguere faite par ceux de la ville de Rouen'.[34] The English did not leave the duchy until August 1450, a further ten months after the fall of Rouen. There were some garrisons still in place in these last months of English rule, and we must ask how, or indeed if, they were paid in the last stages of the occupation. There is clear suggestion that Somerset was trying to fortify the *bailliages* of Caen and Cotentin. We know, for instance, that he ordered artillery to Caen but that it was captured at Bayeux. Some garrison detachments too (from Bayeux, Vire and Caen) were certainly sent to join Kyriell's army as it moved south through the Cotentin, and they may have assisted in the taking of Valognes in late March 1450.

The question of military provision and its financing must necessarily be connected with a further question, that is, whether the English had been able to collect local revenues after the fall of Rouen. The mention of the account of Pellevé might suggest that they had been, although without knowledge of the content of his account, we cannot be certain, nor is it clear how much had been raised as a result of the emergency levy in the *vicomté* of Caen ordered in late October of 1449. But payments were still being made to the English occupiers. The few stray documents which survive for the English administration of 1449 to 1450 stand as the final vestiges of a once elaborate English controlled bureaucracy. One of the last surviving documents of the English administration is a certificate by Andrew Trollope dated 27 March 1450 noting that he has received 150 *livres tournois* from the lieutenant of the *Vicomte* of Falaise 'a seule fin de payer les gens de sa compagnie, lui promettant de lui en faire avoir decharge'.[35] Three days earlier Trollope had acknowledged receipt of 131 *livres tournois* from the *collecteur des aides* at Falaise.[36] Even as late as 22 April 1450 the English were still trying to pay local officials and the garrison at Bayeux from the coffers of the receiver of the *aides* in the *vicomté* of Bayeux, but were relying on the Duke of Somerset's secretary, Jacques de Brucelles, to distribute the monies.[37] Fascinatingly, for this last year of conflict, 1449-50,

---

[34] AN, Collection Lenoir 74, p. 261. I am grateful to Dr Michael K. Jones for this reference.
[35] BNF, pièce originale 2887 Trolop 3.
[36] BNF, pièce originale 2887 Trolop 2.
[37] BL, Add. Ch. 4064.

we see these few English documentary survivals mixed amongst an increasing number of French materials on the administration of Normandy, the latter including, for instance, payments for guarding the Earl of Shrewsbury as hostage in the palace of Rouen before he was escorted to Dreux.[38] The financial system witnessed full continuity as the rulers of Normandy changed from English to French.

But there is a more important conclusion to draw in the light of the loss of Normandy and the resulting political 'fall out' in England. It is likely that many Englishmen who served during Charles VII's reconquest were not properly or fully paid for their services. In this context it is not surprising that Somerset was accused of failing to pay his soldiers' wages in full.[39] As we saw, even in the early part of his lieutenantship, he had paid companies for only two months out of three. We also hear of the poverty-stricken situation of returning soldiers. The petition in French of those expelled from Maine, dated to 1452, notes not only the lack of compensation for their losses, but also the fact that when they retreated into Normandy that area too was captured so that they 'lost all that remained to them of their moveable goods . . . at the moment the majority of them are utterly ruined and in a state of beggary'. At the end of this document, a Latin addition claims that their petition 'was neither conceded nor carried out. And because of this very many soldiers were reduced to very greatest poverty; some for grief became ill and died; others were imprisoned for theft and were condemned to death by justice; while others still remained as rebels in the kingdom of France'.[40] There is the oft-cited example of 100 marks paid to Thomas, Lord Scales to assist a group of veterans.[41] But this is an isolated example, and scarcely

---

[38] BNF, pièce originale 2180 Paignon 5 (17 Dec. 1449).

[39] J. Stevenson, *Letters and Papers Illustrative of the Wars of the English in France during the Reign of Henry the Sixth, King of England* (2 vols in 3, London, 1861-4), ii(2). 721.

[40] Stevenson, ii(2). 598-603, translated in *Society at War. The experience of England and France during the Hundred Years War*, ed. C.T. Allmand (2nd edn., Woodbridge, 1998), pp. 174-6.

[41] As noted in the exchequer issue roll for the Easter term of 1450 on 29 June 1450 a gift of 100 marks was made to Lord Scales, 'qui de desiderio et mandato regis manucepit ad custodiendum et simul retinendum pro certo tempore hos soldarios ligeos et subditos ipsius domini regis nuper venientes de partibus extraneis in regnum anglie': PRO, E 403/780, m. 9, with warrant for issue at E 404/66/187. On 30 June, he was paid part of a further £50 'ad differendum secundum discrecionem suam circa sustentationem solidariorum pro xv diebus ad intencionem quod hospicium Regis disoneretur de dictis solidariis dicto hospicio ad custos grandos inde adherentibus': PRO, E 403/780, m. 10, with warrant for issue at E 404/66/215. See also E 28/80/83 which concerns this same payment, and is noted by B. P. Wolfe, *Henry VI* (London, 1981), p. 239, n. 2.

generous at that. If soldiers had not been receiving pay in Normandy, then they had been living either at their own expense or at the expense of their captains. If the first, then it would scarcely enamour the returning soldiers to the regime in England; Isobel Harvey has already noted that such men were involved in rebellious actions in 1450.[42] If the second, then captains would also have found the final stages of the defence of Normandy a considerable financial drain. Lands in the duchy were no longer worth much, if anything, even if they lay within the ever-shrinking English-held zone. Some men also had ransoms to pay as a result of the final denouement.

Together, or even separately, such factors must have constituted a considerable drain on personal incomes and a major cause of indebtedness. It puts into context, too, Henry VI's desire to offer some recompense to Somerset through the captaincy of Calais. But as Michael Jones has shown, the Duke of York had also suffered financially, even though he was no longer present in person in the duchy.[43] The loss of Normandy cost the crown dear but it also cost those who had been more personally involved in its defence. Whilst we would no longer subscribe uncritically to Postan's suggestion that the financial crisis in which the nobility found themselves as a result of economic changes in the fifteenth century drove them to 'political gangsterdom',[44] we might give more thought to the grave financial implications of the loss of Normandy, and to the need for the crown to offer some sort of compensation.[45] Not only had soldiers and settlers lost their livelihood but they had probably not been enjoying it for most of the last year or more, even before the French moved in for the kill. As the English abandoned the duchy and returned to England, French accountants in Rouen busied themselves with tidying up the last vestiges of the English administration and turned to compiling and auditing what is now British Library Additional Manuscript 11,509. For them it was 'business as usual'. Warriors might come and go, but accountants will always be with us!

---

[42] I. M. W. Harvey, *Jack Cade's Rebellion of 1450* (Oxford, 1991), p. 131.

[43] M. K. Jones, 'Somerset, York and the Wars of the Roses', *EHR*, 104 (1989), 285-307.

[44] M. M. Postan, 'The Fifteenth Century', *Economic History Review*, 9 (1939), 160-7 at 166.

[45] The issue roll for the Easter term of 1450 (E403/780, m. 11) also notes payments on 2 July of 10 marks and £4 respectively to Adam Blandish and Joanna his wife who had previously held a large lordship in Normandy but had to abandon it and return to England because of loyalty to the king.

3 'One of the mooste pryncipall treasours belongyng to his Realme of Englande': Calais and the Crown, c. 1450-1558

DAVID GRUMMITT

> 'But now it is gone, let it go; it was but a beggarly town, which cost England ten times yearly than it was worth in keeping thereof, as by the accounts Of the Exchequer doth plainly appear'.[1]

Thomas Fuller's gloomy account of Calais under English rule has found its echo in the verdicts of most recent historians.[2] Scholars of late-medieval England have concentrated on the cost of maintaining its defences, while to Tudor historians it has seemed an anachronism, diverting the attentions of government from the demands of an emerging 'British' polity. French historians also have largely ignored English Calais, largely no doubt because of the paucity of surviving material in European archives, but also perhaps because of a simple lack of interest in a place under foreign occupation at the very limits of the French state.[3] Thus there is much that is misunderstood

---

[1] Thomas Fuller, *The Church History of Britain: from the birth of Jesus untill the year 1648* (6 vols., London, 1655), ii. 428.
[2] See, for example, G. R. Elton, *England under the Tudors* (1955), p. 222; J. D. Mackie, *The Earlier Tudors 1485-1558* (Oxford, 1952), pp. 558-9.
[3] French histories of English Calais can be found in G. Daumet, *Calais sous les domination Anglaise* (Arras, 1902); F. Lennel, *Histoire de Calais* (2 vols., Calais, 1909-10) Both rely heavily on a limited range of English sources.

about England's last possession of the continental mainland. The aim of this paper is to consider the relationship between Calais and England in the fifteenth and early sixteenth centuries and to assess whether any fundamental changes in the constitutional position of the town and marches occurred in that period. Was Calais regarded as part of the English or French crowns? In particular this essays offers a re-interpretation of the well known Calais Act of 1536. This piece of legislation, passed by the Reformation Parliament, has long been seen as incorporating Calais within the English realm and altering fundamentally the constitutional position of the town and marches.

It is unlikely that any Englishman or woman in the mid fifteenth century would have recognised Fuller's description of Calais as 'a beggarly town' not worth the money that successive English governments poured into it. It had been captured by Edward III in 1347, the lasting achievement of the Crécy campaign, and the territories held by the English king in 1450 were largely those that had been confirmed in 1360 at the Treaty of Brétigny. Crucially the treaty ceded these territories to Edward in full sovereignty.[4] In 1450 the English Pale stretched eighteen miles from near Wissant in Picardy to Gravelines in Flanders and comprised the town of Calais itself, the county of Guînes, the lordships of Marke and Oye and Sandegate and Hammes.[5] From the coastline it extended between eight and ten miles inland. By 1485 the Pale contained twenty-five rural parishes as well as the parishes of Our Lady and St Nicholas within the town itself. The exact borders of the Pale were ill-defined, having been slowly encroached upon by French farmers.[6] The area of English government was known variously as 'Calais', 'Calais and the marches of the same' or 'the town and marches of Calais'. Although probably first employed in 1436, it was not until the 1490s that the term 'Pale' was commonly used to describe those

---

[4] *Foedera*, vi. 219; John le Patourel, 'The Treaty of Brétigny, 1360', *Transactions of the Royal Historical Society*, 5th series 10 (1960), 19-39 at 24.

[5] See the early Tudor map of the Pale, probably prepared in the 1540s, BL, Cotton MS, Augustus I. II, fo. 71 (reproduced in *The Chronicle of Calais in the Reigns of Henry VII and Henry VIII to the Year 1540*, ed. John Gough Nichols, Camden Society, Old Series 35 (London, 1846), pp. xxviii-xxix).

[6] Viscount Dillon's description of the topography of the Pale, from the rental surveys complied in the 1550s, remains the standard work: 'Calais and the Pale', *Archaeologia* 53 (1892), 289-388. This was largely based on his study of the two rental surveys of the 1550s: BL, Harl. MS, 3880 a survey compiled in 1552 and PRO, E 315/371-2, the much larger survey of 1556.

lands around Calais held by the King of England.[7] The western part of the Pale, characterised by numerous small creeks, ponds and waterways, from Calais to Guînes and encompassing the lordship of Marke and Oye was known to contemporaries as the Low Country. It could be readily flooded and served as the principal natural defence of the Pale. The land bordering France, on the other hand, towards Boulogne and Ardres, was known as the High Country, dominated by the Forest of Guînes which in itself proved something of a natural barrier to attack.

Calais's importance to England was thrown into stark relief in the early 1450s, following the ignominious loss of Lancastrian Normandy and Gascony. An appeal by the crown for loans to fund a relief force for the town in 1454 enumerated its benefits to England: first, the Calais Pale formed a frontier and bulwark for the defence of the realm; second, it was essential to the prosperity of English overseas trade; third, it represented a substantial investment by the crown; and, finally, it would be 'the grettist dishonour, rebuke, sclaundre and shame that myght growe to this reame' if it fell.[8] These sentiments were repeated over a hundred years later by the Venetian ambassador when he described Calais as 'the key and principal entrance' to England without which it 'would not only be shut out from the continent, but also from the commerce and intercourse of the world'.[9] Calais, then, was a vital part of the realm's commercial and military strength. But this situation was not by accident, it was the culmination of a policy begun by Edward III and continued throughout the period of English occupation, the aim of which was to ensure that 'Caleys that ryall towne,/ . . . ever yt mot wel cheve/Unto the crown of mery Yngland'.[10]

---

[7] *The Oxford English Dictionary* cites Fabyan's *Chronicle* of 1494 as the first use of the term 'Pale' to describe the English lands around Calais but see David Grummitt, "For the Surety of the Towne and Marches': early Tudor policy towards Calais', *NMS* (2000), 184-203 at 184 for its first official use in 1436.

[8] *Proceedings and Ordinances of the Privy Council*, ed. N. H. Nicolas (7 vols., London: Record Commission, 1834-1837), iv. 352c-d. The document is misdated to 1436, for its correct date see G. L. Harriss, 'Aids, Loans and Benevolences', *Historical Journal* 6 (1963), 1-19 at 4.

[9] H. Ellis, *Original Letters Illustrative of English History* (11 vols., London, 1824-46), 2nd series ii. 226.

[10] *Political Poems and Songs relating to English History, composed during the period from the accession of Edward III to that of Richard III*, ed. Thomas Wright (2 vols., London, 1861), ii. 156.

In 1347 Edward III had vowed to 're-people agayne the towne with pure Englysshemen'. Significantly, in his account of the capture and settlement of the town, Froissart went on to state that the king also expelled many soldiers, replacing them with English civilians, his intention, presumably, to create what the Tudor chronicler Holinshed described as a 'colonie of England'.[11] In August 1347 the king ordered proclamation to be made that houses would be assigned to Englishmen willing to reside there and on 8 October granted property in Calais to 111 Englishmen.[12] By 1365 the local government of town was in the hands of a mayor and eleven aldermen, the same formula as in most English incorporated boroughs, and throughout the Calais Pale the system of *baillis* and *echevins* was replaced by officials appointed by the crown.[13] The most important Anglicising force upon the town, however, were the merchants of the Staple, first established at Calais in 1363 and, despite a brief sojourn at Middelburg in the 1380s, a constant feature of Calais society to 1558.[14] The merchants of the Staple were probably the most important and vocal of late-medieval pressure groups, a pressure they exerted through their ability to lend the crown large amounts of money. Their view of the importance of Calais had a great influence of English policy throughout the first half of the fifteenth century and their influence may be perceived in the arguments that raged between Humphrey, duke of Gloucester and John, duke of Bedford over the relative importance of Calais and Normandy in the prosecution of English war-policy during the 1430s. Gloucester's servants included prominent staplers such as Richard Whittingham and William Cantelowe. Bedford's replacement as captain of Calais by Gloucester in 1435 was a victory for the latter's resolve 'to leave no one . . . in any doubt that whatever Bedford's attitude (to the importance of Calais) may have been, it was still the most precious jewel in King Henry's crown'.[15]

---

[11] In the words of John, Lord Berner's translation: *The Chronicle of Calais*, p. xxiii; R. Holinshed, *Chronicles*, ed. H. Ellis (6 vols., London, 1807-8), ii. 648-9.
[12] *Foedera*, v. 575; *CPR 1345-1348*, pp. 563-5.
[13] Robert L. Baker, 'The Government of Calais in 1363' in *Order and Innovation in the Middle Ages: essays in honour of Joseph R. Strayer*, ed. William C. Jordan (Princeton, 1976), pp. 208-11; *RP*, ii. 358-9.
[14] Eileen Power, *The Wool Trade in English Medieval History: being the Ford Lectures* (Oxford, 1941), p. 88.
[15] Ralph A. Griffths, *The Reign of King Henry VI* (2nd edn. Gloucester, 1998), pp. 202-3. For the strength of the Stapler's position in the early fifteenth century and their ability to dictate policy towards Calais see David Grummitt, 'The Financial Administration of Calais during the Reign of Henry IV', *EHR* 113 (1998), 277-99.

The commercial importance of Calais both necessitated and provided for an English military presence in the town and marches. The Calais garrison was, during the period of English occupation, the largest concentration of military manpower in the dominions of the English king. The ordinary garrison in the Pale, divided between the town and castle of Calais and the outlying fortresses of Guînes, Hammes, Rysbank Tower (in the harbour) and, from the 1520s, Newenhambridge, numbered some 700 men. To this should be added the reinforcements sent to the Pale in times of military or political crisis. These could often double the size of the garrison in royal pay and during the 1540s increased the military establishment to several thousand. A third group was those men in private wages, the servants of the captains and men at arms in the garrison.[16] Thus a large number of Englishmen, including a high proportion of the political elite of southern England, served at some point in Calais. From the 1470s, when William, Lord Hastings became Lieutenant of Calais, the garrison had close links to the royal household, and these links continued to insure that important members of the English political and military elite had first-hand experience of England's French possessions.[17] Moreover, as Luke McMahon and Edward Meek show elsewhere in this volume, the Pale was central to the conduct of English diplomatic relations with France. Members of the garrison, men like Richard Whetehill in the 1460s and Sir John Wallop in the 1530s and 1540s, were frequently employed as representatives of the English crown. Chief amongst these representatives was the governor of Calais, between 1450 and 1471 styled as the captain of Calais, from 1471 the King's Lieutenant and from 1507 the deputy. The decision to style Lord Hastings as King's Lieutenant in 1471 underlined the place of Calais within the English polity, placing it on a par with other dominions like Ireland. As pointed out by one mid sixteenth century observer of royal protocol the

---

[16] The composition and size of the Calais garrison is discussed at length in my forthcoming book *The Calais Garrison: warfare and military service in England, 1450-1558*.

[17] D. A. L. Morgan, 'The King's Affinity in the Polity of Yorkist England', *Transactions of the Royal Historical Society* 5th series, 23 (1973), 1-25; David Grummitt, 'Calais 1485-1547: a study in early Tudor politics and government' (Unpublished University of London PhD thesis, 1997), chap. 3 where the many links between the Calais establishment and the Tudor royal household are explored in depth.

governor of Calais was 'to have all thinges as if the kyng were there in parson . . . (saving he shall not sytt undre the cloth of astate)'.[18]

The military and commercial establishments in Calais were inextricably linked. From the late fourteenth century the wool merchants had met much of the costs of defence. In periods of effective royal government the taxes raised from the export of wool to the Low Countries via Calais had been collected and spent on the garrison in the town itself and in 1466 this arrangement was formalised in the Act of Retainer, whereby the merchants agreed to collect the customs on wool themselves and apply the whole sum to the maintenance of Calais and its garrison. In this way, until the 1520s, Calais became self-financing.[19] The defence of Calais was of the highest priority for fifteenth century English kings. The town survived the Burgundian assault of 1436 and the threat of French attack in the wake of the fall of Normandy and Gascony. After 1453, and especially after 1461, the built defences of Calais were strengthened and new gunpowder weaponry introduced, making the town and marches appear impregnable. In 1480 Louis XI stated in a letter to Lord Hastings: 'je n'y pense oncques, ne le vouldroys faire ne souffoir toucher au moindre villiage de la terre de Callaix: et quant aucun y vouldroit entreprendre, je le vouldroys deffendre à mon povoir'.[20]

Nevertheless, despite its importance to England, Calais's constitutional relationship with the English crown remained ambiguous throughout the fifteenth century. The treaty of Brétigny had ceded Calais and Guînes to the English crown in full sovereignty. But after the accession in 1422 of Henry VI to the thrones of both England and France the opinion that Calais was part of the French crown grew.[21] Despite affirmation in parliament and in popular perceptions – articulated, for example, in the

---

[18] BL, Add. MS, 71009, fo. 29. For the importance of the change of style of the governor of Calais see David Grummitt, 'William, Lord Hastings and the Defence of Calais, 1471-1483' in *Social Attitudes and Political Structures in the Fifteenth Century*, ed. T. J Thornton (Stroud, 2001), pp. 154-5.
[19] For the history of the financing of Calais see the revision of previous negative accounts in Grummitt, 'Financial Administration' and Grummitt, 'For the Surety of the Towne and Marches', 184-203.
[20] Philippe de Commynes, *Mémoires 1464-1498*, ed. E. L. M. E. Dupont (3 vols., Paris, 1840-47), ii. 219n.
[21] Ralph A. Griffiths, 'The English Realm and Dominions and the King's Subjects in the Later Middle Ages' in *Aspects of Late Medieval Government and Society*, ed. J. G. Rowe (Toronto University Press, 1986), pp. 88-9.

Libelle of Englysche Policye – that Calais was an English town, it maintained an anomalous autonomy from the English crown in matters of legal jurisdiction. In September 1347 Edward III had confirmed the charters granted to the burgesses of Calais by the counts of Artois. These gave criminal and civil jurisdictions to the burgesses distinct from the English common law. A petition of 1380, for example, outlined that the mayor had jurisdiction over land disputes in Calais 'according to the law of England' and in disputes over 'trespasses, debts, accounts and other contracts, according to the law and usage customarily practised there of old' and this was confirmed by Richard II and successive English kings by letters patent. One of the reasons given for this anomolous position was the dangers to and vexation of the Calais burgesses crossing to England to answer pleas in the Westminster courts and the threat their absence posed to the defence and good government of the town.[22] In 1379 the king had confirmed the 'ancient laws and customs' of Calais despite an appeal from some of the burgesses of the town that they might override local custom in order that a husband could bequeath any of his chattels to his wife and *vice-versa*. In 1406 the local laws of Calais, as well as of Ireland, Wales and Gascony, had been confirmed by the king in parliament. Appeals arising from judgements in the local courts and in that of the Staple were directed to the king's council and a great many writs of *certiorari* from chancery relating to Calais disputes exist amongst the Public Records.[23] Although writs of error from the Calais courts were supposed to be directed into King's Bench, the decisions of the English common law courts evidently had little effect in the town and marches and the king's council and, later, the court of chancery were the only sources of appeal: this was made explicit in a petition, probably dating from the 1470s, in which two merchants of the Staple appealed to the chancellor's equitable jurisdiction because 'events at Calais [were] not pleadable in bar at Common Law'.[24] Indeed, the growth of the equitable

---

[22] PRO, DL 41/407; *RP*, iii. 87.

[23] *RP*, iii. 67-8, 586. The writs and returns relating to Calais are in PRO, C 47/24/13-7.

[24] PRO, C 1/59/291; Edward Coke, *Fourth Part of the Institutes of the Laws of England*, (London: E. and R. Brooke, 1797), pp. 281-2. The act confirming the liberties of the merchants of the Staple passed in 1449 also provided that no man should be 'excluded of his lawful suit by writ of error' nor should the king's council be excluded from redressing the defaults of the mayor and constables of the Staple: *RP*, v. 149. In 1492 the king's council, in Calais because of the invasion of France that year, exercised its judicial function determining disputed pleas from the town's courts: PRO, REQ 1.

jurisdiction of the court of Chancery in the second half of the fifteenth century was largely fed by appeals from Wales, Calais and other areas of the realm outside the jurisdiction of the common law.

The impact of the loss of Normandy in 1450 and Gascony three years later on the status of Calais *vis-a-vis* the English crown is unclear. The immediate effect of these calamitous events was to sharpen perceptions of English identity within the Pale and to put into sharper focus the notion of Calais as a frontier of England. Sir Thomas Fynderne, Lieutenant of Guînes castle from 1451 until 1460, made this clear when he attempted a crude demarcation of the boundaries of the Pale in the mid 1450s. Almost a hundred years later it was recalled how 'at Cafrere by a pyt summetyme called the wattering place adiuyning to the saide high waye' Fynderne 'caused a post to be set vp hanging from the same by a Cheyne a sword where vpon these wordes were graven: no man be so hardy to take me awaye ffor this ys the right pale between Ingland and ffraunce'.[25] The late-fifteenth century witnessed the erosion of certain French and Flemish customs in the Pale in favour of English ones. By 1474, for instance, the management of the Pale's dikes and waterways was based upon the customs employed in Romney Marsh, Kent, rather than the hitherto employed Flemish system of 'dyke keepers'.[26] The position of those inhabitants of the Pale who were not 'pure English' – that is, either of whose parents were not English – was also called into question. Between 1422 and 1453 there is little evidence that letters of denisation were seen as a requirement by those Calais inhabitants who did not have established English parentage, only two such grants being recorded on the patent rolls in that period.[27] Between 1453 and 1485, however, ten grants of denisation were recorded. Three such grants were made to members of the garrison at Guînes castle after the garrison had seised wool stocks because of the non-payment of its wages in 1457, but it is significant that recipients also included important burgesses, such as Peter Johnson, and royal officials, like Thomas Howbrake, the keeper of artillery

---

[25] PRO, SP 1/168, fo. 185.
[26] PRO, C 76/158, m. 9.
[27] *CPR 1429-1436*, p. 214, grant to Ingelram Slumpart, esq., whose father was a Picard and mother a Fleming; *CPR 1436-1441*, p. 528, grant to Adrian Grenebourgh, born in Calais but presumably not of English parents.

in Calais.[28] This may be evidence of an assertion of a more belligerent and distinctly English identity in the Pale.

This belligerent Englishness found its fullest expression in the policies of the young Henry VIII, with important ramifications for the Calais Pale. In 1513 the king led an invasion of France from Calais to reassert his claim to the French throne. Although the campaign was only of limited military success, it seems clear that Henry's motives were genuine and he wished to emulate the success of Henry V.[29] Nevertheless, it was as the King of England entering an English town that Henry was received at Calais: he wore a brooch depicting St. George in his hat and on his tunic was embroidered the red cross of England.[30] A year earlier, perhaps in an early assertion of the importance of Calais to the renewed claim to the French throne, the king had made a proclamation that the children of those born there were to be regarded as English, provided they remained in the Pale.[31] Calais later became a symbol of the prowess of English arms. The garrison marked the victory at Agincourt annually as 'a solempne tryumphe, goyng in procession, laudyng God, shotyng gonnes with the noyse and melodye of trumpettes and other instruments, to the great reioysng of your subjects beyng aged, the comforte of them that be able men, [and] the encouragyng of yong children'.[32] This sense of Calais's Englishness was also evident in the preparations for the meeting of Henry VIII and Francis I at the Field of the Cloth of Gold in 1520. Originally Francis was expected to lodge in the town but as the meeting drew nearer, the French insisted that the two monarchs met on neutral ground. This acknowledgement of Calais and the Pale as peculiarly English territory continued during the celebrations themselves: Marshall Chastillon complained that the lists planned for the tournament at Campe were upon English ground. The Earl of Worcester, the Lord

---

[28] *CPR 1452-1461*, pp. 419, 434, 638; *CPR 1467-1477*, pp. 86, 214, 307, 393; *CPR 1477-1485*, pp. 42, 100, 506. For Howbrake see PRO, C 76/155, m. 28.

[29] For Henry's motives see S. J. Gunn, 'The French Wars of Henry VIII' in *The Origins of War in Early Modern Europe*, ed. Jeremy Black (Edinburgh, 1987), pp. 28-51; Clifford S. L. Davies, 'Henry VIII and Henry V: the Wars in France' in *The End of the Middle Ages?*, ed. John L. Watts (Gloucester, 1998), pp. 236-32.

[30] Charles G. Cruickshank, *Henry VIII and the Invasion of France* (2nd edn. Stroud, 1990), p. 16.

[31] *Tudor Royal Proclamations*, ed. P. L. Hughes and J. F. Larkin (3 vols., New Haven, 1964-69), i. 93-4.

[32] S. Anglo, 'An Early Tudor programme for plays and other demonstrations against the Pope', *Journal of the Warburg and Courtauld Institutes* 20 (1957), 178.

Chamberlain, later boasted to Wolsey of his success in gaining an English victory in this respect. Professor Anglo dismissed this as petty rivalry but that underestimates the symbolic importance of Calais as England's foothold on the continent.[33]

The relationship of Calais to the English crown in the first years of Henry VIII's reign can be contrasted with that of Tournai. Tournai was captured after a short siege in 1513, the tangible benefit of that year's campaigning. The Emperor Maximillian, Henry's ally in the war with France, insisted that the town declare itself to be obedient to the crown of France and when Henry entered the town in September it was unambiguously as King of France. As Cliff Davies has recently shown, Tournai was consistently treated as part of Henry's French crown: coins were issued on which Henry was described as 'Franciae et Angliae Rex'; the English governors of the town were styled *baillis*; appeals of judgements made in Tournai were not heard in the court of Chancery but in a separate court established in the town; and Tournai was not treated as part of the English realm in parliament.[34] In 1514 parliament had enacted that contracts and actions of debt in Tournai were to be overseen by Chancery but this in practice appears to have been superseded by the special court set up in Tournai to handle appeals formerly heard in the *parlement* of Paris.[35] This was in contrast to Calais which, although it had been described in 1522, like Tournai, Gascony and the Isle of Man as not 'parcel of the realm [of England],[36] was consistently treated in practice like those other 'members' of the early Tudor kingdom, Wales and Ireland, where the common law did not apply.

The assertion of Englishness in Calais also had a profound effect on the Pale's non-English residents. Their position had always been ambiguous whilst the English king had commanded the allegiance of Gascons, Normans

---

[33] *The Chronicle of Calais*, pp. 86-8; Sydney Anglo, *Spectacle, Pageantry and Early Tudor Policy* (Oxford, 1969), p. 149. The lordship of Fynes, where the meeting was held, had always been considered neutral ground in the wars between England and France: PRO, SP 1/166, fo. 186v.

[34] C. S. L. Davies, 'Tournai and the English Crown 1513-1519', *Historical Journal* 41 (1998), 1-26 at 6-12.

[35] Charles Cruickshank, *The English Occupation of Tournai 1513-1519* (Oxford, 1971), pp. 192-3.

[36] Robert Keilway, *Relationes quorundam Casuum*, ed. John Croke (London, 1602), fos. 202-202v; Davies, 'Tournai and the English Crown', 6.

and French. Non-English, as long as there were born in the king's allegiance, had always played an important role in Calais society. For example, during the 1460s, the Gascon Gaillard Duras served as marshall of the town under the Earl of Warwick. The 1466 muster roll shows that about thirty Gascon exiles were serving under Duras in the Calais garrison.[37] Moreover, before the 1450s the use of languages other than English was common place in the law courts of the Pale, particularly in the Dutch-speaking parts.[38] In 1483, however, in response to French threats to the Pale's borders, the council in London ordered the expulsion of all aliens from the Pale. In 1500 Henry VII introduced general anti-alien ordinances in Calais and Guînes and this was repeated in 1511 and 1529.[39] From 1532 the authorities in England and Calais attempted to solve the 'problem' of aliens by forcing them to buy bills of denisation. The commissioners sent in 1535 to enquire into the state of the government of the Pale backed this policy and the Calais act of the following year contained clauses which prevented aliens from taking part in the economic, political and military life of the Pale. It is clear, however, that this policy met with limited success: in 1537 the Calais council estimated that there were still 400-500 aliens in the town out of a population of some 4,000, while the Pale as a whole contained about 6,000 aliens awaiting denisation. The Tudor policy towards aliens should be seen as part of the general assertion of Englishness in Calais. By the late 1530s this was combined with a real sense of conspiracy: the aliens, outside the allegiance of Henry VIII as temporal and spiritual head of the realm of England, threatened to betray the Pale to the adherents of the Pope. This perception was highlighted in the oath of allegiance demanded of the soldiers of Calais in the early 1540s: it required them to take the king's part against all 'earthlie creatures', to defend the Reformation statutes and declare anything that they discovered to the prejudice of the king or the town and marches of Calais.[40] Tudor hostility to the aliens in the Pale reached a climax in 1543: in September the goods of those aliens still resident in Calais who had not taken up the offer of denisation were seised; in October they were forced to leave the town and herded into a camp near St. Peter's church on the outskirts of Calais; and in November they were expelled from the Pale

---

[37] BL, Add. MS, 46455, fos. 58-65v.
[38] P. T. J. Morgan, 'The Government of Calais 1485-1558' (Unpublished University of Oxford D.Phil thesis, 1966), p. 56 quoting Boston MS. 1519.
[39] PRO, E 28/92/57; SP 1/100, fos. 162-3 (*LP* ix. appendix 16); *LP* xii(1). 8.
[40] PRO, SP 1/174, fos. 185-6, printed as appendix B in Grummitt, 'Calais 1485-1547'.

altogether.⁴¹ To the Welsh soldier-chronicler, Ellis Gruffud, this piece of 'ethnic-cleansing' was 'the saddest thing in Calais, crueller than the treatment of the Christians by the Turks', and added that the policy towards the aliens was inspired by the burgesses' envy of the aliens' commercial success.⁴²

To what extent though was this assertion of Englishness, in part manifested through a hostility to aliens in the Pale, part of a grander design to incorporate Calais fully within the English crown, an expression of the territorial consolidation that characterised the Imperial kingship exercised by Henry VIII? The notion that the 1530s in particular saw a process of consolidation throughout the territories ruled by the English king, enforcing English law, language and patterns of administration, formed – along with administrative change – one of the twin pillars of Professor Elton's thesis of a 'Tudor revolution of government'.⁴³ While recent historians have rejected Elton's claims for a programme of administrative reform, engineered by the energies of Thomas Cromwell, the notion that the 1530s witnessed a systematic attempt to consolidate the peripheries of the realm into a unified English state remains. Reform in Calais, it is argued, was part and parcel of a programme that saw the shiring of Wales, the establishment of regional councils in the North and South-West of England, parliamentary and an attack on legal franchises and liberties, incorporating them into the system of English common law.⁴⁴

The means by which this programme of reform was established in Calais, so the arguments runs, was the Calais Act passed by the Reformation parliament in 1536.⁴⁵ On the face of it, its principal points – the institution of a fixed Calais council, the emphasis on the use of the English language and the parliamentary representation of Calais – do seem to conform to the pattern outlined above, but when the genesis and implementation of the act are examined in detail a rather different picture emerges. The act originated out of a commission, appointed on 2 August

---

⁴¹ *LP* xviii(2). 204, 270-1.
⁴² Quoted in Morgan, 'Government of Calais', p. 57.
⁴³ Elton, *England under the Tudors*, pp. 175-7.
⁴⁴ John Guy, *Tudor England* (Oxford, 1988), pp. 174-6; Steven Ellis, 'Crown, Community and Government in the English Territories, 1450-1575', *History* 71 (1986), 187-204 at 202.
⁴⁵ 27 Hen VIII c. 63 (*SR*, iii. 632-50).

1535 and led by Sir William Fitzwilliam.[46] There is little evidence that the commissioners, whose ostensible *raison d'être* was to investigate the effectiveness of royal government in Calais, were sent at Cromwell's instigation. Henry Lacy, one of Cromwell's clients in the garrison, however, wrote 'I pray to god & it be the kenges plesur that it [the commissioners' report] may take gud affecte And thane shalle it surle be naymed ffor yor [Cromwell's] ded: lyke the workes at dovar is'.[47] In fact the Calais act was in a long-established tradition of issuing ordinances for the government of military outposts. For example, the ordinances issued by the Earl of Warwick for Calais in July 1465 were ratified by the king and issued under Great Seal; similarly, on 28 June 1495 Henry VII issued a comprehensive set of ordinances for the government of Jersey.[48] The primarily military character of the reforms codified in 1536 was shown by the re-issue of the existing regulations for watch and ward in the town, as well as defining, in the text of the statute, the captains' responsibilities, the oaths each took on admission to the office and the exact number and terms of service of the men serving in the garrison. Later, in 1544, the regulations governing Calais were adopted for the newly-conquered town of Boulogne.[49]

There is even less evidence that Cromwell saw the commission as an opportunity to include Calais in a general programme of reform by statute. As late as November 1535 Fitzwilliam informed Lord Lisle, the governor of Calais, that the king's council were unsure whether to implement the commission's findings by proclamation or statute.[50] The original plan, it seems, was for the commission to report and its findings to be implemented by proclamation. It was not until Sir William Fitzwilliam made his report that the notion was floated that some items of reform could only be achieved by statute.[51] The preamble of the act recalled that the king considered the town to be 'one of the mooste pryncipall treasours belongyng

---

[46] *LP*, ix. 236/3.
[47] PRO, SP 1/97, fos. 13-4 (*LP* ix. 440).
[48] Warwick's ordinances are enrolled at PRO, C 76/149, m. 14. For Jersey see A. J. Eagleston, *The Channel Islands under Tudor Government, 1485-1642* (Cambridge, 1949), pp. 9-12.
[49] *LP*, xix(2). 801. In preparation for the government of Boulogne the Calais officers' oaths and various decrees regarding the government of the town made since the 1470s were copied and sent to Henry's new conquest.
[50] *LP*, ix. 4, 118, 766.
[51] *The Chronicle of Calais*, p. 130.

to his Realme of Englande' and that he had resolved to stem the decay caused chiefly, it seems, by the negligence of royal officials there. This phrase did not constitute, as Cliff Davies has argued, the 'transfer [of Calais] from Henry's kingdom of France to his kingdom of England' but recalled notions of Calais being part of and belonging to the English crown that, as we have seen, had a pedigree in both official and popular writing that stemmed back at least to the early fifteenth century.[52]

The most oft-quoted provision of the act was to nominate the officers of the Calais council and their precedence within it. This has usually been seen as part of the same policy that established the 'permanent bureaucratic' Council of the North, the Council of the West and even the institutionalised Privy Council of 1540. John Guy, for example, writes: 'The Calais Act of 1536 created an executive council for the government of the town and Calais Pale'.[53] In fact, the Calais council had its origins in the mid fifteenth century as the household counsel of the captain there. During the 1470s letters had been sealed under the common seal of the 'consiliariorum' of the town of Calais.[54] Under the early Tudors the council had signed letters corporately as an executive board as early as 1515. Moreover, the hierarchy of office-holders outlined in the act merely reflected the social status of the incumbents at the time and took little account of their relative importance in the Calais administration. Lord Sandes, the Lieutenant of Guînes, was a peer and Lord Chamberlain of the king's household and could not be expected to rank lower on the council than the arguably more important posts of Lieutenant of Calais castle and high marshal. Conversely, the acting treasurer, ranked five out of eleven, was Robert Fowler – not even a knight. Historically the post of treasurer had been second only to the governor of the Pale. There is little evidence that the provisions in the act for the Calais the everyday government of the Pale.[55] Indeed, it was not until after July 1540, with the appointment of Henry Fitzalan, Lord Maltravers as deputy of council made much impact on Calais, that the Calais council, in close

---

[52] C. S. L. Davies, 'The Cromwellian Decade: Authority and Consent', *Transactions of the Royal Historical Society*, 6th series 7 (1997), 177-95 at 186.
[53] John Guy, 'Thomas Wolsey, Thomas Cromwell and the Reform of Henrician Government' in *The Reign of Henry VIII: politics, policy and piety*, ed. Diarmaid MacCulloch (Basingstoke, 1995), p. 49. See also David Starkey, "Privy Secrets': Henry VIII and the Lords of the Council', *History Today* 37 (August, 1987), 23-31 at 31.
[54] PRO, C 76/165, m. 7.
[55] Grummitt, 'Calais 1485-1547', pp. 65, 127.

cooperation with the Privy Council, became an effective instrument of government for the Pale.[56]

The second point for which the Calais act has been seen as an instrument of Cromwellian reform was the provision for two MPs to be sent from the town. Two MPs were sent from the town, one elected by the deputy and council and one by the mayor and burgesses. Like the MPs representing English boroughs those from Calais were to be allowed 2s a day for their attendance at Westminster 'in suche maner and fourme as within other Cyties and Boroughes within this Realme [of England] is used and accustomed'. To Elton the parliamentary representation of Calais indicated 'how strongly Henry and Cromwell felt that the House of Commons must represent the whole realm'.[57] A recent commentator has even suggested it amounted to 'a tacit rejection of any separate French kingdom', perceiving an official change in the constitutional position of Calais within the Tudor state.[58] If the printed text of the statute, however, reflects the priorities of its authors it is instructive that the clause relating to parliamentary representation covers only sixteen lines out of the eighteen pages of the act. In some respects the presence in parliament of MPs for Calais only reinstated an informal position that had been allowed to lapse in the late-fifteenth and early-sixteenth centuries. In the 1370s the burgesses of Calais had, on at least two occasions, been present in parliament to present petitions relating to the town.[59] In the early 1400s Calais, and its commercial community in particular, was represented in fact, if not in name, by the return to parliament of many important merchants of the Staple. A good example is William Flete, whose election as one of the knights of the shire for Hertfordshire in November 1414 appears to have been engineered in order to allow him to present a petition on behalf of the Staplers.[60]

Similarly, it is difficult to see how other provisions of the act markedly altered the constitutional position of Calais within the realm. The

---

[56] Ibid., pp. 129-37.
[57] Elton, *England under the Tudors*, p. 177. A point stressed in A. D. K. Hawkyard, 'The Enfranchisement of Constituencies 1509-1558', *Parliamentary History* 10 (1991), 1-26 at 7.
[58] Mark Nicholls, *A History of the Modern British Isles: 1529-1603* (Oxford, 1999), p. 176.
[59] *RP*, ii. 358-60; iii. 67, 57.
[60] J. S. Roskell, Linda Clark and Carole Rawcliffe, *The House of Commons 1386-1421* (4 vols., Stroud, 1992), iii. 89. I owe this reference to the kindness of Dr. Hannes Kleineke.

provision 'for kepyng of the courtes of Guysnes, Marke and Oye' allowed those franchises to keep their jurisdiction over civil cases, trespasses and felonies; the only proviso being that the freemen of the lordships were to hold their courts at the Calais exchequer, subject to scrutiny by the treasurer and comptroller 'to see Justice indifferently . . . admynystred unto the Kynges subjectes'.[61] This was driven solely by the desire to curb the inefficiency and corruption that had characterised the government of these areas in the previous decades: in 1521, for instance, Thomas Prout and other freemen of the lordship of Marke and Oye were accused of taking 'upon them self to be Juges . . . And when any of the kinges tenauntes dyed to seese the kinges landes . . . not into the kinges handes but vnto ther owne handes as Juges of the lawe'.[62] Unlike the legislation passed in the same year for Wales, the Calais act said nothing about extending English common law to the town and marches but stressed that the courts were to be kept according to their 'aunciente severall and distyncte custumes'.[63] The only clause in the Calais act which reflected the notion of territorial consolidation was the exhortation to the holders of benefices 'to procure the Englisshe language used within this Realme of England to be spoken' in their parishes. Nowhere is it apparent, as has been argued, that the act represented 'a policy of anglicisation . . . English replacing French as the language of government'. Although some local courts had been held in French, or more likely Flemish, in the fifteenth century, there is no evidence that, by 1500, anything other than English was the language of the Pale's administration.[64]

The remaining clauses of the act related purely to the internal government of the town, measures to improve security and the regulation of entry into the garrison, underlining the principal aim of the act, the better government of the town and marches: for example, there were clauses concerning the 'Buying and Sellyng of Rowmes and Offices', the 'Kepyng of the Welles wythyn the Towne of Caleys', 'Typlyng Houses' and 'The Observacyon of the Olde Ordynances, Decrees and Proclamacions'. Nothing in the act amounted to a conscious effort to change the constitutional status

---

[61] *SR*, iii. 648. Other legislation in the same session had swept away liberties and franchises in England and in 1543 English common law was introduced in Wales.
[62] PRO, E 101/203/27, fo. 16v.
[63] *SR*, iii. 648. The 1536 act for law and justice to be administered in Wales as in other parts of the realm had enacted that inheritance and land transfer be settled according to the laws of England and 'ne after the fourme of any Welshe Lawes or Customes': *SR*, iii., 563.
[64] *The House of Commons 1509-1558*, ed. S. T. Bindoff (4 vols., London, 1982), i. 284.

of Calais with regards to the English crown. The town and marches were already perceived as a part of the realm of England and, in practice, they had existed within the English polity for almost two hundred years.[65]

*   *   *

In 1558, as the prospect of a French attack on the Pale loomed ever closer, the Marian government appealed for troops for the defence of 'a principal member and chief jewel of our realm'.[66] Ten years later the marquis of Winchester wrote to Elizabeth I on the importance of Calais to England and the need to do something about its return. The sentiments he expressed - the town as a bulwark against continental enemies, its importance for commerce and the honour that would be reflected upon the queen by its return - were exactly those expressed by the loan commissioners over a hundred years earlier.[67] The loss of Calais was a body blow to the early Elizabethan polity, contributing to what Norman Jones has called the 'sheer angst of the 1560s'.[68] For over two hundred years, then, Calais was seen as an integral part of the English polity. Steven Ellis's comments on the way in which the fifteenth and early sixteenth century lordship of Ireland interacted with the other parts of the English state are also applicable to Calais: first, it acted as a model for the government of other frontier regions of the realm; second, it contributed new ideas later to be adopted on a wider scale; and finally, 'its political community actively influenced national politics'.[69] From the mid fifteenth century it was increasingly seen not as part of a lost French kingdom but as a 'member' of the English realm, rather as Wales was described in 1536 'as a verrye membre and joynte of' the Imperial crown of England.[70] Although, unlike Wales, it was not fully incorporated into a unified English realm before its fall in 1558, Calais, nevertheless, remained a vital part of the kingdom, 'un petit morceau d'Angleterre *overseas*'.[71]

---

[65] The only other English historian to have taken this point on board was Hilda Chettle ('Calais and the marches had never been considered as a mere fraction or relic of that kingdom of France which the English kings claimed by right of inheritance under the Treaty of Troyes. The inhabitants were English subjects and their statute law was made at Westminster': 'The Burgesses for Calais 1536-1558', *EHR* 50 (1935), 492-501 at 493).

[66] PRO, SP 11/12/6 (*Calendar of State Papers, Domestic Series, Mary I, 1553-1558*, ed. C. S. Knighton (London, 1998), 681).

[67] PRO, SP 12/46/38.

[68] Norman Jones, *The Birth of the Elizabethan Age: England in the 1560s* (Oxford, 1993), p. 2.

[69] Ellis, 'Crown, Community and Government', 198.

[70] 27 Hen VIII, c. 26 (*SR*, iii. 563).

[71] Joseph Calmette and Déprez, *Histoire de Moyen Age* (Paris, 1937), p. 235.

4 The Practice of English Diplomacy in France 1461-71*
EDWARD MEEK

On 8 March 1468, one of Louis XI's diplomatic agents in England wrote to his master recounting a recent journey to London with the Earl of Warwick, Richard Neville. He was able to report that as Warwick passed through town and countryside 'it seemed to the people that God had descended from the skies; and all cried in one voice, Warwick, Warwick!'. The writer of the letter, William Monypenny, concluded that the Earl had never been so well loved by the people of England than he was at that time.[1] Such were the images reaching France of Edward IV's premier Earl. Warwick's European reputation enabled him to play a vital part in the practice of English diplomacy, especially with France; his influence utterly dominated the attempts between 1464 and 1467 to secure an alliance with England's old enemy. As Edward came to prefer a Burgundian alliance, Warwick's continued determination to find an accommodation with the French proved to be one of the most important reasons for the gradual deterioration of relations between Edward IV and the man who had helped him to seize the throne in 1461. The purpose of this paper is to use the practice of English diplomacy in France as a case study, in order to show by whom English diplomacy was carried out, and how diplomacy with France was administered. It is intended that this will shed light on some much neglected

---

* I would like to thank Dr. Rosemary Horrox and also the members of the Late Medieval Seminar at the Institute of Historical Research for their comments on drafts of this paper.

[1] William Monypenny, seigneur de Concressault, was a Scot who had been in French service since the reign of Charles VII: C. L. Scofield, *The Life and Reign of Edward the Fourth* (2 vols., London, 1923), i. 251. Monypenny's letter is printed in H. Morice, *Mémoires pour servir de preuves à l'histoire ecclesiastique et civile de Bretagne* (3 vols., Paris, 1742-6; repr. Farnborough, 1968), iii. cols. 159-61. The letter and Warwick's personal popularity are also discussed in M. A. Hicks, *Warwick the Kingmaker* (Oxford, 1998), pp. 227-8, 265.

aspects of the late medieval English diplomatic polity and especially the diplomatic activities and influence of the Earl of Warwick.

During the reign of Edward IV, there was no consistent use of resident ambassadors by Northern European powers. Even the presence of a resident ambassador at a court in Northern Europe was still a relatively rare occurrence. Francesco Sforza, Duke of Milan, initiated the first series of Milanese residents at the French court in the early 1460s, although it is clear that they were initially regarded by Louis XI with a great deal of suspicion; he feared that they could act as spies.[2] When it was brought to Louis's attention in 1464 that Sforza intended to establish a resident embassy in France, Louis replied that 'the custom in France is not similar to that of Italy because to maintain a resident in these parts is a suspicious thing'.[3] In fact, until the turn of the sixteenth century, special (or temporary) ambassadors were the most common means of formal diplomatic contact between Northern European powers; they tended to carry out the most important diplomatic missions and all formal negotiations. Unlike residents, special ambassadors were usually empowered to treat for certain specified matters and their diplomatic status was annulled after the completion of a particular set of negotiations. Once those negotiations were completed, it was expected that they should immediately return home. Historians such as Garrett Mattingly have thus been able to emphasise the patchy and interrupted nature of high-status relations between North European powers in comparison to the more continuous relations in operation between those Italian states who had adopted the relatively new invention of the resident ambassador.[4] The patchy nature of English diplomacy has been seen as particularly evident when relations with other countries were poor, perhaps owing to the threat of war, war itself, or piracy at sea.

From Edward IV's accession in 1461 until late 1463, relations between England and France were particularly frosty. Despite the fact that three die-hard Lancastrians, the Duke of Somerset, Lord Hungerford and Sir

---

[2] Joycelene G. Russell, *Peacemaking in the Renaissance* (London, 1986), pp. 68-9.

[3] 'la consuetudine de Franza non è simile a quella de Italia, perchè in queste parte a tenere continuamente uno suo ambasatore pare una cosa de suspeto e non de tuto amore, et a casa vostra he el contrario': *Dépêches des ambassadeurs Milanais en France*, ed. B. de Mandrot & C. Samaran (4 vols., Paris, 1916-23), ii. 125. See also *Dispatches with Related Documents of Milanese Ambassadors in France*, ed. P. M. Kendall & V. Ilardi (3 vols., Illinois, 1970-81), iii. xv-xvii.

[4] G. Mattingly, *Renaissance Diplomacy* (London, 1955), particularly chapter 7.

Robert Whittingham, were abruptly arrested by Louis XI at Eu in August 1461, it seems that thereafter Lancastrian envoys were accepted, and to some extent protected, at the French court.[5] In June 1462, Margaret of Anjou herself visited Louis and signed the Treaty of Chinon, by the terms of which Louis lent Margaret 20,000 *livres* in return for a promise that Henry VI would return Calais to France if the loan was not repaid.[6] So French support, however tentative, for the Lancastrian party ensured that formal and direct diplomatic relations between the Yorkist government and Louis XI were greatly diminished. A thorough search of the chancery records at the Public Record Office reveals that no fully empowered and formally accredited ambassador was sent from England to the continent to treat with Louis XI or his officials from 1461 until the conference of St. Omer in October 1463.[7] Whilst Louis did send ambassadors to England, such as the Seigneur de la Barde, it seems that for much of the time these formal diplomatic missions from France were not reciprocated.[8] On the other hand during the same period of around two-and-a-half years the number of English embassies to Burgundy was vastly greater than those to France. Major English embassies were sent to Burgundy in both 1461 and 1462, headed on each occasion by John, Lord Wenlock.[9]

Even if formal relations between England and France were greatly affected by the aid and refuge given to exiled Lancastrians by Louis XI, a considerable amount of informal diplomacy was still being undertaken. Louis Galet was used as a diplomatic agent to conduct diplomacy with the French from mid October 1461 to February 1462.[10] He was not sent as a

---

[5] See A. de Reilhac, *Jean de Reilhac, secrétaire, maître des comptes . . . des rois Charles VII, Louis XI et Charles VIII* (3 vols., Paris, 1886-9), i. 101. Joseph Calmette and George Périnelle, *Louis XI et l'Angleterre* (Paris, 1930), p. 6.
[6] Jean de Waurin, *Anchiennes cronicques d'Engleterre*, ed. L. M. E. Dupont (3 vols., Paris, 1858-63), iii. 176-7.
[7] Even at the St. Omer conference the English delegation seem to have been distinctly unwilling to meet Louis XI in person: Scofield, i. 306-7.
[8] Ibid., i. 238-40.
[9] See for example PRO, E 403/822, m. 8 (26 Sept. 1461); E 403/824, m. 2 (30 Oct. 1461) and also E 403/827A, m. 8 (20 Nov. 1462).
[10] Galet had plenty of diplomatic experience and had been a resident of Calais for many years where he owned some property. It is noticeable that Galet was among those notorious Yorkists at Calais to whom the duke of Somerset was not allowed to grant a pardon in June 1460: M.-R. Thielemans, *Bourgogne et Angleterre: relations politiques et économiques entre les Pays-Bas Bourguignons et l'Angleterre, 1435-1467* (Brussels, 1966), pp. 369-71; Hicks, *Warwick the Kingmaker*, p. 177, n. 40; *CPR, 1452-1461*, p. 585; *Foedera*, v(2). 80.

special ambassador with official powers to conclude any formal agreements with the French, but merely as an informal agent sent to conduct matters that the king had 'charged him with'.[11] These matters were most likely to have been to ensure effective English representation at the French court in a period when Louis was surely under pressure from the representatives of the exiled Lancastrian Queen, Margaret of Anjou.[12] However, it is important to state that exchequer evidence can never provide a full indication of the extent of low-level and informal diplomatic missions sent from England to the continent. Although it is clear from the exchequer records that Warwick Herald was sent to France during November 1461 for unspecified purposes, he also seems to have visited France again in April 1462.[13] One letter of Charles de Melun to the Count of Charolais, written on 14 April 1462 and preserved in the *Bibliothèque Nationale de France*, provides proof that Warwick Herald had indeed visited France for a second time in the spring.[14] A son of Louis Galet had also arrived in Paris in the company of Warwick Herald and the mission of both men seems to have been to deliver letters from Edward IV, the Earl of Warwick and Louis Galet to the French king. Louis XI hoped that since the letters were addressed so humbly to him, if the Count of Foix showed them to the King of Aragon, that king would not trust in any certain support from England.[15] Aside from the delivery of written messages from the king and the Earl of Warwick, Warwick Herald and the younger Galet may also have been asked to gather news of the latest diplomatic developments and report them to the English government upon their return, since Warwick Herald appears to have entered into informal

---

[11] PRO E 404/72/1/104, payment ordered on 13 Feb. 1462. Galet spent 105 days in France.
[12] For Galet's mission and the presence of Lancastrian sympathisers at the French court during the winter of 1461-62 see Scofield, i. 209-10; Calmette and Périnelle, *Louis XI*, p. 16.
[13] PRO, E 403/824 m. 2.
[14] Philippe de Commynes, *Mémoires*, ed. L. M. E. Dupont (3 vols., Paris, 1840-47), iii. 200-2. The letter is ascribed by Dupont to 1463, but has subsequently been dated by Scofield and Calmette to the more likely date of 1462: Scofield, i. 241, n. 1; Calmette and Périnelle, *Louis XI*, pp. 16-8.
[15] Louis XI's letter (also written in Apr. 1462) to the count of Foix, is to be found in *Lettres de Louis XI*, ed. J. Vaesen and E. Charavay (11 vols., Paris, 1883-1909), ii. 37-9.

conversations with Charles de Melun concerning the state of relations between England and Charles of Charolais.[16]

It is curious that firm evidence for payments to Warwick Herald and Galet's son for their missions to France does not remain in the exchequer records at the Public Record Office. Likewise, proof of some of Warwick Herald's earlier missions to Burgundy in early 1461 is only to be found in the accounts of the ducal receiver general housed in the *Archives Départementales* at Lille.[17] One possible explanation for the lack of evidence for Warwick Herald's missions at the Public Record Office is that they may have been paid and organised outside the direct remit of the exchequer. The Earl of Warwick may have paid Warwick Herald directly and may also, in his capacity as captain of Calais, have overseen the payment of Galet's son from his own Calais funds; the younger Galet had probably been sent directly from Calais, a town with which his family had had strong links for many years. So far more low-level and informal missions were undertaken than the sometimes scanty evidence from the English exchequer records would seem to suggest. Those missions organised and sent directly by the Earl of Warwick, and those sent directly from Calais have left very little trace in English archives. Instead, as we have seen, the little evidence that does remain is to be found in diplomatic letters from the *Bibliothèque Nationale* or Burgundian ducal accounts from the Archives at Lille. The Huntington Library in California also provides us with later evidence (from 1477) that a considerable number of diplomatic missions started at Calais and may have been paid for by the captain or lieutenant of the town.[18] Thus, formal ambassadorial missions might have been sent on a patchy basis, especially in times of acute international tension, but it was certainly the case in the later Middle Ages that low-level and informal missions were sent pretty much constantly.

The conference of St. Omer (held first at St. Omer and then Hesdin in September and October 1463) proved to be an important turning point in relations between Louis XI and the Yorkist government. The diplomatic skill of Philip the Good of Burgundy had proved instrumental in bringing the

---

[16] Commynes, *Mémoires*, iii. 201-2. Charles de Melun accused Warwick Herald of being neither 'secret nor sober of language'. The herald had let slip that the English were fearful of the consequences of the death of Philip the Good (who was said to be ill); in England, apparently, Charles of Charolais was believed to be hostile to the Yorkists.
[17] ADN, B 2040, fos. 237, 268.
[18] Huntington Library, San Marino, CA., Ms. HA 13789, fos. 5-6v.

English ambassadors to the presence of the French King; and at last Louis promised not to make war against Edward and promised not to give 'Ayd or Favour to Henry late calling himselfe Kyng of England, Margarete his Wyff, nor her Sonne'.[19] As relations between England and France began to improve from early 1464, evidence for both informal and formal contact on the continent between French and English representatives becomes much more plentiful. We have seen that a few of the previous low-level missions to France were carried out by men connected to the Earl of Warwick, such as Warwick Herald. But from 1464 one can begin to see the stranglehold which Warwick and his officers were able to exert over the conduct of English diplomacy in France.

A series of five letters relating to the early months of 1464 exist to show that in the first few months of 1464 direct contacts took place at Calais, and at nearby Guînes, between French officials and Richard Whetehill, Warwick's Lieutenant of Guînes.[20] In February and March 1464, Whetehill met Louis's representatives to discuss developments in the diplomatic situation. Before 19 February, Whetehill was visited at Guînes by Jean de Tenremonde ('dit le Begue'), one of Louis XI's secretaries; and they probably finalised the arrangements for the mission of Jean de Lannoy to England, which was to take place a few weeks later.[21] On 31 March 1464 another of Louis's officers wrote from Abbeville explaining that he also had been in discussions with Richard Whetehill about the results of Jean de Lannoy's mission to England. The writer of the letter had to admit to the French King, however, that little news had come to Whetehill's attention of the success or failure of those negotiations. They discussed at great length topics such as the return to England of the embassy of Henry IV of Castille.

---

[19] *Foedera*, v(2). 117-8.
[20] The series of letters from 1464 is as follows: Whetehill to Louis XI, from Guînes 19 Feb. 1464 (Appendix III in Scofield, ii. 467); Jean de Tenremonde to Louis XI, from Lille 29 Feb. 1464 (BNF, Ms. Français, 2811, fo. 53); Jean de Tenremonde to Louis XI, from Rochester 19 Mar. 1464 (Appendix IV in Scofield, ii. 468); Jean de Tenremonde to Louis XI, from Paris 25 Apr. 1464 (BNF, Ms. Français, 2811, fo. 63), this letter has no year, but Tenremonde's description of his visits to Calais and Guînes must surely date the letter to 1464 (Jean de Tenremonde, dit le Begue, and this letter are also discussed in A. Lapeyre & R. Scheurer, *Les notaires et secrétaires du roi: sous les règnes de Louis XI, Charles VIII et Louis XII (1461-1515)* (2 vols., Paris, 1978), ii. 303); anonymous letter (known as the Abbeville Letter) to Louis XI written from Abbeville on 31 Mar. 1464 (Waurin, *Cronicques*, iii. 182-6).
[21] See Whetehill's letter to Louis XI, written on 19 Feb. 1464: Scofield, ii. 467.

Whetehill also seems to have complained to Louis's envoy about the actions of a French subject, one 'Pierre Cousinot' who had apparently been involved in the Lancastrian campaign in the North based around the border castle of Bamburgh; evidently Guillaume Cousinot was meant in this case, for he was certainly present at Bamburgh on 22 February, when some diplomatic instructions were issued to him in the name of Henry VI.[22] Although Whetehill's diplomatic activities were little more than informal meetings, rather than fully fledged negotiations, they were nevertheless essential to the continuing improvement and normalisation of relations between England and France.

As Lieutenant of Guînes, Whetehill occupied a vital role in England's diplomatic polity. It was his duty not only to meet with French representatives, but also to channel diplomatic information from France (and other places) to England; he was also responsible for the safe delivery to the Continent of letters coming from England. All the evidence from early 1464 suggests that this was a heavy responsibility, and a considerable burden on his time. Whetehill's own letter of 19 February 1464 tells us that he had passed on Louis XI's previous messages to Edward IV, his chancellor, George Neville, and the Earl of Warwick. Whetehill also promised that Louis's new messages, recently delivered to Calais by Jean de Tenremonde, would be sent to the Earl of Warwick 'in all diligence' by one of the Earl's other officers.[23] Likewise, the writer of the Abbeville letter noted that Whetehill had received a letter from the Earl of Warwick which was then sent directly to Louis. The lieutenant must have taken his responsibilities for the dissemination of diplomatic information extremely seriously as he had even translated the letter from English into French for Louis's convenience. Whetehill also asked that Louis should be informed that the chancellor of England intended to cross the sea in order to attend the conference which had been arranged for 21 April 1464 'pour l'apaisement des differens . . .', although Whetehill hoped that Lannoy's mission would be so successful that another conference would be unnecessary.[24] In addition, Whetehill, as Lieutenant of Guînes, was also responsible for the organisation of a

---

[22] Waurin, *Cronicques*, iii. 182-6. For Cousinot see Scofield, i. 324, n. 1.
[23] Ibid., ii. 467.
[24] '. . . je n'ay peu riens scavoir de luy [Jean de Lannoy] sinon ce qu'il vous pourra apparoir par une lettre que M[onsieu]r de Warvich luy a rescriptes que vous envoie, ensemble la copie d'icelles translatés d'anglois en franchois de la main dudit Richart': Waurin, *Cronicques*, iii. 182.

considerable amount of espionage, presumably mostly carried out against the French.[25]

It is quite clear that many of Richard Whetehill's diplomatic activities were undertaken directly on the behalf of the Earl of Warwick. We have seen already that the lieutenant was constantly forwarding letters from Louis XI to the Earl, and that Whetehill was responsible for the delivery of the Earl of Warwick's own letters to France.[26] Even when Louis's letters were personally addressed to Whetehill, he was obliged to report the contents of the letter to his master, as he reveals in his letter of 19 February 1464.[27] A vast amount of diplomatic business concerned the Earl of Warwick, and emanated from him, because it was with him that continental powers wished to deal. There had been considerable disappointment in 1463, for example, when Richard Neville failed to attend the conference of St. Omer; commitments in the North of England had meant his attendance was impossible. Before the Franco-Burgundian envoy, Jean de Lannoy, left for England in March 1464 Jean le Begue showed him Warwick's letters which Whetehill had given him 'in order that he might be informed of the will of my lord of Warwick'.[28] It was knowledge of Warwick's opinion that was felt to be crucial in preparation for any diplomatic mission to England. In fact Warwick's influence on English policy was felt to be so great that the writer of the Abbeville letter joked that there were 'two chiefs in England, of which the Earl of Warwick is one, and the second chief's name I have forgotten'.[29] Warwick's influence appeared to be all the greater since a foreign secretariat was being operated from Calais by his officers. This secretariat was directly overseen by the Earl, and responsible to him.

At this point, there is no evidence to suggest that Edward IV was anything other than willing to allow the Earl of Warwick such considerable influence over the conduct of English diplomacy with France. If the king permitted Warwick to undertake independent communications with Louis XI through his secretariat at Calais, and allowed virtually all diplomatic contact in France to be carried out by Warwick's officers or associates, it was because Warwick's long diplomatic experience of such matters meant

---

[25] PRO, E 101/197/4, fos. 33v-4.
[26] BNF, Ms. Français, 2811, fo. 53.
[27] Scofield, ii. 467.
[28] BNF, Ms Français, 2811, fo. 53; 'affin q[ui]l soit adverty de la volente de mond[it] S[eigneu]r de Warwych'.
[29] Waurin, *Cronicques*, iii. 184.

that it was convenient for the king to do so. Warwick had, after all, accumulated considerable experience in the art of diplomacy since he had been made captain of Calais in 1455, a post which required frequent diplomatic contact with the neighbouring powers of France and Burgundy.[30] The arrangement between Edward and Warwick was naturally dependent on complete agreement on the direction of foreign policy. In the early years of the reign there was no real possibility of disagreement since the obvious choice of policy was to maintain good relations with Burgundy and thereby arrive at an accommodation with the French through the mediating efforts of Philip the Good. On this king and earl were agreed. If the Lancastrians were to be prevented from gaining aid and refuge from France this course of action was vital, eventually culminating in the agreements at Hesdin in October 1463 and the truce at sea, agreed with France in April 1464.[31] But the first real test of the arrangement between Edward and Warwick came later in 1464 over the vexed question of Edward's marriage. Apparently, during another of Warwick Herald's visits to France in April 1464 the French King had first brought up the proposition that Edward might marry one of his sisters-in-law, another being offered to the Duke of Milan's son, Galeazzo-Maria. According to the Milanese ambassador present, Louis even offered to pay the dowry.[32]

In early July 1464 Warwick's closest associates, John, Lord Wenlock (his lieutenant at Calais) and Richard Whetehill, travelled to Hesdin in order to meet Louis XI and Philip the Good in order to prolong the truce between England and France and to again prorogue the formal conference between England, France and Burgundy to 1 October (it had previously been postponed until 1 July).[33] Wenlock, with eighteen people in his company, stayed at Hesdin for nine days from his arrival on 5 July until

---

[30] For Warwick's earlier career see Hicks, *Warwick the Kingmaker*, pp. 141-9 and also Thielemans, *Bourgogne et l'Angleterre*, pp. 368-9.
[31] *Foedera*, v(2). 121-2; Scofield, i. 325, n. 3.
[32] *Dépêches Milanais*, ii. 75-81; Scofield, i. 326. It is to be noted that evidence for Warwick Herald's mission is again not to be found in the records of the exchequer.
[33] *Foedera*, v(2). 122, 124; Wenlock and Whetehill's commission to treat with Louis was issued on 8 June 1464. Philip was at Hesdin from 23 June until 7 October: H. Vander Linden, *Itinéraires de Philippe le Bon, duc de Bourgogne (1419-1467) et de Charles, comte de Charolais (1433-1467)* (Brussels, 1940), pp. 469-73.

the fourteenth of the month.[34] Philip provided magnificent hospitality and on at least one occasion (on Sunday 8 July) the English ambassadors were lavishly feasted 'aux fontaines du parc'.[35] The mediating influence of Philip the Good again proved valuable, as the truce between England and France, by land and sea, was prorogued from 1 October 1464 until 1 October of the following year.[36] During Wenlock's agreeable sojourn at Hesdin, he, along with Whetehill, made an excursion lasting one day to meet Louis at the castle of Dompierre; an important occasion since this was the first time in Edward's reign that fully empowered English ambassadors had chosen to treat with the French in French territory (rather than in the more neutral settings of St. Omer and Hesdin, in the territories of the Duke of Burgundy).[37] It was at Dompierre that the English ambassadors were introduced to the two sisters of the Queen of France, and again Louis brought up the question of Edward's marriage with Bona of Savoy, and undertook informal negotiations with Wenlock as to the possibility of such a match. Wenlock of course had no powers to agree to the marriage, but, at least according to Georges de Chastellain, he seems to have given Louis the impression that he would argue for the Savoy marriage in England.[38]

Warwick was also quite enthusiastic to pursue the marriage and it was widely believed on the continent that Warwick himself would cross the channel to supervise its negotiation.[39] On 21 September 1464 Alberico Maletta wrote that Duke Philip and the French King were still waiting for Warwick to cross the sea 'per tractare la pace et lo parentato'.[40] All the tentative discussions concerning the Savoy marriage which had been carried out by Warwick Herald, Wenlock and Whetehill during the spring and summer of 1464 were thrown into disarray when Edward dramatically revealed at the Reading council meeting in September that he had already been secretly married on 1 May to Elizabeth Woodville. Although rumours of Edward's marriage had been circulating at the French court for weeks, by

---

[34] ADN, B 2051, fos. 353r-v. The ducal receiver laid out 124*liv*. 15s. 6d. for Wenlock's living expenses.
[35] ADN, B 2051, fos. 127v-8.
[36] BNF, Ms. Français, 6970, fo. 323.
[37] ADN, B 2051, fos. 353-v. It is not actually clear on which day between 5 and 14 July that the English ambassadors actually visited Louis at Dompierre.
[38] Scofield, i. 346. G. de Chastellain, *Oeuvres*, ed. K. de Lettenhove (8 vols., Brussels, 1863-6), v. 24.
[39] *Dépèches Milanais*, ii. 276.
[40] Ibid., ii. 260-1.

10 October the marriage was publicly and officially accepted as a fact.[41] It has recently been pointed out by Michael Hicks that this development did far less to sour relations between King and Kingmaker than is normally assumed; in fact, Warwick was hardly committed to the French marriage and certainly not to an entirely pro-French foreign policy.[42] However, it must at least have been extremely galling for him to find out that Edward's marriage with Bona of Savoy had in fact been out of the question for months, despite the fact that men closely connected to him, such as Wenlock, Whetehill and Warwick Herald, had already carried out informal negotiations for the marriage, and that Warwick himself had been expected to personally arrange the formalities of the marriage with the French King.

When Louis XI told the Milanese ambassador of a rumour he had heard, that there was 'discord between King Edward and Warwick', this was probably an exaggeration of the real state of affairs based on inaccurate gossip and rumour.[43] For when a resigned John Wenlock wrote on 3 October that news of the marriage had caused the 'great displeasure of many of the great lords, and equally to the most part of the whole of the king's council', he also went on to say that the matter had 'proceeded so far' that the marriage should simply be regarded as a *fait accompli* and that one should remain patient.[44] Wenlock further explained that since the announcement had been most unexpected, it was decided that the Earl of Warwick should delay his proposed voyage across the Channel until the king had made his wishes known concerning the matters to be discussed during the earl's mission, namely the further extension of the truce or the possibility of a long-term treaty of peace.

With hindsight it appears that the whole episode indicates a growing self-assertiveness on the part of the king (particularly in terms of diplomatic affairs) that Warwick, in the end, was probably going to be unable to accept. But in the short term, from the autumn of 1464, it appears that diplomacy with France was conducted as it had been before. It was one of the Earl of Warwick's agents who was sent to France in order to explain Edward's marriage, and particularly the reasons for Warwick's decision to delay his

---

[41] Ibid., ii. 276, 292, 'Aviso la V. S^{ria} che de qua publicamente fu dicto e certificato ch'el re de Ingiltera ha tolto per mogliere una dona de Ingiltera, e fu dicto per amore'.
[42] Hicks, *Warwick the Kingmaker*, pp. 260-1.
[43] *Dépêches Milanais*, ii. 304-5.
[44] Wenlock's letter is to be found in BNF, Ms Français, Nouv. Acq., 7634, fo. 69.

trip to the continent.[45] On 23 October Warwick's agent, Robert Neville, arrived in Rouen *en route* to the courts of both France and Burgundy and brought news that relations between Warwick and Edward were not entirely smoothed-over, but that the king was still willing to consider a peace treaty with France.[46] Neville's own letter, written from Lille on 17 November 1464, makes it clear that many of his duties were carried out on the direct behalf of the earl, for the first point that Neville saw fit to make was Louis's avowed affection for the Earl of Warwick. It is also significant that Neville's letter was addressed to Richard Whetehill 'monsieur the lieutenant'; Warwick's foreign secretariat was still operating smoothly from Calais despite the failure of the French marriage.[47]

However, we should not assume that Warwick's capacity for independent diplomatic action threatened the Yorkist polity directly in 1464, for if Warwick was slightly keener than Edward on a firm accommodation with France, he may have felt that the king would eventually be persuaded to his point of view. At this point, and in the following year, Warwick and Edward IV's aims still broadly coincided; namely, that reasonable relations be kept up with both France and Burgundy. In 1465 Warwick was finally able to visit the continent in person; he was the head of an imposing embassy to Calais, sent with full powers to treat with the Duke of Burgundy, his son Charles of Charolais, the Duke of Brittany and the King of France.[48] The membership of these diplomatic commissions cannot have displeased Warwick, for they included men with whom he was extremely close: John Wenlock was included, as was Richard Whetehill. Thomas Kent and Thomas Colt also found their place in the diplomatic sun; Kent was later described as one of Warwick's closest councillors, and Colt was a Neville

---

[45] BNF, Nouv. Acq. Français, 7634, fo. 69: 'mons[eigneu]r le conte de warrewik envoie a p[rese]nt p[ar] devers le Roy [Louis XI] et mons[eigneu]r le duc vng sien serviteur avecques des l[ett]res Remonstrant le cause de sa demoure par de ça..'.

[46] Robert Neville was a member of Warwick's retinue at Calais: BL, Add. MS., 46455, fo. 58. 'Heri giunse qua quello secretario del conte de Veroih, del quale el Re me disse questi dì passati, et anchora se continua che el dicto conte è in division cum el re Odoardo. Alcuni dicono però questo secretario essere venuto per dire a questo re che se luy vole attendere a la pace, che el re Odoardo he contento de mandare perbenché luy habia tolto quella mogliere de Ingleterra e non la cognata de questo re . . . ': *Dépêches Milanais*, ii .323,

[47] Commynes, *Mémoires*, iii. 211; *Dépêches Milanais*, ii. 304-5.

[48] *Foedera*, v(2). 130. (8 May 1465). William, Lord Hastings, the king's chamberlain, was also sent to Calais and was later paid for seventy three days attendance there, from 11 May when he left London until 22 July when he returned: PRO, E 404/73/1/69.

retainer of many years standing. When the Burgundians left Calais around 21 July, nothing had been achieved other than the organisation of another meeting to be held on 1 October 1465.[49] Negotiations with a French representative, Georges Havart, Seigneur de la Rosière, also took place at Calais (a town which not only provided a useful point of organisation for English diplomacy but also a convenient meeting-place for formal embassies).[50] Very little was achieved during the summer's negotiations, most likely because the War of the League of Public Weal provided a considerable complication, none of the opposing continental parties could afford to devote too much time to distracting negotiations with England.[51]

By early 1466 it seems clear that Warwick's growing desires for an Anglo-French rapprochement were being translated into diplomatic action. It is noticeable that it was his agent, Robert Neville, who undertook all of the informal diplomatic missions from England to France at this point. In a schedule of payments listing various sums expended by the treasurer, Walter Blount, Lord Mountjoy, between 24 November 1464 and 1 March 1466, at least four payments were made to Robert Neville for missions to France.[52] But before March 1466, Edward IV received a visitor whose mission was to offer the king a husband for his sister, Margaret of York.[53] The husband was to be none other than Charles of Charolais, heir to the Dukedom of Burgundy. It was this match, and the consequent closeness of Anglo-Burgundian relations, that was to spell the end for Warwick's plans for a long-term treaty with France. The marriage offer made to Edward was not immediately agreed and instead Warwick was again made the head of another embassy to Calais, Boulogne and St. Omer. On 22 March 1466 Warwick was empowered with his close colleagues of the previous year to treat with France, and Burgundy as well.[54] It may not have pleased Warwick that he was expected to treat for a marriage between the Count of Charolais and Margaret of York. In any event the marriage was not agreed; and it may

---

[49] For Kent see Waurin, *Cronicques*, iii. 190; for Colt see Hicks, *Warwick the Kingmaker*, pp. 20, 30, 39. For the negotiations in general, Thielemans, *Bourgogne et l'Angleterre*, p. 416.
[50] A summary of Havart's powers is to be found in *Lettres de Louis XI*, ii. 309-10.
[51] Scofield, i. 380-6.
[52] PRO, E 404/73/1/124B.
[53] Guillaume de Clugny had visited England early in the year and was given a gift of 100 marks: PRO, E 404/73/1/124B; Richard Vaughan, *Charles the Bold* (1973), p. 45.
[54] *Foedera*, v(2). 138-9.

be indicative of Warwick's true ambitions that all that was agreed during the summer was another truce between England and France.[55] Edward equally may not have been pleased that negotiations for the marriage of his sister came to nothing. To remedy the situation he decided upon a course of action that was to split the Yorkist diplomatic polity and threaten the influence of the Earl of Warwick over the conduct of English diplomacy that he had been permitted to have in the early years of Edward's reign.

During the winter of 1466-7 a constant stream of embassies travelled between England and Burgundy; Alard de Rabodenghes and Josse de Halewijn (*souverain-bailli* of Flanders) spent seven months in England from 15 December 1466 until 23 July 1467.[56] Likewise, in March, April and May 1467 an English embassy comprising Richard Beauchamp, Bishop of Salisbury, Thomas Vaughan, an esquire of the body, and William Hatclyff, the king's secretary, spent time in Bruges, Brussels and Ghent undertaking preliminary talks for the Burgundian marriage.[57] It was during the negotiations for the Burgundian marriage that Edward's diplomat *par excellence* came to prominence: William Hatclyff, the king's secretary, was to be almost continually used on diplomatic missions from 1467-76. Lesley Stark has already effectively demonstrated that Edward had deliberately chosen to gather together a new corps of diplomats (such as Hatclyff, Vaughan and Beauchamp) for negotiations with Burgundy.[58] It is quite noticeable that many of those diplomatic envoys who had been associated in the past with Warwick or with his embassies to the continent were conspicuously absent from Edward's commissions for negotiations with Burgundy for the marriage. John Wenlock, Richard Whetehill, Thomas Kent and Thomas Colt, from playing an influential role in English diplomatic practice, now found themselves deliberately sidelined from the negotiations most favoured by the king. Less imposing and more informal missions sent to Burgundy were not carried out by Warwick Herald or by Robert Neville.

---

[55] The truce was signed on 24 May 1466 and was to last until 1 Mar. 1468: *Lettres de Louis XI*, iii. 87-9.

[56] ADN, B 2061, fo. 122v; M. Ballard, 'Anglo-Burgundian Relations, 1464-1472' (DPhil thesis, University of Oxford, 1992), pp. 42-9. This embassy was given £100 in reward by Edward 'It[e]m paied to the Sov[er]ayne of Flaundres and othir Ambassadoures of Burgoine the xix[th] day of March Anno vij° . . . ': PRO, E 404/73/3/73B.

[57] ADN, B 2064, fos. 107, 143v-4, 154v, 176v-7, 209-v.

[58] L. Stark, 'Anglo-Burgundian Diplomacy, 1467-1485' (MPhil thesis, University of London, 1977), chap. 2.

Clearly, Edward was not going to permit his chosen policy of a marriage with Burgundy to be prevented by the more pro-French policies favoured by Warwick and his associates from past missions to France. Continental observers must have felt that Warwick's influence with Edward, and the prestige of his diplomatic colleagues, were not what they had once been, or at least were believed to have been.

In the spring and summer of 1467 a diplomatic battle was being waged in London. The Burgundian embassy of de Rabodenghes and Halewijn had been supplemented temporarily by the presence of Olivier de la Marche and Antoine Lameth.[59] Their mission seems to have been to negotiate a defensive treaty with Burgundy in preparation for the marriage alliance, and to respond to English complaints about Philip's embargo against English cloth.[60] Moreover, a French delegation, which included the French admiral, Louis, Bastard of Bourbon, had also arrived in the city. From Louis's statement to the Milanese ambassador, Emanuele de Iacopo before 18 April 1467, it seems that the French embassy had come to make a counter-offer: an offensive alliance against Burgundy. Richard of Gloucester would marry Louis's second daughter, whose dowry would comprise part of the Burgundian territories, and an alternative match would be found for Edward's sister.[61] Throughout this diplomatic fencing-match Warwick attempted to persuade the king to accept the French offer, for at that time Louis was writing that Warwick 'had always been a friend to his crown' and the French king believed that through Warwick he had already arrived at a secret agreement with Edward. It just remained for Warwick to travel to France 'to conclude everything'.[62] Despite the fact that Louis had clearly misjudged the ease with which Warwick could alter Edward's growing preference for an alliance with Burgundy, Edward was indeed willing to allow Warwick to head another English embassy to France, after all no definite conclusions with the Burgundians had yet been reached and the negotiations with them had dragged on at great length; Edward may simply have been attempting to force Charles and Philip into a deal.

When Warwick arrived at Canterbury with the returning French ambassadors on 27 May 1467, he was accompanied by all of his colleagues

---

[59] ADN, B 2064, fo. 138.
[60] Scofield, i. 410-2.
[61] *CSP Milan, 1385-1618*, no. 119.
[62] Ibid.

who had found themselves surplus to the king's requirements for his negotiations with Philip of Burgundy and his son. John Wenlock, Thomas Colt and Thomas Kent, after a gap of over a year, again found themselves acting as Edward's ambassadors to Louis XI.[63] Setting sail for Honfleur on 28 May, Warwick and the other ambassadors (including an ambassador from the King of Scotland, the Bishop of Aberdeen) along with the earl's numerous esquires, ushers, pages, archers, heralds and trumpets, arrived at La Bouille near Rouen on 6 or 7 of June. Although several of Warwick's servants and his *maître d'hôtel*, Robert Buckland, had already been at Rouen until 29 May arranging the provisions 'pour la venue d'icelui conte de Warwyk son maistre'.[64] Then, after spending six days with Louis XI in Rouen until 16 June, Warwick's party departed for Honfleur via la Bouille, Caudebec and Quillebeuf, eventually putting to sea on 23 June and arriving at Canterbury six days later.[65] Louis XI's hospitality had been immense. Even the most menial of Warwick's many servants were handsomely rewarded; twelve silver cups were given to Jacques de Haye, another *maître d'hôtel* of the Earl. Warwick Herald received 126*liv*. 6*s*., and the earl's archers and trumpets received a further 234*liv*. 7*s*. 6*d*. to share between them.[66]

Louis had hoped that the earl would sign a lengthy peace treaty between England and France in Rouen, for the French King was particularly afraid that a marriage between Charles of Charolais and Margaret of York would, 'par moien dudit mariage', lead on to further alliances between England and Burgundy instead.[67] However, news of the illness of Philip the Good may have cut short the negotiations.[68] So Louis ensured that Warwick was accompanied home by another French delegation consisting of Antoine du Bec-Crespin, Archbishop of Narbonne, the Bastard of Bourbon, William Monypenny, Seigneur de Concressault, Jean de Popincourt, Olivier le Roux

---

[63] *Foedera*, v(2). 144; *Christ Church Canterbury*, ed. W. G. Searle, Publications of the Cambridge Antiquarian Society, 34 (1902), pp. 1-196 at 98-9.

[64] C. de Beaurepaire, 'Notes sur six voyages de Louis XI à Rouen', *Précis analytique des travaux de l'académie impériale des sciences, belles-lettres et arts de Rouen* (1856-7), pp. 284-334 at 327-33 (Pièce Justificative No. 7).

[65] De Beaurepaire, 'Notes sur six voyages', p. 327; *Christ Church Canterbury*, p. 99.

[66] De Beaurepaire, 'Notes sur six voyages', pp. 329-30.

[67] *Lettres de Louis XI*, iii. 144, 154-9.

[68] As suggested by Scofield, i. 425.

and Alexandre Sextre.⁶⁹ But if Edward was willing to let Warwick and his colleagues travel to France to discuss such a peace treaty he was certainly not willing to submit to the proposals which were made to him by the French delegation. This was despite the fact that Louis may even have offered Edward, in return for an offensive alliance against Burgundy, the tempting possibility of papal arbitration concerning Edward's claim over Aquitaine and Normandy.⁷⁰ Although the French ambassadors followed the king from London to Windsor (where they then spent many weeks), it was clear that they were chasing a lost cause.⁷¹ As the French ambassadors were just about to leave, on 14 August, Edward ordered the confirmation of a treaty of amity and mutual defence with Charles the Bold, which bound Edward, his heirs and successors to protect the estate and person of Charles 'contre tous'.⁷² So when Warwick accompanied the French ambassadors to Canterbury for the last time, he can have been in no doubt that, for the moment, Edward was unlikely to be persuaded to adopt the earl's plan for an alliance between England and France.⁷³ The common belief that the Earl of Warwick possessed considerable influence over the direction of Edward's foreign policy and over the conduct of his diplomacy began to alter overnight. Warwick's views on a long-term alliance with France had clearly been ignored. Meanwhile, Warwick's reputation had been badly damaged. Just after the arrival of Louis's returning embassy in August 1467, the French King told an ambassador of the Duke of Milan that 'as a fact he has had nothing but words from the Earl of Warwick' and a few weeks later again complained 'that the Earl of Warwick has made so many promises without fulfilling anything'.⁷⁴

As it turned out, Warwick's embassy of 1467 proved to be the last siseable grouping of English diplomats sent to France until the middle of

---

⁶⁹ *Lettres de Louis XI*, iii. 157-8.
⁷⁰ Scofield, i. 426-7.
⁷¹ PRO, E 403/838, m. 6; E 405/46, rot. 2d.
⁷² Edward's order of 14 Aug. to the keeper of the privy seal ordering him to issue letters to the Chancellor for confirmation of the treaty under letters patent is printed in *Le Cotton manuscrit Galba B.I.*, ed. L. Gilliodts-van Severen (Brussels, 1896), pp. 461-2, no. CLXXXVII. The letters patent were issued by the chancellor on the following day: P. Bonenfant, 'Actes concernant les rapports entre les Pays-Bas et la Grande-Bretagne de 1293 à 1468', *Bulletin de la commission royale d'histoire*, 109 (1943), 53-125 at 106-7. Charles had previously signed the treaty on 15 July: *Foedera*, v(2). 145; PRO, E 30/527.
⁷³ *Christ Church Canterbury*, p. 101.
⁷⁴ *CSP Milan, 1385-1618*, no. 121.

Edward's second reign. Now, relations between England and France returned to the tense situation that had characterised the early part of Edward's reign. From late 1467 to mid 1470 only one accredited ambassador was sent from England to France; and records of only two heraldic missions exist for the same period.[75] However, it is still possible to detect a variety of informal missions sent from England to France (seemingly at the instigation of the Earl of Warwick).[76] Hence we still find that on 24 December 1467 one of Warwick's agents, Robert Neville, had arrived back in England after travelling from France with Louis's agent, William Monypenny.[77] Contrary winds forced them to land in Kent, although they had planned to travel directly to Warwick himself, then based at his estates in the North. When Monypenny wrote to Louis XI on 8 March 1468, he expected that he and Neville would return to France in a few days.[78] The secrecy and informality of Neville's missions meant that the king would have found it very difficult to eliminate them altogether, even if he had determined to do so. Edward may have tolerated them to provide both a useful alternative means of contact with Louis XI, without the possibility of any binding agreements as a result, and also to allow Warwick to save at least some degree of face after the damage to his diplomatic reputation which had already been inflicted. But Edward IV was still concerned that Warwick's capacity for independent diplomatic communication with the French King could be a potent threat. For when Monypenny met Edward before 16 January, the king did seem extremely keen to find out whether Louis's agent was carrying any letters from the French King to the Earl of Warwick amongst his papers. Monypenny replied that he did, but added (perhaps mendaciously) that he was not well informed as to the contents.[79]

---

[75] The ambassador was Thomas Rotherham, bishop of Rochester and keeper of the privy seal: PRO, E 404/74/1/98. Nucelles Pursuivant and Windsor Herald were sent to France in 1468: PRO, E 405/48, rot. 2d.

[76] Hicks, *Warwick the Kingmaker*, p. 268.

[77] 'Sire [Louis XI], maistre Robert Neuille et moy primes terre à Sandevic en Angleterre le jeudy devant Noel, car le vent nous estoit sy fort contraire que nous ne pouvions aller par mer, là où etsoit monseigneur de Varvic; et , de là, primes notre chemin à Londres, où nous trouvasmes le conseil de mon dit seigneur de Varvic . . '.: Waurin, *Cronicques*, iii. 186-9 (Monypenny's letter of 16 Jan. 1468).

[78] Morice, *Mémoires*, iii. col. 160.

[79] 'M'enquist se en avoye aucunes adressantes à monseigneur de Varouic : luy dit que ouy. Me demanda se aucunement savoye du contenu de icelles: luy dit que bien pensoie que aucunement . . .': Waurin, *Cronicques*, iii. 191.

Edward was probably right to be concerned, for later in the year (if a story told many years after the event is to be believed), the Earl of Warwick's agents were involved in a plot to reveal details of Edward's espionage activities to the French King. In October 1468 a certain John Boon was paid for a secret mission to Jean V, Count of Armagnac, to attempt to induce the count to support Edward IV against Louis XI; apparently, Boon was to deliver letters by which Edward 'demandoit à avoir alliance avecques ledit s[eigneu]r d'Armaignac.'[80] According to the story that Boon told at Craon in 1485, whilst being detained by the French, the Earl of Warwick had persuaded Boon to delay his voyage until a herald of the earl's had returned from France. After about a month of waiting at Exeter, Boon was told by Warwick that after delivering Edward's letters to the Count of Armagnac, he should then return via the court of Louis XI, where he should disclose to the French King all that had passed between Boon and the count.[81] Departing from Fowey at some point after Christmas, Boon travelled to San Sebastian and thence to Lectoure, where the count was staying. Boon subsequently gave two accounts of the count's response to Edward's letters. The first, in 1469, stated that the count was willing to support an English invasion of Guienne with around 15,000 of his own men. On the other hand, Boon's second account given in 1485 suggested, instead, that the count had in fact refused to read Edward's letters and that the count's promise of military support for the English had been fabricated afterwards by Louis XI.[82] Although it is not possible to definitely determine what transpired between Boon and Jean V, it is clear that after meeting the count, Boon travelled to Amboise to meet Louis XI, 'ainsi qu'il avoit promis audit comte de Varouyc'.[83] It is in the account of the meeting with Louis XI that Boon reveals that Warwick's herald's mission to France in the autumn of 1468 had been to warn Louis XI of Boon's mission and thereby disclose the whole affair to the French King. The secret activities of Warwick's diplomatic agents were beginning to pose a threat to Edward's own diplomacy.[84]

---

[80] PRO, E 403/841, m. 3; Ian Arthurson, 'Espionage and Intelligence from the Wars of the Roses to the Reformation', *Nottingham Medieval Studies*, 35 (1991), 134-54 at 154.
[81] C. Samaran, *La maison d'Armagnac au XVe siècle et les dernières luttes de la féodalité dans le midi de la France* (Paris, 1907), p. 413 (Pièce Justificative No. 37).
[82] Scofield, i. 466-7. Samaran, *La maison d'Armagnac*, pp. 168-9, 418.
[83] Ibid., p. 414.
[84] By July 1471, John Boon had been delivered into the hands of Edward IV by a certain John White of Dartmouth. In Edward's authorisation for White's reward it was stated that John Boon, 'as an untrue man to us went to the Frenssh king and there discovered oure said

However, throughout 1468, Warwick does seem to have publicly (if grudgingly) accepted the king's prerogative to pursue a royal policy of anti-French alliances; Warwick even accompanied Margaret of York to Margate on her journey to her marriage in the Low Countries.[85] But if Edward did intend to invade France (as parliament was told in May 1468), his allies of Burgundy and Brittany clearly preferred to come to separate arrangements with Louis XI. Charles the Bold signed the Treaty of Péronne with Louis on 14 October after Francis had also come to terms on 10 September by means of the Treaty of Ancenis.[86] So in the late summer of 1468 Edward did not take the opportunity to sever relations with Louis entirely. Thomas Rotherham, keeper of the privy seal, had been sent to France with powers to treat for peace, and stayed there for three months until 4 October.[87] Then, in early 1469, there were signs, according to Michael Hicks, of 'renewed favour towards the Nevilles'.[88] This favour also manifested itself in the diplomatic sphere, for once again, Warwick's agent Robert Neville was sent on an official mission to France on the king's behalf and was paid directly by the exchequer.[89] Edward seemed to be personally willing to once again use Warwick's agent as a means of informal contact with the French court.[90]

However, throughout the turbulent years of 1469-71, Warwick's ambition to completely direct English diplomatic relations with France was continually frustrated. Whilst Edward was in Warwick's power during the autumn of 1469, the earl did seise the opportunity to send 'his ambassador to the Most Christian king [Louis XI] to make an understanding with his Majesty', but in October Edward had to be released from Middleham castle in order to quell growing civil disorder, and would surely not agree to any of Warwick's plans discussed with Louis.[91] The moment had passed. Likewise, after Warwick had fled to exile in France in the summer of 1470 he could

---

l[ett]res [to the count of Armagnac]'. Resisting Boon's bribes, White took him to the king at his own cost and to the king's 'grettest pleasir': PRO, PSO 1/35/1818.

[85] Hicks, *Warwick the Kingmaker*, p. 266. Christine Carpenter, *The Wars of the Roses: politics and the constitution in England, c. 1437-1509* (Cambridge, 1997), pp. 172-3.

[86] There is a good account of both treaties and the diplomacy surrounding them in Vaughan, *Charles the Bold*, pp. 54-8.

[87] PRO, E 404/74/1/98.

[88] Hicks, *Warwick the Kingmaker*, p. 266.

[89] PRO, E 403/841, m. 12.

[90] PRO, E 405/49, rot. 1; PRO, E 403/841, m. 12.

[91] *CSP Milan, 1385-1618*, 132.

hardly negotiate with Louis and with Margaret of Anjou from a position of strength. The queen merely agreed that after a successful invasion of England the earl would be treated 'as a true and faithful subject ought to be treated'.[92] Even in the strange circumstances of February 1471, when Margaret of Anjou was yet to return to England and Edward IV was in exile, the earl was not really in total control of English relations with Louis XI. Warwick was indeed entirely responsible for treating with a delegation of Louis's ambassadors and presumably was pleased to sign a long-term truce and intercourse of merchandise with France on 16 February.[93] Warwick's guarantee that the treaty would be upheld was deemed fundamental by the French delegation.[94] If Warwick now had the authority he wanted to authorise such important diplomatic agreements, the price of Louis's support of Warwick's invasion of England in 1470 still had to be paid. Now, Warwick was clearly expected to provide English support for Louis XI's campaign against Charles the Bold. On 12 February 1471 Warwick felt duty-bound to quickly write to Louis explaining that he had already sent orders to Calais for the commencement of hostilities against Burgundy.[95] But in early 1471 the circumstances for English involvement in a continental war were hardly convenient since Edward IV was expected to invade England at any moment.

Just as Warwick had no firm guarantee that any influence he had on the conduct of English diplomacy in early 1471 would continue during a new Lancastrian government, he had also struggled against Edward IV's final right to direct policy and to choose his own diplomatic personnel. In the

---

[92] Scofield, i. 529-33.
[93] Ibid., i. 563. See also Calmette and Périnelle, *Louis XI*, pp. 323-5 (Pièce Justificative no. 42): this document is a letter from the bishop of Bayeux to Louis XI (written on 6 Feb. 1471). On 21 Feb. 1471, a warrant was issued for the payment of 10 marks to Thomas Smyth, clerk in the privy seal office, for the 'writyng of the trewes and entrecours of marchaundises and other' appoyntementes late taken' betwixt us and oure cousin Lowys of Fraunce': PRO, E 404/71/6/43. See also *English Medieval Diplomatic Practice*, ed. P. Chaplais (2 vols., London, 1982), ii. 717-8.
[94] The bishop of Bayeux enclosed with his letter a copy of Warwick's guarantee of the agreement. All the French ambassadors had deemed Warwick's original letter of guarantee so important that they decided to retain the original rather than sending it to Louis XI, for fear of it being lost 'en chemin': Calmette and Périnelle, *Louis XI*, pp. 324-5.
[95] BL, Add. Ms. 48988, fo. 40. Warwick's letter informs the French king that hostilities had commenced at Calais (apparently members of the Calais garrison had already killed two members of the duke of Burgundy's garrison at Gravelines).

early part of Edward's reign Warwick had been able to use his own diplomatic personnel based around his secretariat at Calais to carry out much of Edward IV's diplomacy with France, especially diplomacy conducted on an informal basis. Perhaps aware of continental taunts as to his reliance on the Earl of Warwick, Edward then chose a foreign policy independently of Warwick's advice and interests. Furthermore, Edward began to develop his own corps of trusted diplomats which he used to further the Anglo-Burgundian alliance. At this point two facts became evident: Warwick was still subject to Edward's final right to choose his own ambassadors, only the king possessed *droit d'ambassade*; and the king alone was able to completely determine the final choice of policy. The conduct of diplomacy, and certainly the direction of foreign policy, was really a matter for kings. This was a lesson which Warwick may have finally learnt as the last frustrated chapter in his career came to a bloody end at the battle of Barnet on Easter Sunday 1471.

5 The Myth of 1485: did France really put Henry Tudor on the throne?*
MICHAEL K. JONES

In late September 1484 Henry Tudor, Earl of Richmond, made a dramatic flight from the duchy of Brittany. Disguised in 'a serving man's apparel' he raced towards the French frontier accompanied by a small body of servants. The man who told the chronicler Philippe de Commynes that since the age of five he had spent his life as a prisoner or fugitive was on the run again.[1] Fortunately Henry and his entire company (the court-in-exile that had gathered around him at Vannes, in southern Brittany) were able to re-assemble in France. The ten month stay that followed was to be the last period of Tudor's exile. He sailed from Honfleur, on the Seine estuary, on 1 August 1485. Three weeks later he had defeated Richard III in battle and was the new king of England. And it is this stay in France (from October 1484 to the end of July 1485) that will be the subject of my paper. It will offer a critical re-evaluation of the belief, long-held in France but more recently adopted by English historians, that Charles VIII's minority government played an important part in putting Henry on the throne.

Henry had been an exile in Brittany for thirteen years, kept in a succession of fortresses. On one occasion, in November 1476, he was handed over to English envoys of the reigning Yorkist monarch, Edward IV. Fearing for his life Tudor had suffered or feigned illness and slipped into

---

* I am grateful to Dr. Steven Gunn and Mr. C. S. L. Davies for their comments on an earlier draft of this article.
[1] The French edition of Commynes that will be used throughout is *Mémoires de Philippe de Commynes*, ed. B. de Mandrot (2 vols., Paris, 1901-3); the conversation with Tudor is to be found at *Mémoires*, i. 457. All quotations in English are from Philippe de Commynes, *Memoirs*, tr. and ed. M. Jones (Harmondsworth, 1972). The details of the escape from Brittany are taken from *The Three Books of Polydore Vergil's English History*, ed. H. Ellis, Camden Society, Old Series 29 (London, 1844), pp. 206-8.

sanctuary at St-Malo. The Breton regime then had a change of heart, and he was escorted back into their protective custody.[2] By October 1483 he had been given his freedom and support in fitting out an expedition that might have claimed the throne of England. Now, some eleven months later, the weathercock of political fortune was to turn again. The Breton treasurer Pierre Landais had struck a deal with the new English king, Richard III, to surrender Tudor. Henry's life was in grave danger, but a timely warning of this plan allowed him to flee towards the border. He was able to reach safety in time. In September 1471 Henry and his uncle Jasper had been intending to ship to France in the aftermath of the Lancastrian defeat at Tewkesbury but had been driven to Brittany by storms. Now at last they had arrived.

His time in France was, according to the account of the Tudor court historian Polydore Vergil, as worrying and problematic as anything he had endured before. During the minority of the fourteen-year-old French king, Charles VIII, the Beaujeu faction (Anne, the daughter of Louis XI, and her husband Pierre, younger brother of the Duke of Bourbon) were running the government and administration of the country. They had been chosen for this task by Charles' father, Louis XI, shortly before his death on 30 August 1483, but were facing considerable opposition from a coalition of noblemen, led by the prince of the blood Louis, Duke of Orléans. The fate of this politically intelligent, astute regime, struggling to ensure its survival was now intertwined with Henry's own.

French historians have been straightforward if brief on this: the Beaujeu regime feared Richard III and saw him as a threat, and as a result equipped an army and a fleet for Henry Tudor in the summer of 1485. Tudor won the throne because of French help.[3] But it has only been in the last fifteen years that English scholarship has followed suit, in a rapid trend already hardening into a new orthodoxy. How has this developed?

The starting-point was Tony Antonovics's 1986 article, appropriately titled 'Henry VII, King of England, "By the Grace of Charles VIII of France"'. Antonovics identified a literary tradition present in the

---

[2] *Polydore Vergil*, pp. 184-6.
[3] P. Pélicier, *Essai sur le gouvernement de la dame de Beaujeau, 1483-91* (Chartres, 1882), pp. 102-3, saw Tudor's victory at Bosworth as 'un succès décisif' for the Beaujeaus' foreign policy. A recent biography of Charles VIII reinforces this view. Y. Labande-Mailfert, *Charles VIII et Son Milieu (1470-1498)* (Paris, 1975), p. 84, notes: 'Les Beaujeu ont placé en 1485 sur le trône yorkiste leur protégé Henry Tudor . . . Charles et les Beaujeu ont fourni tous les éléments de l'expédition'.

French court in the early sixteenth century, emanating from the work of the poet Robert Gaugin, that Henry Tudor was secretly grateful to the French, or at least ought to have been, for their help in 1485. As Gaugin brusquely put it: 'You, an exile, by our help return to your native fields a victor'.[4] Antonovics collected together the relevant printed primary sources, particularly on the reception of Henry in October 1484, when the French government recognised his claim to the throne, and the official support and backing for an invasion plan, finally given in May 1485. This was a cautious appraisal that nevertheless approved the literary tradition: 'if he seemed reluctant to acknowledge it, perhaps Henry of Richmond was, nonetheless, grateful to Charles VIII'.[5]

Caution was less evident in two crucial pieces of work of 1992-3 that advanced the agenda. T. B. Pugh's 'Henry VII and the English nobility' was a major interpretative essay on the reign as a whole, and it did not pull its punches on the Bosworth campaign. For Pugh 'the founding of the Tudor dynasty was the consequence of a shrewd and well-timed French intervention in English affairs'. He added that 'without massive French assistance... Henry Tudor could not have embarked on his great adventure and invaded England in August 1485'. Richard III had underestimated the 'ample resources that Charles VIII's government had so astutely put at his rival's disposal'.[6] These 'ample resources' consisted of no fewer than 4,000 quality troops, a fleet, and 40,000 *livres tournois* (well over £4,000) in money. An earlier attempt to overthrow Richard III, and replace him by Tudor, had been made by Henry Stafford, Duke of Buckingham, but it had attracted scant support among the English nobility. For Pugh the difference between the failure of Buckingham's revolt in 1483 and the remarkable success of the 1485 enterprise was French assistance. Pugh was also struck by the military skill of Philibert de Chandée, the captain of Henry's French troops, whom he believed responsible for the speed of Tudor's march through Wales. This, in his view, caught Richard surprised and inadequately prepared.

Similar figures for the size of the French army and the amount of their financial aid were produced by Sandy Grant, whose 'Foreign affairs

---

[4] Quoted in A. Antonovics, 'Henry VII, King of England, "By the Grace of Charles VIII of France"' in *Kings and Nobles in the Later Middle Ages*, ed. R. A. Griffiths and J. Sherborne (Gloucester, 1986), p. 169.
[5] Ibid., p. 178
[6] T. B. Pugh, 'Henry VII and the English Nobility' in *The Tudor Nobility*, ed. G. Bernard (Manchester, 1992), pp. 50-1.

under Richard III' came out the following year (1993).⁷ Grant looked more closely at the role of the French troops in the battle of Bosworth, particularly during the clash of vanguards at the start of the engagement. He believed the size and military experience of this force enabled them to repulse their English opponents, and provoked the crisis-point of the battle, when Richard charged his rival's position and was cut down in fierce fighting. This justified the French claim that the Tudor dynasty only came to its throne through their help. Noting the anti-French rhetoric of Richard III's proclamations against Tudor, Grant saw Bosworth, with both French and Scottish contingents fighting on Henry's side, as a culmination of the Hundred Years War. He cited the firm declaration of support for Tudor given by Charles VIII's regime, fearful of the threat Richard posed to their own interests, which included the remarkable assertion that Henry had 'the most evident right of anyone in the world to the kingdom of England'.

This re-emphasis has certainly had its effect on mainstream historical opinion, as seen in the vigorous comments of Colin Richmond in a recent (1998) survey: 'the European nature . . . of English politics during the Wars of the Roses is something still not sufficiently stressed: if the battle of Waterloo was won on the playing fields of Eton, the battle of Dadlington [Bosworth] was lost in the anterooms of Blois'.⁸ We have moved a long way from the view of Stanley Chrimes, who in his 1972 biography of Henry VII portrayed a French court 'unable to come to a decisive conclusion as to whether it would give assistance to Henry's project', whose help 'was not on anything but a very modest scale', and whose troops 'were such rabble as he had been able to recruit in Normandy'.⁹ Yet whilst some historians have been more critical of aspects of this new thesis, there has been a remarkable consensus over its broader conclusions.

Ralph Griffiths and Roger Thomas, in their *Making of the Tudor Dynasty*, drew attention to Henry Tudor's landing in the Norman Cotentin in November 1483, following his abortive voyage to England in support of Buckingham's rebellion: 'It is significant that the opportunity was not now grasped to escort Henry Tudor to the French court'. Griffiths and Thomas saw that 'the fiasco of Henry's expedition disillusioned the French' and that

---

⁷ A. Grant, 'Foreign Affairs under Richard III' in *Richard III: a medieval kingship*, ed. J. Gillingham (London, 1993), pp. 113-31.
⁸ C. Richmond, 'Patronage and Polemic' in *The End of the Middle Ages? England in the fifteenth and sixteenth centuries*, ed. J. L. Watts (Gloucester, 1998), p. 67.
⁹ S. B. Chrimes. *Henry VII* (London, 1972), pp. 36-40.

Henry and his entourage were allowed to return to Brittany because Charles VIII's regime 'had not thought it worthwhile to intercept him'.[10] The welcome given to Tudor in October 1484 could be explained by pragmatic factors, the influence of Pierre Landais in Brittany, the plots of the Duke of Orléans, and concern over Richard III's foreign policy. In other words, he was 'a diplomatic pawn'. But the authors stressed the importance of French support from May 1485: 'the French government had provided the resources, the ships and most of the men for the invasion of England . . . Henry naturally felt deeply indebted'.[11]

Cliff Davies, in his 'Richard III, Brittany, and Henry Tudor' (1993), struck a welcome warning note: 'English historians fail to take sufficient account of the preoccupation of the French government with its struggle against the princes and their ducal Breton and Burgundian allies. Support for Tudor... was one of a number of such ploys, though as it turned out an important one'.[12] Two years later, in his 'Wars of the Roses in European context', he returned to the theme: 'Had the French been able to hold out a little longer in Flanders, or had the Breton revolt taken place a little sooner, support for Tudor's dubious enterprise would not have been necessary'. Davies also raised doubts about the size of the army put at Tudor's disposal. He nevertheless concluded: 'Bosworth could not have happened without substantial French aid, and to that extent the French claim that Henry was 'king by the grace of Charles VIII' was justified'.[13]

It has undoubtedly been worthwhile to look at the part played by French troops at Bosworth and the wider role of the minority government of Charles VIII. But the vital question remains: why should the French want to do any English claimant such a favour? Their view of the dynastic upheavals of the Wars of the Roses, expressed at the estates-general at Tours in the spring of 1484, was hardly flattering: a record of 'incessant change' accomplished amidst 'orgies of crime'.[14] Even if this aside played to the

---

[10] Ralph A. Griffiths and Roger S. Thomas, *The Making of the Tudor Dynasty* (Gloucester, 1985), p. 103.
[11] Ibid., pp. 118-9, 170.
[12] C. S. L. Davies, 'Richard III, Brittany, and Henry Tudor, 1483-1485', *NMS*, 37 (1993), 110-26 at 120.
[13] C. S. L. Davies, 'The Wars of the Roses in European Context' in *The Wars of the Roses*, ed. A. J. Pollard (London, 1995), p. 177.
[14] *Journal des états généraux de France tenus à Tours en 1484 sous le règne de Charles VIII, par Jehan Masselin*, ed. A. Bernier (Paris, 1835), pp. 38-9.

gallery, it would be naive to underestimate the self-interested nature of any French intervention. There had been some support for Lancastrian claimants in the reign of Louis XI, but this had been limited in scope and prudent in application. The predilection of Charles VIII's regime was for pretenders. In 1491 the French king and council reportedly offered to help place Edward, Earl of Warwick on the throne because of the wrong they had done in supporting Henry Tudor. This display of contrition did not interfere with their coaching of the pretender Perkin Warbeck in Ireland. Warbeck was escorted to France in 1492 with full honours as 'Duke of York' and 'true heir to the kingdom of England', only to be ditched a few months later after the treaty of Étaples.[15] A comparison between the French treatment of Tudor in 1484-5 and Warbeck in 1492 is instructive, and will be considered later.

Given the pragmatism of French politics there would only be a strong reason to back Henry Tudor if Richard III was perceived as a dangerous threat. This is the thrust of Sandy Grant's article, which suggests that Richard was prepared to reopen war with France and that the French were provoked into launching a pre-emptive strike. This view deserves careful assessment. Two major factors lend it support. Firstly, the Beaujeu government acknowledged Henry Tudor's claim on his arrival in France and recognised him as rightful king of England. Secondly, by May 1485 they had committed themselves to underwriting his invasion, providing men, money and ships. Subsequently, these French troops played an important part in the Bosworth campaign. It seems an unassailable argument, but I wish to turn again to its main components.

Henry Tudor had a claim to the throne before he appeared at the French court. It had emerged during the plotting of Buckingham's rebellion in the autumn of 1483. According to a number of sources he was seen as an acceptable alternative candidate by a broad body of conspirators, Lancastrian and Yorkist, who wished to remove Richard III from the throne.[16] A key element of this plan was that Henry would marry Elizabeth of York, the eldest daughter of Edward IV. This claim had emerged out of an extraordinary political situation: the disappearance of Edward's two sons and his brother Richard's accession on the grounds that they were

---

[15] Ian Arthurson, *The Perkin Warbeck Conspiracy 1491-1499* (Stroud, 1994), p. 15.
[16] *Polydore Vergil*, p. 194; *The Crowland Chronicle Continuation: 1459-1486*, ed. N. Pronay and J. Cox (London, 1986), pp. 162-3. On this see also I. Arthurson and N. Kingwell, 'The Proclamation of Henry Tudor as King of England, 3 November 1483', *Historical Research*, 63 (1990), 100-6.

illegitimate. At Tours in 1484 the French chose to report this in their own acerbic fashion: 'Edward IV's children were murdered with impunity, and the crown transferred to their assassin by the goodwill of the nation'.[17]

A political emergency put the exiled Tudor on the stage. His Lancastrian blood, through his Beaufort lineage, and his French royal descent, from his grandmother Katherine of Valois (which Charles VIII's ministers were well aware of) made him an acceptable choice, on the condition of his marriage to Elizabeth. This reconciled him with members of the Yorkist establishment that had been loyal to Edward IV and united their factions. Ironically, on the failure of Buckingham's revolt, and Henry Tudor's ignominious retreat from the West Country, where he had attempted to land but thought better of it, these ingredients became stronger. Henry was now surrounded by a substantial body of Yorkist exiles and on Christmas Day 1483 at Rennes cathedral they acclaimed him as their king, but only after he had solemnly promised to marry Elizabeth of York on his return to England.[18]

This was a claim of expediency, but it seems not to have impressed the French, struck by the failure of Henry's invasion attempt in 1483, euphemistically referred to as 'Le reboutement en Angleterre de Monsieur de Richemont', and looking to make real political capital out of his arrival.[19] Griffiths and Thomas were right to point out that the French did not intercept Tudor when he landed at St-Vaast-la-Hogue in November 1483 after the collapse of Buckingham's rebellion. Documentary evidence shows an escort was provided from the Norman Cotentin by Henri Carbonnel, an esquire of the stable in Charles VIII's household, who accompanied Henry Tudor as far as the abbey of Saint Sauveur at Redon, on the road to Vannes.[20] In the later literary tradition identified by Antonovics, of which Alain Bouchart's *Grandes cronicques* forms an important part, a different

---

[17] *Journal des états généraux*, pp. 38-9.
[18] *Polydore Vergil*, p. 203. In Vergil's account Henry's intended landing-place is given as Poole in Dorset: ibid., p. 202. *The Crowland Chronicle*, p. 169, places it at Plymouth (Devon), as does the act of attainder of January 1484: *RP*, vi. 245. The information provided in Arthurson and Kingwell, 'The Proclamation of Henry Tudor', 104-6, suggests Plymouth as the more likely destination. I am grateful to Cliff Davies for discussing this point with me.
[19] A. Spont, 'La marine Française sous le règne de Charles VIII', *Revue des questions historiques*, n.s. 11 (1894), 391.
[20] BNF, Collection Clairambault, 473/ 213.

sequence of events was presented: Anne de Beaujeau took the opportunity to welcome Tudor to the French court, where he stayed for a while before returning to Brittany.[21] The account is totally false, and its retrospective gloss warns us of the unreliability of this whole genre.

When Henry made contact with Charles VIII's court in October 1484 he was hoping for a tacit recognition of the claim that had emerged in the autumn and winter of the previous year. As Polydore Vergil put it, Henry sought Charles's assistance, that 'he might return safely unto his own nobility, of whom he was generally called unto the kingdom, so much did they abhor the tyranny of King Richard'.[22] A letter of Charles VIII to Toulon of 3 November 1484 gave an indication of their official response: the English 'were greatly and wondrously divided amongst themselves' and Henry Tudor, Earl of Richmond, and a number of other nobles, with some 500 followers, had come to the king 'in order to recover the realm of England from the enemies of France'. Charles had received them into his service and wished to support them.[23] But the real view they had of this claimant's prospects, as Earl of Richmond, was likely to have been that of Commynes: 'God had suddenly raised up against king Richard an enemy who had neither money nor rights to the crown of England'.[24] Their solution was revealed in a crucial sentence of the letter, where Tudor was described as 'fils du feu roy Henry d'Angleterre'. To increase the prestige of their new guest he was now being passed off as a younger son of the Lancastrian Henry VI.

The remark was extraordinary. The French were well aware who Henry Tudor was. His uncle Jasper had been a pensioner at Louis XI's court from October 1469 to September 1470 and when both Tudors were driven by storms to Brittany in 1471, Louis had sent a number of embassies to Francis II demanding their release.[25] They also clearly understood the Lancastrian succession. Henry VI's only offspring, Prince Edward, had stood as godfather to the Dauphin Charles at Amboise on 30 June 1470. In the Act of Accord that was hammered out at Angers in the following month

---

[21] Alain Bouchart, *Grandes cronicques de Bretagne*, ed. M-L. Auger and G. Jeanneau (2 vols., Paris, 1986), ii. 459-60.
[22] *Polydore Vergil*, p. 208.
[23] The letter is printed in Spont, 'La marine française', 393
[24] Commynes, *Memoirs*, p. 397.
[25] Joseph Calmette and George Périnelle, *Louis XI et l'Angleterre* (Paris, 1922), pp. 115, 178.

provision was made, in the event of the failure of Edward of Lancaster's line to produce heirs, to vest the succession on the Duke of Clarence and his offspring, and this was sworn to in front of the entire French council.[26] To put it simply, the French well knew that Henry VI had no other sons. The comments of the well-informed Burgundian chronicler Jean Molinet make this clear. Henry Tudor was 'assez loingtain de la couronne d'Angleterre'; Edward Plantaganet, Clarence's son, was a far more plausible contender through direct succession.[27]

If the French wanted Henry Tudor to play a part as son of Henry VI, in other words to be a Lancastrian pretender, what was their likely motivation? The position of the Beaujeau regime in the autumn of 1484 was awkward. They had lost the initiative domestically and had temporarily moved the seat of their government to Montargis, whilst Louis of Orléans, in residence in Paris, brought out a series of criticisms of their administration. In this difficult time there were growing fears that Richard III might land a small force in Brittany; indeed, rumours of its arrival were current in September 1484. The appearance of Henry Tudor offered an opportunity to turn the tables on the Orléanists. Few amongst the general French population had heard of Tudor or understood the English plots of 1483, but possession of an apparent Lancastrian heir to the throne had an obvious propaganda value. The letter to Toulon that announced his arrival (probably one of a number circulated to the towns of the realm) was certainly disingenuous. It also referred to *gens de guerre* of the king who had inflicted great damage on English ships intent on raiding the coast of Normandy. It has been recently shown that this 'royal' success was in fact carried out by the Breton privateer, Jean de Coetanlem and his buccaneering fleet; the French admiral, Louis de Bourbon, had simply supplied his ships with additional powder and weapons on their way to the engagement.[28]

The French were prepared to use Tudor, but on their own terms. He had been paraded before the townspeople of the Loire in late October 1484 before he and his followers were moved to Sens. They were far less financially generous than the Breton duke, Francis II. No pensions or

---

[26] *A Chronicle of the First Thirteen Years of the Reign of King Edward the Fourth by John Warkworth*, ed. J. O. Halliwell, Camden Society, Old Series 6 (1839), p. 10.
[27] Jean Molinet, *Chronique*, ed. G. Doutrepont and O. Jodogne (2 vols., Brussels, 1935-7). i. 433.
[28] C. S. L. Davies, 'The Alleged "Sack of Bristol": international ramifications of Breton privateering, 1484-5', *Bulletin of the Institute of Historical Research*, 67 (1994), 230-9.

allowances were granted to Henry or the leading members of his company. And the one-off payment of 3,000 *francs,* issued by the French council on 17 November, may only have been authorised after Henry had agreed to play the part of a pretender.[29] A similar rhetoric would accompany Perkin Warbeck's cleverly staged arrival and reception in the summer of 1492. Warbeck himself wrote to Isabella of Castille describing how he 'came to the king of France, who received me honourably, as a kinsman and a friend', whilst Charles VIII told his subjects that he had sent ships to Ireland to fetch 'our cousin the Duke of York' because he was 'true heir to the kingdom of England'.[30]

The possibility of such a scenario is supported by letters sent by Henry to England in early November 1484, where for the first time he formally claimed the crown. It was a very significant step. Neither Henry Bolingbroke in 1399 or Edward IV himself in 1471 had declared their aims in advance of their return from exile; they had simply asserted their wish for a restoration of their aristocratic inheritances. And the example of Richard, Duke of York, who does seem to have advanced his own claim in September 1460, but was rebuffed in parliament later that year, was hardly encouraging.[31] In October 1483, as he embarked for Buckingham's ill-fated rebellion, Henry had avoided any overt statement or use of the royal style, and his receipt of a loan from Francis II at Paimpol on the Breton coast instead used his aristocratic signature, 'Henry de Richemont'.[32]

---

[29] *Procès-verbaux des séances du conseil de régence du roi Charles VIII*, ed. A. Bernier (Paris, 1836), p. 164. The more generous treatment of Henry by Francis II is described in B. A. Pocquet du Haut-Jussé, *François II, duc de Bretagne, et l'Angleterre* (Paris, 1929), pp. 249-53.
[30] Arthurson, *Perkin Warbeck*, pp. 51-5.
[31] Bolingbroke's initial refusal to claim the throne is considered by James Sherborne, 'Perjury and the Lancastrian Revolution of 1399', *The Welsh History Review*, 14 (1988), 217-41; the case of Edward IV in 1471 is discussed in Charles Ross, *Edward IV* (London, 1974), p. 163. For a recent appraisal of Richard, Duke of York's claim in 1460 see Michael K. Jones, 'Edward IV, the Earl of Warwick and the Yorkist Claim to the Throne', *Historical Research*, 70 (1997), 342-52.
[32] BL, Add. MS., 19398, fo. 33 (30 Oct. 1483). This document, signed by Henry Tudor and his uncle Jasper, Earl of Pembroke, is badly faded in places. Nevertheless P. M. Kendall, *Richard III* (Trowbridge, 1955), pp. 482-3, followed by Chrimes, *Henry VII*, p. 26, n. 3, was wrong to ascribe it to 31 Oct: the text reads 'Le penultime jour d'octobre'. Its location at Paimpol is a reasonable deduction, but the *quittance* only gives 'pres brehat en bretagne' [the Île de Bréhat, north of the bay of Paimpol].

Tudor's letter of November 1484 appealed to his supporters in England. He was ready 'to pass over the sea with such force as my friends here are preparing for me'. The letter was signed with the regal 'H', a style he was to continue to use as king (up to 1492). Elements of his text may have been carried through from the 1483 conspiracy, with its emphasis on the usurpation of Richard III, such as the phrase 'for the just depriving of that homicide and unnatural tyrant'. However the central passage contained something quite new, speaking of 'the furtherance of my rightful claim, due and lineal inheritance of that crown'.[33] This may have been a compromise agreed with the Beaujeu regime. A specific claim as son of Henry VI would have had no credibility in England, yet the formula of 'lineal inheritance' could allow them to circulate Tudor's letters and maintain their own deception for as long as it suited them. It seems that this ploy was referred to by Commynes. 'Tudor', he said later, 'was a member of the House of Lancaster, but he was not the closest claimant to the crown, whatever one may say about it, at least as far as I understand it'.[34] Commynes, who had served on the French council between 1484-5 and had met and talked to Henry shortly before his invasion attempt, was in a position to know.

The formula of 'inheritor of the crown' was used by Tudor right up to his departure from France. A document drawn up on his behalf in Paris on 13 July 1485 used the style 'heritier du royaulme d'engleterre'.[35] But once he arrived in Wales it was dramatically dropped, never to reappear. A letter to the Welsh gentry shortly after his landing at Milford Haven used the far more general 'for the adoption of the crown unto us of right appertaining', and this form of words was followed in a letter to Sir Roger Kynaston of 14 August 1485.[36] This suggests that the use of rightful

---

[33] The text of this letter survives from a seventeenth-century copy in BL, Harleian MS., 787, fo. 2v, and has subsequently been printed in a variety of sources. It is undated, and the attribution to Nov. 1484 follows Griffiths and Thomas, *Tudor Dynasty*, pp. 125-6, as does the identification of the signature as 'H' rather 'HR'. Richard III seems to be referring to its distribution in England in a letter to the mayor of Windsor of 6 Dec. 1484: BL, Harleian MS., 787, fo. 2v.

[34] Commynes, *Memoirs*, p. 354.

[35] AN, MC: Et/XIX/1/ rés. 269.

[36] The letter to the Welsh gentry is found in *The History of the Gwydir Family, written by Sir John Wynn*, ed. J. Ballinger (Cardiff, 1927), p. 28. It is addressed to John ap Meredyth, but is likely to have been one of a number circulated after his landing. The letter is undated, but its wording makes clear it was released after Henry's arrival at Milford Haven. Henry expressed: 'the great confidence that we have to the nobles and comons of this our principality of Wales, we be entred into the same'. For the second letter, to Kynaston, see G.

inheritance as a basis for assuming the royal title was imposed on Henry by the French, and that he jettisoned it as soon as he could.

It was not in Tudor's interests to put his claim in writing, and to base it on lineal descent, which to an English audience could only have meant the Beaufort descent through his mother, and thus a Lancastrian restoration. For him to recover the realm he had to unite the political community, recognising the rightful titles of both Henry VI and Edward IV. The Crowland Chronicler made the following revealing comments on Tudor's claim in the aftermath of his victory at Bosworth: 'in this parliament [November 1485] the king's royal authority was confirmed as due to him not by one but by many titles . . . to rule rightfully over the English people not only by right of blood but victory in battle and of conquest. There were those who, more wisely, thought that such words should rather have been kept silent than committed to proclamation . . .'.[37] The chronicler chose to stress the importance of the marriage to Elizabeth of York, 'in whose person, it seemed to all, there could be found whatever appeared to be missing in the king's title'.

To English observers it may well have seemed that Henry had reneged on the agreements of 1483, and was now claiming the throne in his own right, through his Lancastrian blood-link. The arrival of John de Vere, Earl of Oxford, in Tudor's camp in November 1484 would have fuelled such suspicions. Oxford had never recognised the Yorkist regime after 1471, and according to Molinet was an enthusiastic proponent of the new claim.[38] Richard III was able to exploit the contents of Henry's letter to considerable effect. In a proclamation of 7 December 1484, re-issued and enlarged on 23 June 1485, he poured scorn on Tudor: 'which of his ambiciones and insociable covetise encrocheth and usurpid upon hym the name and title of royall estate of this Realme of England, where unto he hath no maner, interest, right or title or colour, as every man wele knoweth', adding that 'if he shulde acheve his fals entent and purpose . . . shold ensue the disherityng

---

Grazebrook, 'An Unpublished Letter by Henry, Earl of Richmond', *Miscellenea Genealogica et Heraldica*, 4th series, 5 (1914), 30. Both are discussed in R. Horrox, 'Henry Tudor's Letters to England during Richard III's Reign', *The Ricardian*, 80 (1983), 155-8.

[37] *The Crowland Chronicle*, p. 195.

[38] *Molinet*, i. 433-4; C. Scofield, The Early Life of John de Vere, 13th Earl of Oxford', *EHR*, 29 (1914), 228-45.

and distruccion of all the noble and worshipfull blode of this Realme'.[39] Richard was able to play on the fears of the Yorkist establishment in the event of a wholesale restoration of Lancastrian titles and estates. He also accused Tudor of bargaining with the French king and council, and of being willing to surrender Calais to gain their support. This was a shrewd counter, that tarnished Henry with the opprobrium of earlier Lancastrian negotiations at the secret treaty of Chinon in 1462.[40]

According to Rosemary Horrox, in her recent study of Richard III's reign, the claim to the throne sent out in November 1484 'demonstrated the enhanced credibility of Henry Tudor, who from being a last-minute expedient in 1483 had become a persuasive alternative candidate'. Noting evidence of a conspiracy in November 1484 to encourage Tudor in a fresh invasion attempt, she emphasised how it was 'his endorsement by France which made overt resistance to Richard III a more feasible option'.[41] But the nature of the endorsement, combined with the evident Lancastrian sentiment of the November plot, which arose in the Earl of Oxford's Essex heartlands, was in fact likely to strengthen Richard's hand. He had the opportunity to pursue a policy much like that of his brother Edward IV in the spring of 1471, when Yorkists suspicious of the Readeption government of the Lancastrian Henry VI were enticed back into the fold. Similarly, Richard could now exploit the uncertainties inherent within the broad coalition that supported Tudor. Henry's apparent 'Lancastrianism' could be used against him, in an attempt to win over the Woodville faction, his main Yorkist allies. This strategy was to come very close to success.

Having committed himself to an attempt to win the English crown very much on French terms, Henry was forced to endure an anxious wait. Any hesitation could only be damaging to his prospects. Polydore Vergil indicated this as a very difficult time for Henry and his company of exiles. In

---

[39] The full text of the first proclamation of 7 Dec. 1484 is given in *British Library Harleian Manuscript 433*, ed. R. Horrox and P. W. Hammond (4 vols., Gloucester, 1979-83), iii. 124-5. The second, of 23 June 1485, is provided in *The Paston Letters*, ed. J. Gairdner (6 vols, London, 1904), vi. 81-4, from which the quotations are taken. My view of Richard's anti-French rhetoric differs from Grant, 'Foreign Affairs under Richard III', 125-6, in interpreting its primary objective as the undermining of Yorkist support for Henry Tudor within England.

[40] In the treaty of 24 June 1462 the Lancastrians promised to hand Calais over to the French in return for Louis XI's support in recovering the throne for Henry VI: Calmette and Périnelle, *Louis XI et L'Angleterre*, pp. 283-4.

[41] Rosemary Horrox, *Richard III: a study in service* (Cambridge, 1989), p. 281.

a clear reference to the struggle between the Beaujeau and Orléans factions in the winter of 1484-5, he related how 'Earl Henry . . . was compelled to go and make earnest suit unto every man particularly'.[42] After having announced to his English supporters that he would shortly be crossing over with his army, he could ill-afford any delay. Yet the French remained non-committal. Vergil emphasised that after the return of Charles VIII's regime to Paris (in February 1485) Henry again pressed the government for help, 'and sought there to bring to pass his suit, requesting King Charles again to take him wholly to his tuition'. Richard III learnt of the demoralising effect of the Beaujeaus' procrastination through his spies, hearing how 'Henry, hindered amongst the French by reason of the time, grew weary with continual demanding of aid, that he profited nothing, nor that any thing went forward . . . '.[43]

The uncertainty endured by Henry Tudor in the spring of 1485 was caught well in the *Dunes Chronicle* of Adrien de But. It told of speculation over the destination of an army being prepared by the French marshal Esquerdes. Some observers thought it might be used to help Tudor, others for an attack on Calais. In the event it was sent to reinforce the Flemish towns against the Archduke Maximilian.[44] Support for Henry was dependent on the Beaujeaus' careful calculation and the priorities of their foreign policy. It seems likely that a sudden, renewed threat of English intervention in Brittany prompted the final commitment to Henry's cause, set out in a royal decree of 4 May 1485.[45] This at last announced Charles VIII's backing for Tudor's invasion.

The regime was seeking financial help from the estates of the kingdom (to meet at Rouen from 20 May) to implement its policies. One of the items in this long statement of intent concerned the minority government's support for Henry. The estates were reminded that this claimant had come to the French court seeking help to recover the realm of England, and it had been decided to offer him military assistance ('avons appoincte l'estat de luy et de ses gens'), for which a considerable sum of money would be needed. This was deliberate propaganda, which elaborated the pretence embarked upon in November 1484, that Tudor had a clear and

---

[42] *Polydore Vergil*, pp. 209, 214.
[43] Ibid., p. 213.
[44] Davies, 'Richard III, Brittany, and Henry Tudor', 120.
[45] The extract from the *ordonnance* is printed in Pélicier, *Le gouvernement de la dame de Beaujeau*, p. 254.

direct right to the English crown ('considerant que c'est la personne de tout le monde qui a le plus apparent droit oudit royaulme d'Angleterre'). In pursuit of this aim, the Beaujeaus accorded Henry the style and precedence of a prince of the blood in all public ceremonies within the city of Rouen, where the royal entourage was now based. This was demonstrated in the order of the procession marking the feast of the Ascension, on 12 May 1485. Tudor was given the rank of *princeps Anglie,* and placed directly after the French princes of the blood, the Dukes of Orléans, Bourbon and Lorraine.[46]

The French government encouraged Henry to assume openly the English royal title, first used by him in his November 1484 letter, in all his transactions within the town. When Tudor made an offering to the cathedral chapter on 30 June 1485, as he began preparations for his expedition, he gave it under the style of *dominum regem Anglie.*[47] Henry had waited six months for such firm support. The signs of a real commitment are confirmed by documentary evidence. The account of Jean Lallement, receiver of finances in Normandy, recorded an authorisation by the Beaujeau government for a grant of 40,000 *livres tournois* (about £4,400) to cover the costs and expenses of Tudor's army.[48] This grant was made shortly after Charles VIII's formal entry into Rouen, accompanied by Henry, on 14 April 1485, and was almost certainly that referred to in the 4 May *ordonnance.*

The French ensured their promised assistance was widely publicised. Molinet described how Charles VIII delivered to Tudor 60,000 *francs*, 1,800 troops and artillery and ships for his invasion army. Commynes saw this aid swelling Henry's force to 3-4,000 men; the French king gave these men 'a large sum of money and some artillery'.[49]

The information was circulated abroad. A newsletter of Diego de Valera to Ferdinand and Isabella of Spain, dated 1 March 1486, informed

---

[46] C. de Robillard de Beaurepaire, *Entrée de Charles VIII à Rouen en 1485* (Rouen, 1902), pp. 23-4. When Henry attended deliberations with the cathedral chapter (28 Apr. 1485), alongside the Beaujeaus and other prominent members of the French court, he was also styled *princeps Anglie*: ibid., p. 22.

[47] The offering was made by Tudor shortly before his return to Paris. It was recorded by the cathedral chapter as follows: 'delato seu reportato capitulariter scuto uno auri de Aquitania per Dominum regem Anglie, principem de Richemont, in capella Beate Marie': ADSM, G 2143. An open assumption of the royal title is also found in a contemporary record of Charles VIII's entry into Rouen on 14 Apr., where Henry is described as 'le conte de Richemont, soy disant roi d'Angleterre': Beaurepaire, *Entrée*, p. 9.

[48] BNF, Nouvelles Acquisitions Françaises 7642, fos. 159v-60.

[49] Molinet, i. 434; Commynes, *Memoirs*, p. 355.

them that in response to Tudor's appeal for help, Charles VIII 'displaying the liberality which is befitting in great princes, granted him two thousand combatants paid for four months, and lent him fifty thousand crowns, and gave him his fleet in which to make the passage'.[50] This official view became the basis of the literary tradition of the French court in the early sixteenth century, that help from the minority government of Charles VIII put Tudor on the throne. As Alain Bouchart put it: 'par le moyen de ladicte madame de Beaujeau furent audit Richemond baillez navires et gens de guerre en si bon nombre qu'il conquist son royaulme d'Angleterre'.[51]

There is a need to distinguish, however, between the rhetoric, the propaganda that Charles VIII's administration chose to release for its own purposes, and the political reality. Significantly, there was a sharp discrepancy between French and English sources over the scale of assistance that Tudor received. According to Polydore Vergil Henry received only a 'slender supply' from Charles VIII; he left the French court on his own initiative 'with 2,000 only of armed men and a few ships'. In the *Song of Lady Bessy* (an early sixteenth century source originating from the Stanley family), when Tudor went to Paris to request from the French king the men, money and ships that had been earlier promised, he was met with a flat refusal.[52] And curiously Commynes, in another section of his work, also struck a different tone, describing how Tudor 'with a little money from the king, and some three thousand of the most unruly men that could be found and enlisted in Normandy, crossed over to Wales ...'.[53] To reconcile these contradictions it has been suggested that the English accounts, which date from early in Henry VIII's reign, chose to deliberately play down French involvement in the 1485 campaign at a time of renewed hostilities between the two countries. It is a possible explanation, but not an entirely satisfactory one.

The all-important issue here is the amount of money Henry Tudor actually received from the French. Lallement's account roll registered the

---

[50] The text of this letter is given in W. J. Entwistle, 'A Spanish Account of the Battle of Bosworth', *Bulletin of Spanish Studies*, 4 (1927), 34-7 at 35. A more detailed discussion of the source is provided by A. Goodman and A. Mackay, 'A Castilian Report on English Affairs, 1486', *EHR*, 88 (1973), 92-9.
[51] Bouchart, *Grandes cronicques*, ii. 460.
[52] *Polydore Vergil*, pp. 215-6; *Bishop Percy's Folio Manuscript*, ed. J. W. Hales and F. J. Furnivall (3 vols., London, 1868), iii. 350.
[53] Commynes, *Memoirs*, p. 397.

outright grant to Tudor of 40,000 *livres tournois* for the expenses of his army. But only a first instalment of 10,000 *livres* was to be paid immediately.[54] This was a deliberate move, to provide enough for Henry to start his preparations, but no more than that. The Beaujeau regime could monitor the likelihood of English military intervention in Brittany, which Tudor's planned invasion was intended to counter. Lallement's financial records are confirmed by the French receiver-general's accounts for 1484-5. They prove that Henry did indeed receive this first quarter's payment, but offer no indication that the rest of the sum ever arrived.[55]

New evidence has come to light concerning this crucial shortfall. It takes the form of a private contract of 13 July 1485, drawn up by the notary Pierre Pichon of the Rue Saint-Antoine, Paris. The arrangement was between Henry Tudor and Philippe Luillier, Seigneur de Saint-Jean-le-Blanc and Captain of the Bastille. Luillier agreed to lend Tudor 20,000 *écus d'or* (30,000 *livres tournois*) such was the urgency of his need ('pour subvenir a ses tres grans et urgens affaires'), but only on the most stringent conditions.[56] Thomas Grey, Marquis of Dorset and John Bourchier, Lord FitzWarin, who under the terms of agreement had to remain in France as pledges for the loan, also provided their letters of obligation on the same day. Henry had not been given the remainder of his promised grant. He now had to borrow it.

The timing of this arrangement was significant. The letters of commission for Richard III's aid to Brittany, a force of 1,000 archers, have been convincingly redated to 25 June 1485, and on the same day Charles VIII's government warned its subjects that an English army was preparing to invade the realm.[57] But dissident Breton rebels, sheltered by the Beaujeaus, had already invaded the duchy (on 24 June) and the army raised against them refused to fight. By the end of the month Landais's regime had collapsed. A warrant for his arrest and trial was issued on 3 July 1485. He was quickly interrogated and then executed. By mid July the threat of English military intervention in Brittany no longer existed.

The content of the document of 13 July reflected these political circumstances. Tudor desperately requested coin of the realm of France,

---

[54] BNF, Nouvelles Acquisitions Françaises 7642, fos. 159v-60.
[55] BNF, Ms. Fr. 23266, fo. 45.
[56] The contract is found in the records of the Minutier Central des Notaires de Paris: AN, MC: Et/XIX/1/ Rés. 269.
[57] Davies, 'Richard III, Brittany, and Henry Tudor', 119-22.

money of account no longer being adequate. As surety for the loan he would surrender all his personal goods and possessions ('toutes ses biens et meubles'). As a more substantial guarantee was needed, Henry also agreed to leave behind the Marquis of Dorset and Lord FitzWarin as pledges, and promised to reimburse Luillier for the additional costs of their captivity in the Bastille Saint-Antoine. The obligations of Dorset and FitzWarin were chivalric, the oath of a knight of the Order of the Garter and baron and *noble personne* to honour fully their part in the agreement, such was the great need ('grant besoigne et necessite') of their master, Tudor.

This surety was mentioned by Polydore Vergil. Since the Marquis of Dorset had earlier fled Henry's camp, only to be overtaken at Compiègne and persuaded to return, it has usually been assumed that Tudor thought Dorset's loyalty unreliable and wanted Charles VIII to keep him locked up. Yet the incident needs to be seen in a larger context. According to Vergil, Dorset was 'called home of his mother [Elizabeth Woodville], partly despairing for that cause of Earl Henry's success, partly suborned by king Richard's fair promises'.[58] Henry's alliance with the Woodvilles was collapsing. In July 1485 he was to learn of the marriage of Cecily, the second surviving daughter of Edward IV, to Ralph Scrope of Upsall, an esquire of the body in Richard III's household. Rumours that Richard himself might marry Elizabeth of York were so alarming that they 'pinched Henry by the very stomach', to use Vergil's vivid phrase.[59] He may have reassured Dorset that his promise to the Yorkist exiles at Rennes in December 1483 would be honoured, and reminded him of John Morton's mission to the papal curia, to secure the dispensation for the marriage.[60] But his broader appeal to Yorkists as a viable claimant was now in real jeopardy.

Such an interpretation is supported by the agreement of 13 July 1485, that indicated the choice of Dorset and FitzWarin as pledges was forced upon Henry by the French. Luillier, one of Charles VIII's councillors, knew that if the invasion attempt failed, his possession of the only two

---

[58] *Polydore Vergil*, p. 214. Richard's overtures to the Woodvilles, which had commenced in Dec. 1484, are discussed in Horrox, *Richard III*, pp. 293-6.

[59] *Polydore Vergil*, p. 215. The marriage between Cecily and Ralph Scrope is considered in more detail in Michael K. Jones, 'Richard, Duke of Gloucester and the Scropes of Masham', *The Ricardian*, 134 (1996), 454-60 at 458.

[60] C. S. L. Davies, 'Bishop John Morton, the Holy See and the Accession of Henry VII', *EHR*, 102 (1987), 2-30.

Yorkist lords in Tudor's army represented his best chance of getting the money back. It is also borne out by the speed of Tudor's actions in freeing the two men after his victory at Bosworth; a sign that he saw their imprisonment as a debt of honour, rather than a device to muzzle an unreliable ally.[61] The absence of Dorset and FitzWarin made it far less likely that Henry could land his army in the West Country, where the two had considerable support, and pushed him into the riskier option of disembarking in Wales. An invasion that needed to gather adherents from all sections of the community, now had Henry claiming his royal title through 'lineal inheritance' and his Lancastrian blood and no Yorkist peers. There was not a lot here to be grateful for.

The document of 13 July showed that the French government had withdrawn support for Henry Tudor's enterprise, despite its earlier promises. It was content to let Henry raise a small mercenary army, and hire the necessary shipping for its transport, but on terms that undermined his chances of any real success.[62] He was now regarded as expendable, a possible distraction for Richard III, but little more. Seven years later, in the summer of 1492, the French court cultivated another pretender amidst fresh fears of an English invasion. Perkin Warbeck, honoured with the title of 'Duke of York' and 'true heir to the English kingdom', was then ruthlessly discarded at the treaty of Étaples and had to flee Paris for Flanders.[63] As Tudor left the French capital for the Seine estuary in late July 1485 he would surely have reflected on the gap between rhetoric and harsh political reality. This *volte-face* more plausibly accounts for the contradictions between French and English sources. The firm offer of support for Tudor was intended for public consumption. This was repudiated at the eleventh hour, leaving Henry only what he could gather together on the basis of his hard-won loan. It is very real disillusionment that is caught both by Polydore Vergil and the *Song of Lady Bessy*.

Henry Tudor was fortunate that quality troops were available for hire. He had some Scots and Bretons with him, along with his group of exiles. But his main recruitment came from Esquerdes's disbanded army

---

[61] Spont, 'La marine Française', 399.
[62] The hire of French ships, under the vice-admiral Guillaume de Casenove, for Tudor's expedition more readily accounts for the acts of piracy on their return voyage: ibid., 394; Goodman and Mackay, 'Castilian Report', 95, n. 2.
[63] Arthurson, *Perkin Warbeck*, p. 55.

from Flanders and the remnants of the war camp at Pont-de-l'Arche. This camp, a creation of the last years of Louis XI, had been scaled down at the beginning of Charles VIII's minority and was in the process of being disbanded. As a result, the number of men available for Tudor's campaign was limited, and was unlikely to have amounted to much more than a thousand.[64] Nevertheless, companies of trained pikemen were still in existence in Normandy in the summer of 1485, and some had been used by Esquerdes in his campaign in Flanders. These unpaid soldiers were a problem for the regime, and Tudor's expedition offered an opportunity to find a use for them. One such man was Colin Lebeuf, from the *bailliage* of Amiens. He had been in the war camp at Pont-de-l'Arche, and served in Tudor's enterprise, the *voiage d'engleterre,* in the retinue of the Gascon Perrot, one of Esquerdes' captains. This and other companies had returned to France in September 1485.[65] These soldiers were unruly and a nuisance to the civilian population but they had been well-trained and drilled, in the Swiss fashion, and their formation against mounted attack was to serve Henry well at Bosworth.

Tudor's small force had sailed from Honfleur on 1 August 1485, reaching Milford Haven in South Wales six days later. It was a hazardous undertaking. Henry had not been able to organise an uprising to coincide with his landing, and was instead forced to rely on the secret promises of his supporters. Only a relatively small number actually joined his army on its march towards Bosworth. Yet Henry's hired French troops may have played a crucial part in deciding the battle. A letter written by one of their captains, at Chester on 23 August, the day after the engagement, provides a vivid testimony.[66] According to this account, when Richard III charged Henry's

---

[64] A. Spont, 'La milice des Francs-Archers (1448-1500)', *Revue des questions historiques,* 61 (1897), 474-7. The most recent assessment of the size of the expedition is found in Davies, 'The Wars of the Roses in European Context', 244, n. 30, which gives the strength of Tudor's fleet as seven ships. This was the number of vessels that accompanied Casenove in his attack on the Venetian galleys on 20 Aug. 1485: Spont, 'La marine Française', 394. Even if the original fleet were slightly larger, Davies believes it was unlikely to have carried many more than 1,000, of whom 500 would have been English exiles. On this basis, the number of French soldiers available to Tudor has been consistently overestimated.

[65] This information is drawn from a *lettre de rémission* of May 1486: AN, JJ 218, fo. 11.

[66] Extracts from this important letter are cited in Spont, 'La milice de Francs-Archers', 474. The positioning of French troops in the vanguard of Tudor's army is noted in *The Crowland Chronicle*, p. 181; Molinet, i. 435.

position in a bid to kill the Tudor claimant, he was accompanied by his entire division ('vint a tout sa bataille'). Faced with this onslaught Henry dismounted and surrounded himself with a phalanx of French pikemen (perhaps drawn from the flanks of his vanguard): 'voult estre a pye au milieu de nous, et en partie fusmes cause de gaigner la bataille'. The letter then reports Richard's cry of despair as the force of his attack was blunted, 'ces traitres francois aujourduy sont cause de la perdicion de nostre royaume'. This bears the mark of a genuine recollection.

The stirling performance of these soldiers was also briefly remembered in a later source, a poetic epitaph to the marshal Esquerdes by Nicaise Ladam.[67] But its description of this vehemently anti-English commander as an 'arbiter' of Tudor's fate was a retrospective enlargement, consistent with the broader, literary tradition adopted by the French court in the early sixteenth century. There is no contemporary evidence that Esquerdes ever joined Henry's army, and it is unclear whether he even assisted in its recruitment. The requirements of French foreign policy had changed, making any official involvement with Tudor's expedition unlikely. The leader of Henry's mercenaries, the Savoyard Philibert de Chandée, was a professional soldier of fortune who had no connection with the Beaujeu government. By the summer of 1486 he had been attracted to a new martial enterprise, in the service of Ferdinand and Isabella of Spain.[68]

Henry Tudor was always willing to honour a debt of loyalty to those who had done him service in his exile. He was genuinely grateful to his French mercenaries, who had fought so well for him at Bosworth, and this is shown by his reward to their Captain, De Chandée, whom he elevated to the Earldom of Bath.[69] But the tradition that Charles VIII's regime put him on the throne would have been met with the same cynicism and sardonic humour that governed most of his political affairs. We should do well to follow suit.

---

[67] L. Thorpe, 'Philippe de Crèvecoeur, Seigneur d'Esquerdes: two epitaphs by Jean Molinet and Nicaise Ladam', *Bulletin de la commission royale d'histoire*, 119 (1954), 201.
[68] Chandée's military skill is described by Bernard André, *Vita Henrici VII*, in *Memorials of King Henry VII*, ed. J. Gairdner (London, 1858), p. 25. His wish to serve Ferdinand and Isabella is found in Entwistle, 'A Spanish Account', 36-7. Chrimes, *Henry VII*, p. 40, suggests that Tudor first met him during his Breton exile.
[69] Goodman and Mackay, 'Castilian Report', 94-5. On Henry's sense of loyalty see M. Condon, 'The Kaleidoscope of Treason: fragments from the Bosworth story', *The Ricardian*, 92 (1986), 208-12.

6 'To Traffic with War'? Henry VII and the French campaign of 1492

JOHN M. CURRIN

Henry VII's 1492 invasion of France, launched late in the campaigning season, is often depicted not as a serious military campaign, but as an elaborate political exercise for salvaging the king's honour following defeat over Brittany, as an excuse for imposing taxes, and as a means for extorting from the French King a financially rewarding peace.[1] Sir Francis Bacon, the first 'modern' historian of the reign, helped fix this view, writing that Henry 'shewed great forwardness for a war', but secretly intended 'no purpose to go through with any war upon France'; and 'did but traffic with that war to make his return in money'.[2] Bacon drew his basic information from the *Anglica Historia* of Polydore Vergil, but Vergil thought that Henry earnestly desired to wage war against France, with his resolve and determination strengthened by news that Maximilian I, King of the Romans, also planned

---

[1] For this view, see J. Gairdner, *Henry the Seventh* (London, 1889), pp. 87-101; W. Busch, *England under the Tudors: King Henry VII (1485-1509)*, tr. A. M. Todd (London, 1895), pp. 61-6; A. F. Pollard, *The Reign of Henry VII from Contemporary Sources* (3 vols., London, 1913-4), i. li-vi; J. D. Mackie, *The Earlier Tudors* (Oxford, 1952), pp. 105-11; R. B. Wernham, *Before the Armada: the emergence of the English nation, 1485-1588* (New York, 1966); S. B. Chrimes, *Henry VII* (London, 1972), pp. 281-2; P. S. Crowson, *Tudor Foreign Policy* (London, 1973), pp. 61-2; M. V. C. Alexander, *The First of the Tudors: a study of Henry VII and his reign* (Towowa, N.J., 1980), pp. 101-3; S. Doran, *England and Europe, 1485-1603* (London, 1986), p. 16.

[2] Francis Bacon, *The History of the Reign of King Henry the Seventh*, ed. J. Weinberger (London, 1996), p. 102. Gladys Temperely thought Bacon had overstated the case. She argued that Henry was serious in his intention to make war on France, and driven by an out-of-date anti-French sentiment among the English, but in the end realised that he was being used by his allies and settled for an honourable peace: G. Temperely, *Henry VII* (New York, 1914), pp. 103-11. R. L. Storey doubted that a military show of force to compel a peace from France 'on a cash basis' was Henry's aim at the time of his war parliament in 1491: R. L. Storey, *The Reign of Henry VII* (New York, 1968), pp. 79-80.

to wage war against France. Vergil claimed that circumstances changed when Henry, with his military preparations nearly completed, suddenly learned from Christopher Urswick and Sir John Rysley, his envoys returning from Maximilian's court, that the King of the Romans was unprepared for war. Knowing that he could not wage a war against France alone, or abandon it without provoking charges of cowardice and of seeking to extract money deceitfully from his subjects, Henry went forward with it, welcoming at the same time peace overtures from King Charles VIII of France. Crossing the Channel with his army, Henry besieged Boulogne-sur-Mer until Anglo-French negotiators had arranged the Treaty of Étaples, allowing the king to exit the war honourably.[3]

Suspicion that Henry had conducted a sham campaign emerged at the end of the 1492 campaign. It is stated emphatically in a 1507 biography of Wilwolt von Schamburg, Captain of the *Landsknechte* sent to assist the English at Boulogne-sur-Mer. The anonymous author of *Die Geschichten und Taten Wilwolts von Schamburg* recorded rumours that Henry had taken from his subjects 'eighteen times a hundred thousand gulden', promising to carry on the hereditary war against France; and that after giving a hundred thousand gulden to the King of France, he was allowed to attack and sack a couple of towns near Calais. The author stated also that there was 'acknowledgement between the two kings, that the King of France shall have given to the King of England ten tons in gold crowns for his stuff and effort, even labour, out of England'. Moreover, according to the author, both kings had placed in a great hall several barrels, each full of ashes and topped by a layer of gilded copper coins, meant to fool the English knights and nobles into thinking that their king had won from the French King 'ten times a hundred thousand gold crowns'.[4] Schamburg's story at least underscores the feeling in Habsburg circles at the time that Henry had conducted a sham war for money. But countering suspicion of a sham war is evidence suggesting, as Vergil does, that at first Henry intended to wage a serious and vigorous campaign against the French in conjunction with allies, above all with Maximilian I; and that the king's plan, which miscarried in the end, may

---

[3] *The Anglica Historia of Polydore Vergil, A.D. 1485-1537*, ed. Denys Hay, Camden Society, New Series, 74 (London, 1950), pp. 49-57. Quotation is taken from Hay's translation. Unless noted otherwise, all translations are those of the present author.

[4] 'Die Geschichten und Taten Wilwolts von Schamburg', ed. A. von Keller, *Bibliothek des Litterarischen Vereins in Stuttgart* 1 (1859), pp. 136-7. I am grateful to Dr. S. J. Gunn for bringing this work to my attention.

have included the briefly-held dream of recovering the lost Plantagenet territories of Normandy and Guyenne and restoring the Lancastrian 'dual monarchy'.

The diplomatic ground for the war was prepared in September 1490 with the three treaties of Woking for defensive and offensive alliances against France. The offensive alliance between Henry and Maximilian, concluded on 12 September, bound the two kings to declare war against France within three years at the latest, 'or at sometime sooner if it seems useful and conducive to both of the kings themselves'. Each king would personally invade France to recover his right, and continue the war for two years, making neither truce, peace nor alliance with Charles VIII without the consent of the other king.[5] To his ratification of the 1489 Treaty of Medina del Campo, Henry added a new treaty modifying the terms of the previous Anglo-Spanish alliance to mesh with his new Habsburg alliance, bringing Ferdinand and Isabella into the war against France on the same terms.[6] By joining England, Spain, and Austria-Burgundy in a war against Charles VIII, Henry hoped to force surrender to the allies territories they claimed, including the lost Plantagenet lands in France'.[7]

In various public documents, such as the commissions for collection of the Benevolence of 1491 and statutes enacted by the parliament of 1491-92, Henry, setting out his reasons for war, justifying it as a matter of honour and peace, for the recovery of 'our kingdom of France', including the lands of Normandy, Anjou, Touraine, and Aquitaine, and for the thwarting of Charles VIII's malicious designs against England.[8] The council ordinance of 1492 establishing a regency government while the king was campaigning in France repeated the defensive and offensive aims of the treaties of Woking, stating that Henry was fighting 'for the recoveryng of his right

---

[5] *Foedera*, xii. 397-407.

[6] *Foedera*, xii. 413-9. Bergenroth erroneously calendared the treaty of 20 Sept. 1490 as Henry's ratification of the Treaty of Medina del Campo: *CSP Spain, 1498-1531*, 53.

[7] The text of the new Anglo-Spanish treaty made reference to Henry's grand design, saying 'how useful and opportune it might be if the three kings themselves, of the Romans, of Castile, Leon, Aragon and Sicily, and of England were joined, united and confederated against the Prince of the Gauls himself, and if there were struck between them such a treaty, and similarly, if there be kept a method of war against the aforesaid Prince of the Gauls, by which every single one may be able to recover promptly and quickly his right, and attack all the more in person the Prince of the Gauls': *Foedera*, xii. 414.

[8] For examples, see the commission for the Benevolence of 1491: *Foedera*, xii, 446; *SR*, ii. 549, 556.

within his seid realme of Fraunce, and for the defence of other his allies and confederates as he is obliched to doo'. The ordinance makes specific mention of the English claims to 'the crowne and regally of Fraunce', and to 'the duchies of Normandy, Guyan', Turayn', and the countie of Mayne'. As in the treaties of Woking, 'thinsaciable covetise and voluptuous desire' of the king of France was denounced, and in addition to the English claims, the causes of war given included Charles's seizure of Brittany 'by oppression and force', his taking as his wife Duchess Anne of Brittany (whom Henry still recognised as Maximilian's lawful wife), his stirring of rebellion in Flanders and Ireland, his attempts to subvert and invade England and Calais, and his inciting the King of Scotland to make war against Henry.[9]

The later Plantagenets used their claim to the French crown to force French kings into recognising their full sovereignty over Normandy and Gascony,[10] but most Tudor historians do not think it likely that Henry was attempting the same. Margaret Condon, for example, argues that Henry was enough of a 'realist' to know that the old claims in France were unattainable, and so the statements about recovering his rights in France in the ordinance of 1492 were merely window dressing.[11] Such language would have served as justification for levying new taxes to boost royal income and as a tool for intimidating Charles VIII into making a cash settlement for peace. But the war against France did not originate within the exclusive context of royal finances; it emerged from Henry's diplomacy between 1489-90, which aimed at establishing a triple alliance between England, Spain, and Austria-Burgundy that would not only defeat French attempts to absorb Brittany, but also help the allies recover their various claims in France.[12] The Benevolence of 1491 and the war taxes granted by parliament that year perhaps should be considered not simply as revenue-raising devices, but as part of Henry's effort to translate the offensive alliance of Woking into military action.

---

[9] The ordinance, PRO, C82/329/53, is printed in M. M. Condon, 'An Anachronism with Intent? Henry VII's Council Ordinance of 1491/2' in *Kings and Nobles in the Later Middle Ages*, ed. Ralph A. Griffiths and James Sherborne (Gloucester, 1986) p. 244.
[10] C. S. L. Davies, "Roy de France et Roy d' Angleterre': the English claims to France, 1453-1558', *Publication du centre Européen d'études Bourguigonnes (XIVe-XVIe)* 35 (1995), 123-4.
[11] Condon, 'Anachronism', p. 229.
[12] On this diplomacy, see J. M. Currin, 'Henry VII and the Treaty of Redon (1489): Plantagenet ambitions and early Tudor foreign policy', *History* 81 (1996), 343-58 at 346, 352-3; D. Potter, 'Anglo-French Relations 1500: the aftermath of the Hundred Years War', *Journal of Franco-British Studies* 28 (1999/2000), 41-66 at 47-51.

Checking extension of French rule over Flanders and Brittany, disrupting the Franco-Scottish alliance, and ending French support for the pretender Perkin Warbeck were vital to Henry's dynastic security and England's national interest; but Henry also lived in an age when royal policy and regal honour entailed defending and asserting dynastic territorial claims. By reviving the symbols of the Lancastrian 'dual monarchy', Henry emphasised his claim to rule the separate kingdoms of England and France. He personally handed to his printer, Richard Pynson, a woodcut for the 1492 printed statutes and ordinances of war symbolising the 'dual monarchy': the juxtaposed shield of the three leopards and three *fleurs-de-lis* of the later Plantagenet kings and shield of the three *fleurs-de-lis* of the Valois kings. During the preparations for the invasion in 1492, William Pawne, Henry's clerk of the stables, purchased for the king's horses harnesses covered in blue velvet, with gilt *fleur-de-lis* and pendants decorated with *fleur-de-lis*. These items, it seems, were for the ornamentation of the caparisons and trappers of the royal horses, suggesting that in France Henry intended to ride with his army arrayed as *le roy de France*.[13] Henry also had prepared for circulation in France a special gold ryal, with the image of the king wearing the 'closed' imperial crown on the obverse, and the arms of France set in the middle of a Tudor rose on the reverse.[14] These elaborate iconographic displays seem very excessive for mere window-dressing, and so may have been manifestations of Henry's dream – his fantasy – that he was on the verge of reviving the 'dual monarchy' in emulation of Henry V.

Henry VII's mental world was strong in belief of the supernatural, of magic, alchemy, astrology, and prophesy,[15] and so political weight may have been given to the prognostication of Alsons Frysauce foretelling an English victory over France, which circulated in England in early 1492. The author claimed to have received his vision in 1415, while a clerk to the astrologer of the Ottoman Sultan, and to have written it down in 1431. In

---

[13] PRO, E 36/125, p. 191. In the fifteenth-century *Le grand armorial équestre de la Toison d'or*, there is an illustration of '*Le Roy de France*', riding a horse in caparison and trapper of blue decorated with gold fleur-de-lis. Bibliothèque de l'Arsenal, Paris, MS 4790, fo. 47v.

[14] C. E. Challis, *The Tudor Coinage* (Manchester, 1978), p. 52.

[15] On the political importance of prophesy at the early Tudor court, see Keith Thomas, *Religion and the Decline of Magic* (London, 1971), pp. 289-91, 415-6. On Henry VII's reliance on prognostications, see C. A. J. Armstrong, 'An Italian Astrologer at the Court of Henry VII' in *Italian Renaissance Studies*, ed. E. F. Jacob (London, 1960), pp. 433-53.

fact, the prophecy was written in late 1491 at the earliest, with Henry VII in mind. Casting the Tudor king in the messianic role of 'Son of Man', the prognostication foretells of Henry's conquest of France by right and might, succoured by the King of the Romans, and of his destiny to rule as a great king:

> And Westeurope shall' have mych to doo, for within that tyme the Son of Man, which is the kyng of Englande, shall demaynde his right of the crowne of Floure de Lice [i.e., France], the which he shall have sone after . . . And that tyme the son of man of Westeurope, that is of Englande, shalbe crowned Kyng of Fraunce and shalbe [the] furst that shall' cause pease to be publisshed in Christendome, and he shalbe a grete justiciar' to yaim that be under hym, and he shalbe a grete enemy to traytors. . . . And in the yer' of oure Lorde a thousand CCCC. IIII^{xx} and XII. the kyng of England shall enter' the lande of the Floure de Lice, with a grete pusaunce, without departyng thens unto the tyme that he shalbe crowned, and that coronacion and victory shall' come to hym bye yaim of Esteurope [i.e., Maximilian], which shall' come to hym for socoure. And the peopul' of the Floure de Lice shall have that yer' strongly to do and suffer, and [it] shall cost the life of mony a man or ever it be doone, for the treson shalbe so mych and so grete that the realme of Floure de Lice wilbe glade to be quyte of yaire king.[16]

This prophecy may have been meant to build support for Henry's war and help establish legitimacy for his claim to France; but Henry, who seems to have believed in the power of prophesy, may have been convinced by it that he had a destiny to fulfil in asserting his claim to France.

The late date of Henry's 1492 invasion, often taken as evidence of his lack of serious military purpose, was not part of the king's initial plans. In fact, as the treaties of Woking indicate, Henry at first anticipated a war lasting at least two years, if Charles did not surrender to the allies the territories they claimed. Although these treaties required the allies to commence hostilities by September 1493, Henry began his invasion of France more than a year earlier, which was allowed under the terms of the treaties of Woking, because of the deteriorating military situation in Brittany in 1491. Henry, who had acted as protector of Duchess Anne since sending

---

[16] Printed in HMC, *Report on the Manuscripts of Lord Middleton* (London, 1911), pp. 264-5.

the first military expedition to Brittany in 1489, was unable to counter the vigorous French offensive during the summer of 1491, and was thus compelled to withdraw the remnant of his army from the duchy. By November, with Brittany effectively under French control, Duchess Anne, no longer trusting promises of protection and help from either Henry or her proxy husband, Maximilian, made peace with Charles VIII, agreeing to marry the French king in December.[17]

Henry began his financial preparations for war in the summer of 1491, while the French were overrunning Brittany, with collection of the 'Benevolence'. In November, parliament granted two fifteenths and tenths, with the first fifteenth and tenth payable on 1 April 1492, and the second on 11 November. Parliament also authorised the levying of a third fifteenth and tenth, payable on 11 November 1493, should the king's army stay abroad for eight more months, through the winter of 1492-3.[18] Because Henry disbanded his army by the end of 1492, the third fifteenth and tenth was never levied. If one of Henry's motivations for the invasion was to have a pretext for levying taxes, then why did he not conclude a truce and keep at least a token force in France to justify levying the third fifteenth and tenth, and then make peace with France?

Instead of creating pretexts for raising money, Henry's diplomacy at the time was attempting to translate the strategic vision of the treaties of Woking into military action. The alliance with Maximilian, who was also regent in the Netherlands for his son, Archduke Philip, was seen, especially by the French, as a revival of the Anglo-Burgundian alliance that had helped Henry V defeat France earlier in the century. In the view of Tudor historians, following Vergil, Maximilian was too mercurial and impotent to carry through his military obligations, and thus left Henry to fight France on his own. Indeed, compared to other monarchs, Maximilian was politically and financially weak but that ought not to be overemphasised. At the time, the French did not think him so impotent.

Maximilian and his father, Emperor Frederick III, could not do much in Europe without political backing and financial aid from the princes and electors of Germany. Nevertheless, between 1488 and 1492, Maximilian

---

[17] A. Dupuy, *Histoire de la réunion de la Bretagne à la France* (2 vols., Paris, 1880), ii. 221-32. On Henry's military interventions in Brittany, see J. M. Currin, '"The King's Army into the Partes of Bretaigne": Henry VII and the Breton wars, 1488-1491', *War in History* 7 (2000), 379-412.

[18] *RP*, vi. 442-4; *SR*, ii. 555-6.

had strengthened his political position in both Germany and the Low Countries. In the Low Countries, Maximilian contended with a widespread rebellion led by the Three Members of Flanders (Ghent, Bruges, and Ypres), which was supported by the French and by Philip of Cleves, the son of Adolphe, Lord Ravenstein. In 1490, he joined the succession war over the kingdom of Hungary, and established his dynastic interest in Brittany by marrying Duchess Anne by proxy. Maximilian entrusted the task of suppressing the rebellions in Flanders to his *statthalter*, Duke Albrecht of Saxony, and to Count Engelbert of Nassau. Although the Three Members had capitulated by June 1492, Philip of Cleves, a superb naval tactician, kept on fighting from his fortified base at Sluis, attacking shipping in the North Sea and English Channel. Cleves became a close ally of France, and member of Charles's *conseil du roi*. His hold on Sluis not only allowed him to disrupt trade and communication between England and the Low Countries, but also permitted France a strategic foothold in Flanders. Consequently, dislodging Philip of Cleves from Sluis became a common cause shared by Henry and Maximilian.

Maximilian was also seeking to overthrow the 1482 Treaty of Arras, in which he had been compelled to accept a marriage between his daughter, Marguerite, and Charles VIII, when Marguerite came of age, and to cede to France as Marguerite's dowry the counties of Artois, Burgundy, and the Franche-Comté. The rapid success of the French in Brittany during the summer and autumn of 1491 forced Maximilian into a negotiated settlement over Hungary in early December so that he could concentrate his attention on recovering Brittany and his son's Burgundian patrimony.[19] Charles VIII's jilting of Maximilian's daughter and his marriage to Maximilian's proxy queen came as a double insult, grievous injuries for which honour demanded revenge. In Germany, a French agent warned the king about the deepening hatred for France among the Germans.[20] In January and February, Charles's agents in Germany reported that the princes and communities of Empire had turned against France, and were determined to support Maximilian, who, intending to attack Burgundy, was amassing an army at Strasbourg.[21]

---

[19] H. Wiesflecker, *Kaiser Maximilian I: Das Reich, Österreich und Europa an der Wende zur Neuzeit* (5 vols., Munich, 1971-86), i. 302.
[20] BNF, MS Français 15541, fo. 166; Wiesflecker, i. 333-6.
[21] BNF, MS Français 15541, fos. 121v, 163, 166.

Henry VII tried to exploit this anger, sending in February 1492 a letter to the electors and Princes of the Empire, in which the Tudor king condemned Charles VIII for marrying Anne of Brittany and for supporting the rebels in Flanders in order to subvert Maximilian's authority. In language similar to the treaties of Woking, Henry warned the electors and princes of the lust for power and domination that gripped the King of France. By illicitly marrying Maximilian's solemnly betrothed queen, Henry said, Charles VIII had shown contempt not only for the Church, but also for the King of the Romans and for the entire German Empire. Henry urged the electors and princes to take vengeance for these 'very atrocious and very accursed injuries', lest 'everlasting disgrace and opprobrium' befall the electors, princes and lords of the Empire.[22] Henry aimed his remarks at the emotions of the electors and princes of the Empire, at their sense of honour, so that, out of their anger, they would back a Habsburg war against France. Henry's letter reads as a well crafted and calculated diplomatic move to help build the political support that would enable Maximilian to undertake an offensive war against France. It seems excessive and unnecessary if all Henry wanted was the mere pretence of war.

Fearing that Charles would marry Marguerite to a French nobleman in an attempt to hold on to Artois, Burgundy and the Franche-Comté, Maximilian made the return of his daughter and these territories his principal concern in 1492.[23] Between 8 April and 5 July, the Count of Nassau and the president of Flanders negotiated in France for the return of Marguerite and her lands and an end of French support for Philip of Cleves, all of which the French refused.[24] In June and July, Charles's agents in the Empire again sent warning that Maximilian was assembling an army to attack France, and that he had received men and money from the King of Bohemia and from the new King of Hungary.[25] By mid July 1492, when Henry finally committed himself to the invasion of France, Charles VIII and his councillors fully expected attacks not only from Henry, but also from Maximilian.

Vergil's claim that Henry began assembling his forces in the belief that Maximilian was doing the same is supported by the historical evidence;

---

[22] Johann Philip Datt, *Volumen Rerum Germanicarum Novum Sive de Pace Imperii Publica Libri V* (Ulm, 1698), pp. 502-3.
[23] Wiesflecker. i, 335.
[24] ADN, B 2144, fo. 123; *Chroniques de Jean Molinet*, ed. J.-A. Buchon (4 vols., Paris, 1828), iv. 199-200.
[25] BNF, MS Français 15541, fos. 140, 159.

but his story, repeated by Bacon and others, that while assembling his army he first learned from his ambassadors of Maximilian's lack of military preparation does not seem credible. Throughout 1491-2, and even during the English campaign in France, Henry and Maximilian exchanged envoys and messengers frequently, suggesting that at the very least Henry should have been aware of Maximilian's level of preparation well before he committed himself to the invasion. Pierre Puissant, Maximilian's secretary, resided at the Tudor court between February 1490 and October 1492.[26] Henry sent François du Pou, one of his French secretaries, to the Habsburg court on two long missions between October 1491 and February 1493.[27] Accounts of the receiver-general for Flanders and of the English exchequer show that between October 1491 and November 1492 messages were exchanged 40 times between the Tudor and Habsburg courts and between Henry VII and Maximilian's officers in the Low Countries. Some of these messages were described as 'touchant matiers et affaires secretz', or as 'touchant les affaires d'entre les deux rois'.[28] These included messages Henry sent through his heralds directly to Maximillian and Archduke Philip.[29] The exchanges continued after Henry invaded France. On 13 October 1492, during the siege of Boulogne, a messenger delivered letters of Puissant and King Henry to Maximilian 'touchant l'aliance des deux rois'.[30] Also in October 1492, members of the council of Flanders, led by the president, the Duke of Saxony, the count of Nassau, and the governor of Lille, met with Henry and his councillors on matters relating to the Tudor-Habsburg alliance.[31] Despite frequent communication, Henry and Maximilian, except in the case of Sluis, coordinated their political and military actions poorly because of differing strategic objectives. Henry invaded France in October to capture Boulogne-sur-Mer, while Maximilian invaded in December to conquer Burgundy and the Franche-Comté.

---

[26] ADN, B 2144, fos. 150v, 163, 168r-v; PRO, E 404/81/1, 3 Jan. 7 Henry VII; E 405/78, rot. 42.

[27] PRO, E 404/81/1, 19 Oct., 25 Nov., 27 Mar., 7 Henry VII; E 404/81/3, 19 Apr. Temp. Henry VII; E 405/78, rots. 36, 42, 57; E 36/130, fo. 144v; E 36/125, p. 239.

[28] ADN, B 2144, fos. 82, 91, 92r-v, 93r-v, 95v, 101, 102v, 106v, 107, 110, 111v, 113v, 114r-v, 119v, 121, 125-28v, 132v, 135, 137, 140v; B 18844/29564; PRO, E 404/81/1, 3, 12, 15, 23 Jan., 3 Feb., 31 Oct., 12 Nov. 7 Henry VII; E 36/130, fo. 64; E 405/78, rots. 39-40, 42-4.

[29] PRO, E 404/81/1, 12 Nov., 1, 3, and 5 Jan. 7 Henry VII; E 405/78, rot. 42.

[30] ADN, B. 2144, fo. 128v.

[31] ADN, B 2144, fos. 128r-v, 132v, 135.

In reaction to the French success in Brittany, Henry intended to invade France in the spring of 1492. His military preparations began in the late summer of 1491, soon after the nobility affirmed the king's decision for war in a Great Council.[32] Between late August 1491 and April 1492, artisans set to work in royal workshops and elsewhere manufacturing bills, bows, arrows, and a variety of ordnance. Commissioners purveyed wood, coal and saltpetre for producing gunpowder; wheat, flour, oats, beans, beef, bacon, cheese, beer, wine, and salt for feeding the king's soldiers; and pipes, barrels, carts, carriages and horses for transporting weapons, munitions, and supplies. Henry sent agents abroad to hire 500 ships and 300 crossbowmen, and purchase guns, harnesses and other supplies from the Low Countries. Food and weapons, escorted by 'wafters', were brought to Portsmouth and Southampton, the staging areas for the army. The king had a gunpowder factory constructed at Southampton, and a 'bere hous' built at Portsmouth 'for the surtie and wele of the Kynges navy'.[33] In December 1491, Henry ordered one of his sea captains to survey ports from Southampton to Land's End and along the Severn and locate ships available for service.[34] In February 1492, one of the yeomen of the crown contracted for the king's service ships from Essex, Norfolk, and Suffolk.[35] A Milanese agent at Henry's court reported in mid January that the king was giving his whole attention to the war against France, and having spent much already on the military preparation, he was not about to abandon it. Moreover, according to the agent, Henry believed that some leading Frenchmen would join him when they saw the effect of the war,[36] which was also foretold in the prophecy. Between March and May, Henry contracted, by formal indentures for war, with various nobles and gentlemen for the retinues that would make up the bulk of his army. The indentures stipulated that the retinues would muster at Windsor, Guildford, Winchester or Portsmouth in late May and early June, and then proceed to Portsmouth for embarkation.[37]

---

[32] *The Great Chronicle of London*, ed. A. H. Thomas and I. D. Thornley (London, 1938), p. 224; P. Holmes, 'The Great Council in the Reign of Henry VII', *EHR* 101 (1986), 840-62 at 844-5.
[33] PRO, E 36/285, fos. 18v-50v, 73; E 36/130, fo. 151v; E 404/81/1, 27 Oct. and 23 Nov. 7 Henry VII; E 405/78, rots. 39-41, 45, 47; E 101/72/3/1064, 1068; C 76/175, mm. 19, 21; *CPR 1485-94*, pp. 392-7, 414-5.
[34] PRO, E 404/81/1, 7 Dec. 7 Henry VII; E 405/78, rot. 47.
[35] PRO, E 36/285, fo. 62v.
[36] *CSP Milan, 1385-1618*, 454-6.
[37] For the extant indentures for war, see PRO, E 101/72/3/1065-67, 1069-95; E 101/72/4/1096-1115; E 101/72/5/1121-1145; E 101/72/6/1146-1162; BL, Add. Charter

The selection of Portsmouth for the embarkation suggests that Henry initially intended to land his army in Brittany or Normandy, and did not yet consider Brittany lost to France. He had postured since 1489 as the duchess's 'bon père', as her protector; however, after Anne's marriage to Charles VIII in December 1491, Henry became patron of a conspiracy of disgruntled Bretons to overthrow the duchess and install in her place a new duke.[38] He feared that the acquisition of Brittany would increase the wealth and naval power of France.[39] Perhaps believing that the Bretons did not want to be subjected to France, Henry tried to exploit among the Bretons a quasi-nationalistic sense of being 'Bon Breton' for his own political ends.[40] Pierre le Pennec, a lawyer from Morlaix, an official under Duke Francis II, and servant of Jean de Rieux, Marshal of Brittany, organised the conspiracy on Henry's behalf.[41] Pennec, who seems to have entered Henry's service around June 1491,[42] drew into the plot men who had lost power and status in Brittany as a result of the new regime, men who wanted revenge against rivals, or men who simply wanted money. Most significant among the conspirators were Marshal Rieux, whom the duchess had long disliked and mistrusted; Jean, Vicomte de Rohan, a claimant to the duchy, who, having helped the French conquer Brittany, now found himself cast aside;

73951. Some of these are in *Foedera*, xii. 478-80.

[38] *Le complot Breton de M. CCCC. XCII*, ed. A. de la Borderie (Nantes, 1884); J. M. Currin, 'Pierre le Pennec, Henry VII of England, and the Breton Plot of 1492: A Case Study in "Diplomatic Pathology"', *Albion* 23 (1991), 1-22.

[39] 'Henrici VII Angliae Regis ad Maximilianum Regem Romanorum & Imperij Ordines, in Comitiis Confluentiae habitis Anno MCCCCXCII. Legatio' in *Germanicarum Rerum Scriptores aliquot Insignes*, ed. Marquard Freher (3 vols., Frankfurt and Hanover, 1611-37), iii. 37-8.

[40] On this national Breton sentiment, see J. Kerhervé, 'Aux origines d'un sentiment national. Les chroniqueurs bretons de la fin du moyen âge', *Bulletin de la société archéologique du Finistère* 108 (1980), 165-206; M. Jones, "Mon Pais et Ma Nation': Breton identity in the fourteenth century' and "Bons Bretons et Bons Francoys': the language and meaning of treason in later medieval France' in *The Creation of Brittany: a late medieval state* (London, 1988), pp. 283-307, 329-50.

[41] It seems that Pennec first became acquainted with Henry during the Tudor's exile at the court of Duke Francis II. Pennec acted as liaison between Marshal Rieux and the commanders of the English army to Brittany in 1490: Currin, 'Pierre le Pennec', 4-6; P.-H. Morice, *Mémoires pour servir de prevues à l'histoire ecclésiastique et civile de Bretagne* (3 vols., Paris, 1742-6), iii. col. 657.

[42] PRO, E 404/80/3, 30 June 6 Henry VII.

Guillaume Carreau, Captain of Brest, and Maurice du Mené, Captain of Morlaix. Henry indicated support for the claim of Rohan against Duchess Anne.[43] The plan entailed delivery of Brest and Morlaix into English hands so that Henry could land his army in Brittany. Henry needed to win over Captain Carreau if he were to get control of Brest. Henry offered Carreau, who was receiving from Charles VIII a modest annuity,[44] more money and an honourable command. He proposed sending Lord Willoughby de Broke, steward of the royal household and commander of the English expeditions to Brittany, with a sum of cash and authority to grant Carreau whatever he asked.[45] In late February, Henry set 20 May as the date when his 'Roial Armye' would invade 'his Royaume of Fraunce'.[46] In early April 1492, Henry, assured by Pennec that he 'would have the whole country', declared that he would invade France around 8 June. He also assured the Bretons that he would have neither peace nor truce with the French; that, with help from God, he would free Brittany from the 'captivity' of France, so that they could enjoy their liberty and franchises 'under a prince of their nation'.[47]

The king planned to land at least part of his army in Brittany from his own ships, hiring in March 1492 a Breton 'lodesman' for his great carrack, *Regent*.[48] But Henry also needed Breton ships. Merchants from Tréguier, Lannion, St-Brieuc and Paimpol, declaring their desire to be 'good and true Bretons', offered the use of their ships. On 21 April, Henry told Chancellor John Morton that these Breton merchants were 'willing to sende over suche shippes as they have to helpe and conveye over the see part of our Armee. But because theire mynd and entent maye not be knowen unto our auncient ennemyes and adversaries the frenshemen, they must feyne to come in merchandise into this oure Reame, and thereuppon to have oure several letteres of safeconduitt. . .'. An enclosed bill listed 68 Breton ships, giving in most cases the names of the ships, their owner and master, their portage, and port of origin. Of the vessels listed, 27 were between 25 and 50 tonnes; 35 ships were between 60 and 120 tonnes; and six ships were between 160 and 300 tonnes, making available to Henry a total portage of

---

[43] *Le complot Breton*, nos. 12, 13; Currin, 'Pierre le Pennec', 11-2.
[44] BNF, MS Français 32511, fo. 409.
[45] *Le complot Breton*, no. 25; Currin, 'Pierre le Pennec', 15.
[46] PRO, E 101/72/3/1064, 1068.
[47] *Le complot Breton*, no. 25; Currin, 'Pierre le Pennec', 20.
[48] BL, Add. MS, 7099, fo. 4; S. Bentley, *Excerpta Historica* (London, 1831), p. 89.

about 5,400 tonnes.[49] This list was modified before the letters of safe conduct were issued by the chancery on 24 April, when the total number of Breton vessels was increased to 71 ships. Of these, 36 ships were between 20 and 55 tonnes; 24 ships were between 60 and 120 tonnes; seven were between 160 and 300 tonnes, and four were of unknown portage.[50] The total tonnage to be made available to Henry was still around 5,000 tonnes, perhaps not enough to convey the whole English army and their horses, guns, and other weapons but sufficient to land a sizable force to secure Brest and Morlaix. In the end, Henry had to abandon plans to invade through Brittany. His indiscreet agent had oversold support for the English in the duchy, and Captain Carreau, who may have been a French agent all along, turned Pennec's correspondence over to Jean de Chalon, Prince of Orange and Charles VIII's lieutenant-general in Brittany. Fully apprised of the plot, the Prince of Orange and the chancellor of Brittany spent May and June preparing local defences to resist the English.[51] Henry postponed the invasion to 12 August, abandoning plans for an invasion of Brittany.[52] He mustered his army at Canterbury in middle and late September, and embarked it from Sandwich and Dover to Calais.[53]

Division and discord in France had been the key to previous English victories, and Charles VIII was not about to repeat past mistakes. In September 1491, he had some of the leading nobles in France, those who had been at odds with each other, swear to a new league for the defence of the king and the kingdom from foreign enemies and for the healing of internal discord. The king reconstituted this league in July 1492 to include his new queen, Anne of Brittany.[54] These measures sent a clear message to Henry and his allies that they would not profit from a divided France. However, Charles and his councillors believed that they might benefit by stirring

---

[49] PRO, C 82/92, 21 Apr. 7 Henry VII.
[50] PRO, C 76/175, mm. 13-6.
[51] *Le complot Breton*, nos. 33-8; Bertrand d' Argentré, *L'histoire de Bretagne jusques au temps de Madame Anne, dernière duchesse* (Paris, 1618), p. 694. Chancellor Montauban issued a mandate, dated 10 June, establishing posts between Dinan and Brest 'to know and learn the things that the English and enemies of this country might wish and intend to do, so that they might be attended to more promptly': Morice, iii. col. 903.
[52] PRO, E 101/72/6/1163.
[53] PRO, E 36/285, fos. 18v-50v.
[54] For the declarations of these leagues, see T. Godefroy, *Histoire de Charles VIII, roy de France, par Guillaume de Jaligny, André de Vigne & autre historiens de ce temps-là où sont descrits les choses les plus memorables, etc.* (Paris, 1684), pp. 616-7, 625-7.

120 *The English Experience in France*

discord and division in England.

The government of Charles VIII pretended that they had placed Henry Tudor on his throne, and that Henry had turned ingrate by opposing French ambitions in Brittany and in Flanders and by reasserting the Plantagenet claims.[55] Beginning in the summer of 1490, Charles VIII, through an English agent named John Taylor, encouraged first the pro-Yorkist Hayes Conspiracy to liberate and crown the Yorkist clamant, Edward, Earl of Warwick, and then the Perkin Warbek Conspiracy, in which, at Taylor's urging, Warbeck took on the role of Richard, Duke of York, the missing son of Edward IV. Charles VIII sent into English and Irish waters a flotilla under Adam Nyvletet to assist Taylor and the conspirators. Henry placed evidence of the Hayes Conspiracy before parliament in 1491 as proof of the French king's deceit and maliciousness.[56] The developing Warbeck Conspiracy, although a distraction, did not deter Henry's war preparations. In the spring of 1492, Charles VIII had Warbeck brought to France while he and his councillors decided how best to use the impostor against Henry.[57]

By mid January 1492, news of Henry's military preparations at London, Southampton, Poole and Fowey had reached the French court.[58] The elderly Jean d'Estouteville, seigneur de Torcy, told Charles VIII that it was prudent to be on guard, but the English threatened war out of 'the fear that they have that we might encroach upon them, because they see that you have now the country of Brittany, and that you can have many ships'.[59] Charles was not so sure. Between February and May, he made several requests for financial aid to raise an army of 24,000 men. He told his subjects that the King of England was assembling a great number of men, ships, and artillery, intending shortly to land in person in Normandy or elsewhere; and that the King of Romans and other 'adherents and allies who have an understanding with the said King of England' were also preparing to invade France 'to pillage and divide it between them, or rob and destroy and put our subjects in captivity'. In addition to Normandy, Charles's

---

[55] See above Michael K. Jones, 'The Myth of 1485'.
[56] *RP*, vi. 454-5; Ian Arthurson, *The Perkin Warbeck Conspiracy, 1491-1499* (Stroud, 1994), pp. 16-21.
[57] A. Spont, 'La marine française sous le règne de Charles VIII', *Revue des questions historiques*, n.s. 11 (1894), 418-9; Arthurson, *Perkin Warbeck*, pp. 21-3, 50-1.
[58] BNF, MS Français 15541, fo. 113.
[59] Ibid., fo. 117.

government anticipated attacks in Brittany, Guyenne, Picardy, Languedoc, Burgundy and Champaign.[60] In May, Jean de Chalon and Philippe de Montauban urged action to strengthen defences in Brittany, but the king feared more an English invasion through the Pas-de-Calais or Guyenne.[61]

In early May, English ships appeared off Honfleur, but did not attack. Their mission may have been to reconnoitre the costal defences. Later the same month, however, English ships seised and brought to Portsmouth five Norman ships laden with wheat.[62] About 9 June, Laurens Breton, an Italian merchant arriving in France from England, was interrogated by Norman officials. Breton told the French that he had seen eight large and small ships at Portsmouth, 60 vessels at Southampton, but no soldiers, apart from those guarding the ships. Nevertheless, said Breton, 300 Dutch ships were expected to arrive soon. The French asked about Henry's artillery. Breton replied that he had counted 35 pieces. The French also asked about Henry's finances, about recently seised prises, about the location of Henry's great ships, *Regent* and *Sovereign*, about support among the English for 'the son of King Edward', about Henry's whereabouts, and about news of any new agreements between England and Spain. Breton replied that the English had taken five Flemish ships off Boulogne-sur-Mer; that the *Regent* and *Sovereign* were at sea with other ships; that Henry was still in London; and that there was no news of any new Anglo-Spanish agreements. This information suggested that the English were not ready to invade at this time, otherwise Henry would have moved to one of the ports.[63]

A week later, officials at Dieppe interrogated the crew of a captured English ship. The prisoners told the French that on 2 June, 100 ships were anchored at Southampton, and an additional 100 ships had arrived the same day. They said that there were another 100 ships at Portsmouth, including a great vessel of between 300 and 400 tonnes, and ten barks, each of 180 tonnes. Furthermore, the ships at Southampton were to transport carts and

---

[60] AN, K 74, no. 34; BNF, MS Français 25717, nos. 122-5, partly quoted in Spont, 'La marine française', 423; *Lettres de Charles VIII, roi de France*, ed. P. Pélicier (5 vols., Paris, 1895-1905), iii. nos. 660 and 671.
[61] *Lettres de Charles VIII*, iii. no. 671; BNF, MS Français 20615, no. 34.
[62] Spont, 'La marine française', 424-5; C. de la Roncière, *Histoire de la marine française* (6 vols., Paris, 1899-1934), ii. 430.
[63] BNF, Français 15541, fo. 158r-v, partly printed in Spont, 'La marine française', p. 429. See also the letter of Louis, Duke of Orlèans to Charles VIII, 9 June 1492, printed in Godefroy, *Histoire de Charles VIII*, p. 613.

122 *The English Experience in France*

victuals. They added that 200 to 300 Flemish ships were expected, and that 100 Spanish ships had arrived in Southampton, one of which was a great vessel, of 300 tonnes, manned by 280 sailors. The English also said that Henry would amass in his kingdom 1,000-1,100 ships. They told the French that Henry was at Sheen, near London; yet rumours were about that the king's army would be ready by the Feast of St John the Baptist (24 June), with more than 1,000 carriages for guns. The French asked again about the *Regent* and *Sovereign*, and the whereabouts of Lord Willoughby de Broke, commander of the English army. The English replied that Willoughby de Broke was at sea on the *Regent*, off Honfleur and Villerville, blockading the mouth of the Seine.[64] In late June, three Bretons who had escaped from an English prison told French officials that 60 large Spanish ships, carrying Spanish soldiers, had arrived in England, along with Flemish ships; that 300 ships were ready to sail, and that the English were intending to land troops in two places somewhere in France.[65]

On Friday 15 June, Willoughby de Broke's fifteen ships attacked vessels off Honfleur, burning 45 Breton salt ships that tried to escape into Barfleur. The next afternoon, the French repelled the English when they tried to land near Barfleur. Willoughby de Broke ordered two more assaults the following afternoon, involving between 1,200 and 1,500 men, which the French again repelled. Willoughby de Broke may have intended to seise Barfleur with his sea-borne force, have the ships gathered at Southampton and Portsmouth ferry over additional troops and supplies, and secure Barfleur as the bridgehead for an English invasion into Normandy.[66] The English fleet remained at sea during July, but made no further raids on Normandy.[67] Early the following month, Guillaume Carreau and Jean de Porcon, receiving news that Henry had dismissed his army until next spring, proposed sending a well-armed fleet of 40 to 50 ships to attack the English fleet and deter further raids on France. Breton officials urged Charles VIII to approve this plan, but the king wanted his ships held back to defend the

---

[64] BNF, MS Français 15541, fos. 153-4 (Spont, 'La marine française sous Charles VIII', 430).

[65] Spont, 'La marine française', 430-1.

[66] BNF, MS Français 15540, fo. 132; BNF, MS Français 15541, fo. 97. Both letters are printed in *Le complot Breton*, nos. 39, 41. See also Spont, 'La marine française', 427-8; Roncière, ii. 432. The French commanders counted 34 English ships, but the accounts of Henry's treasurer of war list 15 ships: PRO, E 36/285, fo. 60.

[67] PRO, E 36/285, fo. 60r-v.

French coast.⁶⁸

By June, Henry's strategic concerns had shifted from Brittany and Normandy to the Low Countries. The Duke of Saxony began the long siege of Sluis on 18 May, and Henry sent naval and land forces to assist him. He appointed Sir Roger Cotton admiral of a fleet of twelve ships and 1,000 soldiers and sailors, and in August, put Sir Edward Poynings in command of a land army of about 900 men.⁶⁹ Charles VIII instructed Philippe de Crèvecœur, seigneur d'Esquerdes and his governor in Picardy, to succour Cleves by land and sea, but ships of Duke Albrecht and the English blockaded Sluis. French reinforcements for Sluis were held back to deal with the threatened invasions of Henry and Maximilian. By the end of September, Philip of Cleves commenced negotiations with Duke Albrecht. On 2 October, as Henry was landing in Calais, Philip and Duke Albrecht concluded a peace.⁷⁰ The victorious siege of Sluis was the only success to come from the Tudor-Habsburg alliance, ending the rebellion and depriving France of a valuable client and foothold in Flanders.

Henry's peace overtures to France during the summer of 1492 may have been a Tudor ruse. On 12 June, a few days before Willoughby de Broke attacked Barfleur and shortly after sending Cotton to assist in the siege of Sluis, Henry empowered Bishop Richard Fox, Giles, Lord Daubeney, lieutenant of Calais, and Sir James Tyrell, lieutenant of Guînes, to negotiate peace with France.⁷¹ On 11 and 16 June, Tyrell wrote to Marshal d'Esquerdes requesting, on behalf of Daubeney, that the French king send an embassy with sufficient powers to negotiate peace.⁷² The treaties of Woking allowed Henry to conclude a truce with France, unless war had commenced. It is uncertain whether Henry informed or consulted Maximilian. He knew about the count of Nassau's mission to France, and so in sending an embassy to France, Henry was doing no less than

---

⁶⁸ BNF, MS Nouvelles Acquisitions Françaises 1232, fos. 254r-5v; BNF, MS Français 15541, fos. 65, 99 (*Le complot Breton*, nos. 42-43); 3 Aug. 1492, *Lettres de Charles VIII*, iii. no. 687; Spont, 'La marine française', 431; Roncière, ii. 433.
⁶⁹ PRO, E 36/285, fo. 26v-7, 33v-4v, 58v; E 36/208, fos. 66-85. For Sir Roger Cotton's appointment as admiral of the fleet at Sluis, see PRO, C 82/94, 18 June 7 Henry VII. For Sir Edward Poynings appointment as commander at Sluis, see PRO, C 82/94, 24 Aug. 8 Henry VII.
⁷⁰ For different accounts of the siege of Sluis and English involvement, see Molinet, *Chroniques*, iv. 288-318; 'Die Geschichten und Taten Wilwolts von Schamburg', 116-28.
⁷¹ *Foedera*, xii. 481-2.
⁷² BNF, MS Français 15541, fos. 88, 174.

Maximilian.⁷³ Marshal d'Esquerdes, forwarding to Charles VIII Tyrell's letters, doubted English sincerity, saying that 'the effect of their display be more for invasion'.⁷⁴ On 26 July, Charles authorised d'Esquerdes to communicate with Daubeney, and he empowered ambassadors to negotiate with the English.⁷⁵ Fox's peace embassy is taken as evidence that Henry wanted not war, but an honourable and profitable peace from France; yet, on the eve of his invasion, he seems to have rejected just such a peace.

As he had done two years earlier, Henry demanded a large sum of money, 1,000,000 *écus d'or*, and the French, as before, refused it. Charles told d'Esquerdes that his council and the *Parlement de Paris* found Henry's demand 'trés grande et excessive', adding that 'the King of England ought to be well contented that we should pay him what is said to be due him on account of Brittany'.⁷⁶ Charles VIII, however, did not want an end to the negotiations. In late August 1492, he further instructed d'Esquerdes to learn from Daubeney what sum of money he intended should be paid for all time. If Daubeney persisted in the demand for 1,000,000 *écus d'or*, then d'Esquerdes was to conclude a truce for two or three years, or for however long it could be arranged. In turn, the King of France would pay a larger sum of 80,000 to 100,000 *francs*, for one time only. Henry, however, had rejected a similar offer in 1490. So, Charles told d'Esquerdes, if the English found unacceptable his offer to repay Henry's expenses for Brittany, then d'Esquerdes was to find out from them 'the limit of that to which they would come to, one time for all, of which sum would content them, diminishing from that which they had demanded, in order to advise the king of it, so that he [i.e., Charles VIII] might make known to him [i.e., d'Esquerdes] his good pleasure about it, for he means to work in this matter without holding it in delay or dissimulation, nor that it should end in rupture'.⁷⁷ Charles was trying to be flexible on the issue of money, offering to pay Henry a sum that was less than the demanded 1,000,000 *écus d'or*, as a one-time payment so it would not appear as if he was paying tribute. In short, Charles was willing

---

⁷³ On 27 May, Maximilian sent a message 'a toute diligence' to Daubeney, with the request that it be forwarded to Henry. It is not known if this message had anything to do with the negotiations with France or the siege of Sluis: ADN, B 2144, fo. 105v.

⁷⁴ BNF, MS Français 15541, fo. 91.

⁷⁵ *Ordonnances des rois de France de la troisième race, receillies par order chronologique*, ed. D.-F. Secousse, et al. (21 vols., Paris, 1723-1849), xx. 347-8.

⁷⁶ *Lettres de Charles VIII*, iii. Pièces Justificatives, no. 25.

⁷⁷ See note 96.

to pay most of what Henry demanded, including reimbursement for his costs in Brittany. In the treaty of Étaples, Charles agreed to pay Henry over several years 745,000 *écus d'or*, or three-quarters of Henry's initial demand. If Henry's invasion of France was mostly for the purpose of extorting from Charles a profitable peace, then he could have obtained it in late August 1492, avoiding the trouble and added expense of an actual military campaign only to end up concluding in November an agreement that he could have had three months earlier. Henry's ambitions, it seems, were more than financial.

When news that the English had landed in Picardy reached him, Charles VIII concluded that Henry had deceptively used the peace negotiations to put him off his guard. He expressed this view to his subjects, saying:

> We had been content to agree to a certain treaty and negotiation which, on the part of and at the request of the King of England, we had made. And although his demand was very excessive, nevertheless, to avoid the great evils and inconveniences that can come on account of war, we willingly condescended to most of his demand, of which, as much as by reason, he ought to have been content. And under engagement and semblance, he had made to want to agree to the said good of peace, withdrawing his army in his country and giving leave to the ships he had, to better colour his malice and to surprise and deceive us. After he knew that we had retreated into the marches here, he suddenly sent to Calais part of his army, and furthermore, we are very certain that he comes there in person and in great power, deliberately, with some of our enemies, to burden us, and our said realm and subjects by all ways and means that they can do ...[78]

On 18 July, while Henry's officials ostensibly negotiated peace with Charles's officers, Henry, announcing that he was now to undertake his 'voyage', ordered the barons of the Cinque Ports to provide, as they were obligated to do, 57 ships, sufficiently manned and arrayed, to serve for 40 days; and to have these ships ready to go to sea with the king's army by the end of August.[79] By proclamation of 2 August, Henry commanded all able-bodied

---

[78] *Lettres de Charles VIII*, iii. no. 692. A slightly different version of this letter, from the Archives de Harfleur, is quoted in Spont, 'La marine française', 433-4. For other versions, see Potter, 'Anglo-French Relations 1500', 50.
[79] *CPR 1485-1494*, p. 390.

subjects with harness to be ready 'upon an hour warning, to serve . . . in such manner and form as the case shall require'.[80] Ordnance, victuals and horses were purveyed and brought to the new staging areas of Sandwich and Dover.[81] The spiritual requirements of war were included as well. Henry invoked, through the intercession of the Virgin Mary and St. George, God's favour on his army; and in the retinue of Sir John Savage, two 'oratours' continually prayed for the success of the campaign.[82] Henry gathered English ships from as far west as St. Ives and Penzance, and he hired Dutch vessels. His fleet numbered 707 ships, of which 355 were Dutch. There were some Spanish ships, but no Breton vessels.[83] It was not enough. Henry seised the Flanders Galleys of Venice to transport his great guns from Southampton to Calais, over the protests of the Venetian Captain, and the doge and senate.[84] On 15 September, the king was at Canterbury for the mustering of the retinues. Ten days later, at Dover, he oversaw the embarkation of the first elements of his army to Calais, and on 2 October, he crossed the Channel on *The Swan*.[85] Contemporaries estimated the size of Henry's army to be between 20,000 and 25,000 men. It was probably between 12,600 and 14,000 men, but still the largest English army sent to France during the fifteenth century, and certainly a major military undertaking.[86] Charles VIII expected the English invasion, but was unsure if it would come in Brittany, Normandy, Guyenne or Picardy. On September 30, while ordering ships to sea, reinforcements into the Breton marches, and ships and men to Ireland 'toward our cousin the Duke of York', news

---

[80] *Tudor Royal Proclamations*, ed. P. L. Hughes and J. F. Larkin (3 vols., New Haven, 1964-9), i. 30-1.
[81] PRO, C 76/176, m. 6; *CPR 1485-1494*, pp. 404, 414-5.
[82] PRO, PSO 2/3, undated petition of Henry Whitford and Florence Lee. Whitford and Lee had also served as orators in Lord Willoughby de Broke's army in Brittany.
[83] PRO, E 36/285, fos. 59v-72v.
[84] *CSP Venetian 1202-1509*, 621, 622, 624, 625. The galleys suffered damage when entering the port of Calais, and after off-loading Henry's guns, had to return to Southampton for repairs.
[85] PRO, E 36/285, fos. 18v-50v. Henry's progress at the time can be traced through the warrants and signet letters he sent to the Chancery. The king's last warrant from Dover was issued on 2 October, and his first warrant from Calais is dated 4 October: PRO, C 82/98, 99. Henry's chamber accounts document his arrival in Calais on 2 October: Bentley, *Excerpta Historica*, p. 91.
[86] *CSP Milan, 1385-1618*, 464; Molinet, *Chroniques*, iv. 325; K. E. Lacey, 'The Military Organisation of the Reign of Henry VII' in *Armies, Chivalry and Warfare in Medieval Britain and France*, ed. M. Strickland (Stamford, 1998), p. 244.

reached the French king that the English had landed in France. 'Presently we have been warned', Charles wrote to his secretary, 'that a great band of the said English have descended at Calais, awaiting the King of England, who ought to arrive there shortly with the rest of his army; and that the King of the Romans is disposed to be joined with him from the other quarter'.[87]

Henry's decision in mid July to proceed with his invasion came soon after the failure of Nassau's embassy in France, when Maximilian appeared to be moving toward war. In September, at a meeting of the *Reichstag* in Koblenz, Maximilian requested financial aid for war against Charles VIII. In October, through du Pou, Henry sent another message to Maximilian and to the electors and princes of the Empire, urging them to reject peace with France. He told the electors and princes: 'Everyone ought to know that the faith of Frenchmen is a poor bet, because whatever they swear or promise, it is always out of fraud and deception, and they do not hold or observe anything unless by arbitration and at their pleasure'. Henry again condemned the French for all sorts of evil deeds, such as subverting the Dukes of Brittany and Burgundy, stirring discord in Germany, promoting rebellion in Flanders, and even instigating Richard III's usurpation and murder of his nephews. Henry reminded the *Reichstag* of Charles VIII's disgraceful snatching of Maximilian's proxy wife, and of his bad faith in rejecting the request, made through Englebert of Nassau, for the return of Marguerite of Austria and her lands. If these injuries were not avenged, said Henry, then 'the greatest vice, scandal, ignominy, and disgrace shall accrue and flow back not only to the King of the Romans himself, but also to all the Holy Roman Empire, its princes, and its allied kings and princes'.[88] After Henry's peace with France, these remarks could only have angered the Habsburgs as the words of a false hypocrite. If, as many Tudor historians believe, Henry intended to make peace with Charles VIII at the time of his landing in France, which was when he sent this message to Maximilian and the princes and electors of the Empire, then he was indeed a hypocrite.

To members of the *Reichstag*, Brittany, Burgundy, and Flanders mattered less than the tax burden they would have to bear for Maximilian's war. Nevertheless, they granted him a *Reichshilfe* of 94,000 florins, although only 16,000 florins were actually paid. In November, following the conclusion of the *Reichstag*, Maximilian left Koblenz for Metz. He planned

---

[87] BNF, MS Français 25717, no. 133.
[88] 'Henrici VII Angliae Regis ad Maximilianum', pp. 36-8.

an attack into Burgundy and Champagne to recover the lands lost earlier to Louis XI, and, perhaps, then march north to join with the English at Boulogne. Marshal d'Esquerdes could have been caught between the English and Habsburg armies had Henry and Maximilian coordinated their attacks. But Maximilian invaded the Franche-Comté with 4,000 horse and 2,000 Swiss mercenaries on 21 December, weeks after Henry had made peace with Charles VIII and had disbanded his army. Without money to continue the war, Maximilian soon had to make peace with Charles VIII as well.[89] Maximilian did not abandon Henry as the Tudor authorities claim. He sent a mercenary force of 4,000 foot and 2,000 horse, under the commands of Wilwolt von Schamburg and Louis de Bauldreh, to assist the English at the siege of Boulogne. But Schamberg, first seizing the opportunity to attack and take Arras from the French, arrived at Boulogne after Henry had made his peace with France. Henry received Schamburg coolly, and the captain became convinced that Henry and Charles VIII had conspired together.[90]

Schamburg's suspicions seem plausible to historians who see no strategic purpose to Henry's rather late invasion of the Boulonnais. But Henry, who made the decision to go ahead with the invasion against the advice of his council, may have had a limited strategic goal in mind.[91] The Boulonnais was a frontier region, facing the English at Calais and the Habsburgs in Flanders; and Boulogne-sur-Mer anchored a line of frontier defences running from Boulogne along the coast northeast to Ardres, south to Montreuil, southeast to Abbeville, and east to Doullens, Péronne, St-Quentin, Guise and Mézières. Boulogne was also the portal to Upper

---

[89] Molinet, *Chroniques*, iv. 326; Wiesflecker, i. 337-9.
[90] The size of the force sent to aid Henry at the siege of Boulogne is given in ADN, B 2144, fos. 138v, 181-182. For Schamburg's diversion to Arras, see 'Die Geschicten und Taten Wilwolts von Schamburg', 128-36. See also H. Ulmann, *Kaiser Maximilian I: Auf urkundlicher Grundlage dargestelt* (2 vols., Stuttgart, 1884-85), i. 162-3.
[91] 'The Requestes and Supplications of the Capitayns of Englande made unto King Henry the seventh for a Peace to be concluded between France and England', stated that at a council of war held in the Palace of Westminster, Henry 'was instantlie required and prayed to respite this present journey until a moor covenable season, and that such his allies, as had promised his Grace of mutuall ayde, wer in a moor redines'. Henry rejected the requests because of the promises he had made to Maximilian and to his own subjects. The original 'Requestes and Supplications', PRO, E 30/612, is badly damaged, and the signatures of most of the captains are illegible. A copy exists in BL, Cotton MS, Caligula D VI, fos. 13-7 (*Foedera*, xii. 490-4).

Normandy and the Île de France.[92] The chronicler Jean Molinet reported that Henry intended to take Boulogne and then 'draw beyond and conquer the duchy of Normandy'.[93] If Boulogne could be taken before the onset of winter, then Henry would have an expanded foothold in France, an advance-base from which, in the spring, with full strength and perhaps the support of his Woking allies, he could launch an offensive into Normandy. Henry already had the grant of a third fifteenth and tenth should his army remain abroad that could have helped sustain a core force through the winter and prepare for a spring campaign.

Apart from Maximilian's ability to follow through on his military commitments, such a strategy depended on taking Boulogne before winter. In July, when Henry decided to invade through the Pas-de-Calais, Boulogne seemed vulnerable. On 18 June, Marshal d'Esquerdes complained to Charles VIII about the delay in his request for materials he had ordered for the fortification of Boulogne. He feared that without time or additional help the defences would not be ready if the English invaded, as he expected them to do any moment.[94] Sir James Tyrell may have learned about Boulogne's weak defences, and when arranging the peace talks between Esquerdes and Daubeney, he may have entered the town. Various reports convinced Henry and his captains that Boulogne, 'a feble fortified town easy t'aproch and obtaign' could be taken in three or four days. During the actual siege in October, however, they discovered that it had been fortified to become 'oon of the strongest townes of Picardye, so that it is not prennable without long continuance and jeopardie of losse of great number of men'. Henry's army captured only a few of the smaller castles around Boulogne. The king's captains realised that worsening weather and diminishing supplies would soon compel the king to give up the siege and withdraw his army, 'which should not be honorable to his Grace'.[95] By late October, Henry, urged on by his captains, shifted his strategy to salvaging his honour, gaining as much profit as he could. Marshal d'Esquerdes, concerned about the loss of Arras and Maximilian's threat to Artois, this time welcomed the new English overtures. He visited Henry, and even ate and drank with the king.[96] On 3

---

[92] Sir Charles Oman, *A History of the Art of War in the Sixteenth Century* (New York, 1937), p. 16; A. Lottin, et al., *Histoire de Boulogne-sur-Mer* (Lille, 1983), pp. 103-4.
[93] Molinet, *Chroniques*, iv. 323.
[94] BNF, MS Français 15541, fo. 91.
[95] This is according to 'The Requestes and Supplications': *Foedera*, xii. 493.
[96] For an account of the siege of Boulogne, see Molinet, *Chroniques*, iv. 323-6.

November, with the conclusion of the peace of Étaples, Henry's campaign ended.

In English equivalents, Charles agreed to pay Henry about £145,000 to cover the £124,000 he spent in defence of Brittany and the arrears of the pension Louis XI had granted to Edward IV. To dispel the whiff of dishonour, the king's captains, in their 'Supplication', put to Henry the case that acceptance of the peace would 'conserve greatelie his honeour'.[97] Whatever profit Henry gained from France, it came at the price of turning Maximilian from an ally into an enemy. English ambassadors defending Henry's policy to the Habsburgs claimed that their king had acted honourably, and had given aid and succour to Maximilian in Brittany and at Sluis. Moreover, they said, when Henry made his descent into France, the English did not find Maximilian ready for war; nevertheless, in the peace with Charles VIII, Henry, with difficulty, included Maximilian and Archduke Philip, and their territories. Responding for the Habsburgs, the chancellor of Flanders accused Henry of violating the treaties of Woking, specifically the promises that the two kings would wage war against France for the recovery of their rights, and that neither king would cease waging war, or make truce or peace with France, without the consent of the other. Maximilian, said the chancellor, did have an army ready in the marches of Luxembourg and along the frontier of Champaign, and that his captains brought troops to assist the English at Boulogne, even though the treaties of Woking did not oblige Maximilian to commence the war until next season. Apart from violating the treaties of Woking, the Habsburgs did not think that Henry's peace with Charles protected their interests, for it ignored the return of Marguerite and her dower lands.[98]

It is evident from the chancellor's response that if Henry's policy all along had been to 'traffic' with war and make a return of his money, then it was foolishly short-sighted, and played Maximilian for a fool. If true, then it should not have surprised Henry that Maximilian would take up the cause of Warbeck as revenge. It is more likely, however, that Henry miscalculated in his campaign. His strategic plans depended on taking Boulogne before winter, and when this proved impossible, the king concluded the war as honourably as he could. Henry included Maximilian and Philip in the peace with Charles, probably thinking that he could win their approval if he

---

[97] *Foedera*, xii. 493.
[98] ADN, B 18824/23771 and 23772.

showed that he had taken steps to protect their territories. But Henry again miscalculated how much the Habsburgs felt betrayed when they learned of his violation of the treaties of Woking, and this second miscalculation drove an angry Maximilian to support Perkin Warbeck against Henry. The sudden peace with France was for Henry the most honourable way to extricate himself from the war, but it convinced many, like Wilwolt von Schamburg, that the King of England, in collusion with the King of France, had been acting deceptively all along. In trafficking with this war, Henry made his return in money, but he also found himself back where he started in 1485: isolated in Europe, dependent on the goodwill of France, and mistrusted by the Habsburgs.

7 'Une haquenée ... pour le porter bientost et plus doucement en enfer ou en paradis': the French and Mary Tudor's marriage to Louis XII in 1514

CHARLES GIRY-DELOISON

Recounting the last days of King Louis XII of France, the French chronicler Robert de La Mark, Seigneur de Fleurange, quoted the quip the clerks of the Parisian law courts (the *basoche*) circulating in Paris in November 1514 regarding his marriage to Princess Mary the previous month: 'le roy d'Angleterre avoit envoyé une haquenée au roy de France, pour le porter bientost et plus doucement en enfer ou en paradis'.[1]

Of course, the quip was meant to amuse. Louis was 52 and in poor health ('fort antique et débile' as Louise de Savoie so pleasantly wrote in her

---

When quoting from Cotton MS Caligula D VI [hereafter Caligula D VI], I have used the original foliation to allow easier cross reference.

[1] 'The King of England had sent a hackney to the King of France to carry him more swiftly and more sweetly to Hell or to Paradise': Robert de La Mark, Seigneur de Fleurange, *Histoire des choses mémorables advenues du reigne de Louis XII et François Ier ... depuis l'an 1499 jusques en l'an 1521 ...*, ed. Joseph-François Michaud et Jean-Joseph-François, Nouvelle collection des mémoires pour servir à l'histoire de France depuis le XIIIe siècle jusqu'à la fin du XVIIIe, 1ère série, 5 (1838), 45. Brantôme quotes a slightly different quip: 'Aussi disoit-on pour lors quand il l'espousa, qu'il avoit pris et chevauchoit une jeune guilledine [hackney] qui bientost le mèneroit en paradis tout droict, et plus tost qu'il ne voudroit, son grand chemin': Pierre de Bourdeille, abbé de Brantôme, *Oeuvres complètes*, ed. Ludovic Lalanne (11 vols., Société de l'Histoire de France, Paris, 1864-1882), ii. 369. See also, ibid., iii. 8 n. 3. The spousals took place in Abbeville on the 9 October.

Journal[2]) and had married a very pretty but very young girl, 33 years his junior.[3] It was common knowledge throughout the European courts that the king had been severely ill a few years before and was still suffering from gout.[4] In December 1514, his doctors, who had put him on a very strict regime, were furious to learn that he was spending most of his days (and

---

[2] Louise de Savoie, *Journal*, ed. Joseph-François Michaud et Jean-Joseph-François, Nouvelle collection des mémoires pour servir à l'histoire de France depuis le XIIIe siècle jusqu'à la fin du XVIIIe, 1ère série, 5 (1838), 89. Louise had no particular sympathy for Louis XII and was eager to see her beloved son François, Duke of Angoulême on the throne. Should Mary bear a son for her husband, Louise's life-long dream would be shattered. The duchess of Savoie and her daughter-in-law, Claude de France, kept Mary under close supervision in awe that the 'merveilles' Louis claimed to have done on the night of his 'amoureuses nopces' were not just the boast of an ageing man. In a letter dated 13 Oct. 1514, the two English ambassadors, Charles Somerset, earl of Worcester and Dr Nicholas West reported to Henry VIII that 'the Quene is continually with hym [Louis XII], of whom he maketh asmuch, as she reporteth to us herself, as it is possible for any man to make a Lady': BL, Caligula D VI, fo. 199 (H. Ellis, *Original Letters Illustrative of English History* (11 vols., London, 1824-46), 2nd series, i. 243). Claude stayed with Mary as much as possible and obtained that one of her close servants, Madame d'Aumont (Françoise de Mailli, wife of Jean V, sire d'Aumont), should be lady-in-waiting to the queen and sleep in her room. Francis, who had also been opposed to the marriage, clearly appeared to be less worried. Two days after the ceremony in Abbeville, he told Fleurange: 'Advantureux, suis plus joyeux et plus aise que je fus passe vingt ans; car je suis seur, ou on m'a bien fort menti, qu'il est impossible que le Roy et la Royne ne puissent avoir enfans' and added 'qui est faict a mon advantage': Fleurange, *Histoire*, p. 44.
[3] Mary's date of birth is not precisely recorded but Walter C. Richardson, *Mary Tudor: the White Queen* (London, 1970), p. 273 claims that the fragmentary evidence available suggests 18 Mar. 1495. Maria Perry, *Sisters to the King: the tumultuous lives of Henry VIII's sisters – Margaret of Scotland and Mary of France* (London, 1998|), p. 8 gives the same date, relying on the inscription in the margin of Lady Margaret Beaufort's Book of Hours dated 18 March: 'Hodie nata Maria tertia filia Henricis VII, 1495'. Mary would therefore have been nineteen when she married Louis XII of France. She had been married by proxy to Charles of Castile in London in Dec. 1508 but the contract was repudiated on 30 Jul. 1514 and two weeks later emissaries were sent to France.
[4] Jean d'Auton tells us that, in Feb. 1505, Louis XII was taken ill in Paris and was ordered by his doctors to leave the city, as they believed that its notorious humidity and the winter cold air heightened his chronically poor health: 'ses médecins luy dirent que le changement d'air et l'esloing de ce lieu où il estoit luy allègeroyent son mal'. The king left for Blois but in early Apr. his health deteriorated suddenly ('En l'entrant du moys d'april, en l'an mille cinq cens et cinq, le Roy, de rechief, se trouva tout debille et fort mallade': Jean d'Auton, *Chronique de Louis XII*, ed. René de Maulde La Clavière, (4 vols., Société de l'Histoire de France, Paris, 1889-95), iii. 360) and he was so close to death that masses and processions were held throughout the kingdom in a last attempt to save him. When in May he finally did recover, it was held by all to be a miracle: ibid., iv. 1-9.

nights) with his newlywed: 'et lui disoient bien les médecins que s'il continuoit il en mourroit pour se jouer'.[5] Indeed Louis fell ill the day after his wedding for, as Fleurange put it, 'il avoit voulu faire du gentil compaignon avecques sa femme; mais s'abusoit, car il n'estoit pas homme pour ce faire'.[6] Although he attended the receptions in Paris in November, the king was unable to journey to the Loire valley, as had been planned. Instead the court went to Saint-Germain-en-Laye for three weeks, before returning to Paris in December to stay at the Hôtel des Tournelles[7]. The words also rang very true. In French, a hackney is a medium size mare, of the 'ambelinge stood'[8] that proceeds at the leisurely pace fit for a woman. When Mary met Louis outside Abbeville on 8 October, she was riding such a hackney. The king went towards her, according to Fleurange, on his 'grand cheval bayard, qui saultoit'.[9]

But in reality, the *basoche* were out to ridicule the king and to discredit the new queen: in French, as in English, hackney also meant a filly or, worse, a prostitute.[10] They were voicing the persistent rumours that, despite her marriage to Louis XII, Mary was engaged in relationships with Charles Brandon, the dashing Duke of Suffolk, and Francis, Duke of Vendôme (or of Bretagne as the English nobility liked to style him) and heir apparent to the crown of France. It is also quite likely that the *basoche* were taking revenge on Louis. If we are to believe Brantôme, the King of France, then married to Anne of Brittany, had warned them to be careful of what

---

[5] Fleurange, *Histoire*, p. 45.
[6] Ibid., p. 45.
[7] Richardson, *Mary Tudor*, p. 123. The Hôtel des Tournelles was situated in the rue Saint-Antoine.
[8] See for example the description of the different horses owned by the duchess of Suffolk in Apr. 1547 in 'The booke of such horses as my Lades grace hathe at Grimstrope or elles where the 28 of Aprill, anno primo Ed. VI .. '., Historical Manuscripts Commission, *Report on the Manuscripts of the Earl of Lancaster preserved at Grimsthorpe* (1907), pp. 453-6. The booke lists 'mares of the ambelinge stood' and 'mares for the trottinge stood'.
[9] Fleurange, *Histoire*, p. 43.
[10] It is interesting to note that the English and the French differ on the origins of the word hackney. For the latter it comes from the Middle-English 'aquenei' which is derived from the name of the village Hackney (now East London), the horses bred there being particularly renowned. According to the *Dictionnaire étymologique de la langue française*, the word first appeared in the French language c. 1367. But Henry Bradley's *Middle-English Dictionary* and the *Oxford English Dictionary* state that it comes from Old French.

they said in their plays about him and his court, and certainly never to mention his wife on pain of being sent to the gallows:

> ... lui [Louis XII] estant raporté un jour que les clercs de la basoche du Palais, et les escolliers aussi, avoient joué des jeux où ils parloient du roy, de sa court et de tous les grandz, il n'en fist autre semblant, sinon de dire qu'il falloit qu'ilz passassent leur temps, et qu'il leur permettoit qu'ils parlassent de luy et de sa court, non pourtant desreglement, mais surtout qu'ils ne parlassent de la reyne sa femme en façon quelconque; autrement qu'il les feroit tous pendre.[11]

With Mary, they probably thought they were on safer ground because of the popular dislike of the English and of the king's age.

Of course, Mary's secret marriage to Suffolk a month or so after her first husband's death, fuelled the speculations that she had cuckolded Louis. The allegations are recorded in the *Mémoires* of the French chronicler, Brantôme. Writing over 50 years after events he had not witnessed,[12] Brantôme tells of a complex affair where Mary did her upmost to become pregnant so that she might 'vivre et règner reyne mère peu avant et après la mort du roy son mary'. Having found little, or no, satisfaction with Louis, she attempted to charm Francis with her 'caresses and mignardises' but the sudden death of her husband forced her to spread the rumour that she was expecting Louis's child and to 's'enfloit par le dehors avecques des linges peu à peu'. It was only due to Madame la Régente's perspicacity (who, after all, Brantôme tells us, was a 'Savoysienne qui sçavoit que c'est de faire des enfans'), that the plot was discovered and Mary exposed and sent back to England.[13] Two other French chroniclers, contemporaries of Louis XII, are far more cautious. They both report that it was thought that Mary might be pregnant, but neither alluded to Suffolk. Martin du Bellay talks of a rumour going about only after Louis's death and quickly halted by Mary herself; he mentions neither Charles nor Francis: 'Après sa mort, on eut quelque

---

[11] Brantôme, vii. 316.
[12] Pierre de Bourdeille, abbé de Brantôme was born in 1540 and died in 1614. It is quite possible that he learnt of the rumour from his father who went to England in 1520 to take horses to Henry VIII: Brantôme, x. 53-5.
[13] Ibid., ix. 640-2.

soupçon que la royne Marie fust grosse; mais soudain on fut asseuré du contraire par le rapport d'elle-mesme'.[14] Fleurange states that Francis only did his kingly duty by comforting Mary whom he called his 'bele-mère'.[15] But a month or so after Louis's death, he felt compelled to ask Mary if he could style himself King of France because he did not know if she was pregnant or not. Mary answered that he could, 'car elle ne pensoit point avoir fruict au ventre qui l'en peust empescher'.[16] Nevertheless, the rumour of a pregnancy was known to foreign emissaries: on 4 February 1515, Mercurin de Gattinare wrote from Compiègne that 'pour ce que la royne qu l'hon dict estre grosse estoit demeurée à Paris'.[17]

I

Princess Mary's marriage to Louis XII was a major political event, not only in the tortuous course of Anglo-French relations, but also for the future of the Valois-Orléans dynasty. It was, equally, an important cultural event at a time when the new Italian artistic influences were slowly being assimilated by French artists. The entries, the receptions, the jousts and the jewellery lavishly laid upon Mary were all part of an exercise in propaganda designed to impress the English, to demonstrate Louis's magnanimity and the wealth of the kingdom and to restore French pride after the Battle of the Spurs. All the French and English chroniclers of the day covered the event, Although not all as briefly as Louise de Savoie who curtly recorded in her *Journal*: 'Le 9 d'octobre 1514, furent les amoureuses nopces de Louis XII, roi de France, et de Marie d'Angleterre, et furent espousés à dix heures du matin, et le soir couchèrent ensemble'.[18] Nevertheless, the novelty lies elsewhere, in

---

[14] Martin du Bellay, *Mémoires de Messire Martin du Bellay . . . depuis l'an 1513, jusques au trespas du roy François Ier . . .*, ed. Joseph-François Michaud et Poujoulat, Nouvelle collection des mémoires pour servir à l'histoire de France depuis le XIIIe siècle jusqu'à la fin du XVIIIe, 1ère série, 5 (1838), 121.

[15] Interestingly, Francis told Henry that he was 'acoustume' to visit 'la royne ma[r]ye ma bele mere v[ot]re bonne seur . . . pour savoyr sy ele avoyt aucune chouse afere en quoy luy pense fere plesyr et ayde': BL, Cotton MS. Caligula D VI, fo. 256.

[16] Fleurange, *Histoire*, p. 46.

[17] *Négociations diplomatiques entre la France et l'Autriche durant les trente premières années du XVIe siècle*, ed. André J.G. le Glay (2 vols., Documents Inédits sur l'Histoire de France, Paris, 1849) ii. no. 14.

[18] Savoie, *Journal*, p. 89.

the immediate production of two different types of narrations of the major ceremonies that marked Mary's travel through northern France and her arrival in Paris: chapbooks and illuminated manuscripts. The cheap prints were small octavos written in haste, with no pretence to literary elegance, on standard sixteenth-century rag paper, sometimes embellished with woodcuts and sold a few days after the events they described, for a couple of pence, to the general public who could read. The illuminated manuscripts were destined for an entirely different category of readers, those who could commission and afford such costly objects which were as much artistic as literary productions. Mary's was not the first royal wedding to be recorded in manuscript or to be put into print.[19] Nor was it either Mary or Louis's first experience of the media. There is a manuscript account by André Delavigne of the French king's marriage to Anne of Brittany, and their subsequent entry into Paris in November 1504.[20] And in 1508, Richard Pynson (a Frenchman from Rouen who had emigrated to London) printed Pietro Carmeliano's narrative of Mary's betrothal, by proxy in London, to Charles Prince of Castile, the son of the Emperor Maximilian.[21] On that occasion, Pynson published two versions of Carmeliano's work: a luxury Latin edition, on vellum in a large type and illustrated with four fine woodcuts and a cheap, and partially abridged, translation, in English, with only two cuts of lesser quality. The Latin edition was intended for the more educated and refined public; the English one for a broader and more humble

---

[19] The first royal entry to have been printed in France is that of Charles VIII into Rouen in 1485: Charles de Beaurepaire, 'Entrée et séjour du roi Charles VIII à Rouen en 1485', *Mémoires de la Société des antiquaires de Normandie*, 20 (1854),

[20] André Delavigne, *Comment la Royne à Sainct Denys sacrée fut dignement en grand solempnité; Pareillement comme estoit acoustrée, Quant à Paris elle fit son entrée* . . ., ed. Henri Stein, 'Le sacre d'Anne de Bretagne et son entrée à Paris en 1504', *Mémoires de la Société de l'Histoire de Paris et de l'Île-de-France*, 29 (1902), 268-304. Jean Nicolaï wrote an account of Anne's previous marriage to Charles VIII and entry into Paris in Feb. 1492: ed. J. de Gaulle in the *Bulletin de la Société de l'Histoire de France*, (1848-56), 111-20.

[21] Petrus Carmelianus, *The Solempnities & triumphes doon & made at the Spouselles and Mariage of the Kynges doughter the Ladye Marye to the Prynce of Castile Archeduke of Austrige* (London, 1508) in 'The Spousells of the Princess Mary, Daughter of Henry VII, to Charles, Prince of Castille, a.d. 1508', ed. James Gairdner, *Camden Miscellany IX*, Camden Society, New Series, 53 (London, 1893).

audience.²² The 1514 documents belonged to the same vain – although the luxury versions were only available in manuscript.

Descriptions of four of Mary's entries have survived: those into Boulogne on 2 October, Montreuil on Thursday 5 October, Abbeville on 8 October and Paris on 6 November 1514. Apparently unknown to English historians, the Boulogne entry was recorded by Jacques Leest, abbot of Saint-Wulmer of Boulogne. It was still to be found in the municipal archives of the city at the end of the nineteenth century (*Terrier de Saint Wulmer*, 1505) and was edited in 1863 by abbé D. Haigneré.²³ Interestingly, it dates Mary's arrival in Boulogne to September 'à dix heures devant disner', though not giving a precise date. D. Haigneré argues that it must have been 30 September since news of Mary's landing had reached Abbeville by the morning of 3 October.²⁴ Nevertheless, I do believe Hall's account to be accurate: 'Thus the ii. Daye of October at the hower of foure of the clocke in the morenynge thys fayre ladye tooke her ship . . . and her shippe with greate difficultie was brought to Bulleyn'.²⁵ First, because he makes no mistake on the date of her entry into Abbeville, and, second, because Andrea Badoer, writing to the Venetian senate on 14 August 1514 gives the same date.²⁶ Jacques Leest and his abbey were heavily involved in the organisation of the entry: the abbey had built and decorated the ship which was the main element of the pageant, the prior Leurens Framery had composed the verses, and all the monks took part in the procession that greeted Mary before the gates of Boulogne. The account appears to have been written as a record of the hard work done by the abbey, not as a full report of the entry; it stops

---

²² For a discussion on the related subject of 'deluxe presentation copies' of books in the sixteenth century and on Petrio Carmeliano, see David R. Carlson, *English Humanist Books. Writers and Patrons, Manuscript and Print, 1475-1525* (Toronto, 1995).
²³ Jacques Leest, *Entrée solennelle de Marie d'Angleterre seconde femme de Louis XII en la ville de Boulogne le . . . septembre 1514*, ed. abbé D. Haigneré, *Almanach de Boulogne*, (Boulogne, 1863), pp. 85-90.
²⁴ *LP* i(2). 3331.
²⁵ Edward Hall, *The Union of the Two Noble and Illustrious Families of Lancaster and York*, ed. H. Ellis (London, 1809), p. 570. According to Polydore Vergil, the dreadful meteorological conditions in which Mary arrived in France were interpreted by the French as a terrible omen: 'It was widely reported among the people that this event [Mary's quick widowhood] had been portended by a terrible storm which suddenly arose on land and sea while she was crossing to France' (*The Anglica Historia of Polydore Vergil, A.D. 1485-1537*, ed. Denys Hay, Camden Society, New Series, 74 (London, 1950), p. 225).
²⁶ *CSP Venetian, 1509-1519*, 482.

when the monks leave Mary at the Eglise Notre-Dame to return to the abbey of Saint-Wulmer. Mary entered Montreuil on 5 October 'environ quatre heures apres midy' and left the town for Rue two days later. The description of her entry, entitled *Monstreul*, is to be found in the British Library and was edited by Francis Wormald in 1957.[27] Contrary to the Boulogne document, *Monstreul* is a full account of Mary's entry and stay in the city until her departure. The Boulogne and the Montreuil descriptions remain in manuscript and have no woodcuts.

There are four surviving different anonymous accounts of Mary's entry in the rain into Abbeville on 8 October,[28] and of her marriage to Louis the next day. Two are to be found in the Bibliothèque Mazarine: *Sensuit lordre qui a este tenue a lentree de la royne a Abeville* and *Lentree de la royne a Ableville*,[29] and two in the Bibliothèque Nationale: *Lentree de la royne a Ableville*[30] and *Lentrée de la royne de France à Abeville le neufiesme jour d'octobre.*[31] The first two were edited in 1859 by Hippolyte Cocheris. Although all four accounts are in print and are dated 9 October from Abbeville, they differ in their presentation and in their contents. The first three, comprising four pages recto-verso, are of a better finish: the paper is of good quality with regularly cut edges, and the text is printed in small gothic type and clearly laid out in paragraphs. They all have a woodcut on the front and back page. *Sensuit lordre. . .* has a richly attired lady riding a horse through a forest looked upon by an embraced couple on the title-page, and the traditional representation of the emblem of the Order of Saint Michael (an escutcheon bearing the arms of France, crowned by the royal crown, and encircled by the collar of the Order of Saint Michael)[32] on

---

[27] BL, Add. MS. 45132, fos. 1-5. Francis Wormald, 'The Solemn Entry of Mary Tudor to Montreuil-sur-Mer in 1514', in *Studies Presented to Sir Hilary Jenkinson*, ed. J. Conway Davies (Oxford, 1957), pp. 475-9. The text of the entry is preceded by a song composed for the marriage: BL, Add. MS. 45132, fos. 8v-9, Wormald, 'Solemn Entry', pp. 474-5 (hereafter, anonymous song).
[28] 'Of water from heaven there was no lack until evening [8 Oct.], which caused some regret': *CSP Venetian, 1509-1519*, 511.
[29] Bibliothèque Mazarine, ms 22028.
[30] BNF, RES LB29-50, hereafter *Lentree de la royne a Ableville* (BNF).
[31] BNF, RES LB29-49.
[32] For examples of illuminated manuscripts of the Order of Saint Michael in the early sixteenth-century, see *De L'ordre de saint-michel à la Legion d'honneur*, catalogue of the exhibition '5ᵉ centenaire de la création, à Amboise de L'ordre de saint-michel', held at Amboise 7 June – 20 July 1970, particularly pp. 17-40.

the back page. Both *Lentree de la royne a Ableville* have, on the front page, a group of horsemen before the drawbridge and crenellated gate of a town, and, on the last page, two mounted knights tilting before the royal couple, the knight on the left having been thrown to the ground. The Bibliothèque Nationale edition of *Lentree de la Royne a Ableville* has a second woodcut at the end of the text which depicts a different group of horsemen entering a walled town. On the other hand, *Lentree de la Royne de france*... is of lesser quality, the pages are unevenly cut, there are no paragraphs and the text is printed in large gothic type. Furthermore it has no woodcuts. Finally the texts differ, but not as one would have expected: those of the two *Lentree de la Royne a Ableville* and *Lentree de la Royne de france*... are all identical and give less details on the wedding ceremony on 9 October than *Sensuit lordre*... Only the *Lentree de la Royne a Ableville* now in the Bibliothèque Mazarine has an imprimatur.

Mary's entry into Paris and the receptions that followed quite logically generated more literature. Six descriptions of the entry survive: five in print, one in manuscript. Of the printed editions, one is in the Bibliothèque Mazarine, *Le[n]tree de tres excellente princesse ma dame Marie Dangleterre & Royne de France. En la noble ville cite et universite de paris faicte le lundy vi iour de Novembre. Lan de grace Mil cinq cens & quatorze*, and has been published by Hippolyte Cocheris.[33] The other four are to be found in the Bibliothèque Nationale: *Lentree de tresexcellente Princesse ma dame marie dangleterre Royne de france en la noble ville cite & universite de paris facste le lundy vi iour de novembre lan de grace mil v c xiiij*,[34] *Lentree de tresexcellente Princesse dame Marie Dangleterre Royne de france en sa noble ville cite & universite de paris faiste le lundy vi iour de novembre lan de grace mil cccc. Xiiij*,[35] *Le[n]tree de tres excellente princesse ma dame Marie Dangleterre & Royne de france. En la noble ville cite & universite de paris faicte le lundy vi iour de Novembre. Lan de grace Mil cinq cens & quatorze*,[36] and *Lentree de tressexcelle[n]te*

---

[33] Rés. 35484, in *Entrée de Marie d'Angleterre, Femme de Louis XII, à Abbeville et à Paris*, ed. Hippolyte Cocheris (Paris, 1859), pp. 21-34, hereafter *Lentree de tres excellente*... (BM).
[34] BNF, Res LB29-51 (hereafter 1).
[35] BNF, RES LB29-51A (hereafter A). It has been edited, but without the woodcuts, by Charles Read Baskerville, *Pierre Gringore's Pageants for the Entry of Mary Tudor in Paris* (Chicago, 1934), pp. 19-31, hereafter *Lentree de tresexcellente*... (BNF).
[36] BNF, RES LB29-51B (hereafter B).

pri[n]cesse ma dame Marie Dangleterre Royne de france en la noble ville cite et universite de Paris faicte Le lundi vi iour de nove[m]bre Lan de grace Mil cinq cens et quatorze.[37] All five texts are identical, the only variations being the number of abbreviations. But, as for the Abbeville documents, there are some minor differences in their presentation. Versions 1 and A are the only ones to have an imprimatur. Version 1 comprises six pages non-folioed, the first five are printed recto-verso, the sixth, only on the verso. The text is disposed in well centred paragraphs and printed in a gothic type slightly larger than those used in the four other versions. Version A has eight recto-verso, gilt-edged, non-folioed pages of good quality paper, and the text is printed in small gothic type and clearly laid out in paragraphs, although badly centred. Version B is of slightly lesser quality (no gilt-edging) and printed in a different small gothic type. Version C is the cruder of the five: it comprises only four recto-verso non-folioed pages, the print is a very small gothic type and there are no paragraphs. All five versions have woodcuts. *Lentree de tres excellente* . . . (BM) and version B have, on the title-page, two horsemen addressing a bearded soldier before the crenellated walls of a city, and, on the back page, the same woodcut as in both the *Lentree de la Royne a Ableville*. The only woodcut in version 1 is identical to the one on the front page of both the *Lentree de la Royne a* Ableville. Like the Bibliothèque Nationale edition of *Lentree de la Royne a Ableville*, version A has three woodcuts: one on the title-page (two horsemen facing a walled city on their left, one of the horses with a cross of Saint George on its rear right flank) and two on the last page (on the recto a knight in armour, a lady facing him, and on the verso, two mounted knights tilting but, contrary to version B, neither dismounted and there is no royal couple looking on). Version C has only three small vignettes at the top of the title-page, representing fantastic animals on a background of lilies and roses.

The manuscript edition is now in the British Library and has been edited by Charles Read Baskerville.[38] Entitled *De la reception et entrée de la illustrissime dame et princesse Marie d'Angleterre (fille de Hen. VII) dans la ville de Paris, le 6. Nov[emb]re 1514. Avec belles peintures*, it was composed by Pierre Gringore, who had devised some of the pageants of the

---

[37] BNF, RES LB29-51C (hereafter C).
[38] BL, Cotton MS Vespasian B II, fos. 3-15; Baskerville, *Pageants*, pp. 2-15 (hereafter Pierre Gringore). Unfortunately, the miniatures are in black-and-white.

142 *The English Experience in France*

Parisian entry.³⁹ The main feature of the manuscript is the seven beautiful 'peintures' of the pageants. The manuscript is of very fine quality, with illuminated paragraph marks and capitals at the beginning of each paragraph.⁴⁰ Pierre Gringore gives not only a very detailed description of the different pageants with the verses that accompanied each one, but also his own interpretation of the tableaux.

Two other events related to Mary's entry into Paris were also recorded in manuscript or print:⁴¹ the oration given to Mary by Maître du Breul in the name of the University of Paris on 26 November, and the jousts that lasted ten days, from 13 to 23 November 1514. A deluxe manuscript version of the oration, with a miniature of Mary standing in a room under a canopy surrounded by the members of the university and being presented a crown bearing lilies and roses, was prepared by the university for the queen. It is composed of fourteen folios and, like Pierre Gringore's manuscript, there are illuminated paragraph marks and capitals at the beginning of each paragraph. The margins of the title-page are decorated with lilies and roses and, in the lower margin, with the arms of the Sorbonne. Initially, the first capital letter encircled the arms of England but, at some stage, those of the Bourbon family were superimposed.⁴² There is a contemporary manuscript copy of the text, in French, although without any miniature or decoration, in the British Library⁴³ but I have found no printed version of the oration. The two manuscripts differ slightly from each other in the spelling and the abbreviations. As for the jousts held in the rue Saint Antoine, Gilbert Chauveau, Montjoie king-of-arms, wrote a detailed account of them which was printed in Paris in 1514. The book is of similar quality to the ones mentioned above: the 44 non-folioed recto-verso pages are gilt-edged and the text is printed in small gothic type, but it has no woodcuts nor imprimatur.⁴⁴ The jousts must have attracted much interest as several manuscript copies of

---

³⁹ For Pierre Gringore, see Baskerville, *Pageants*, pp. xi-xxxii.
⁴⁰ See the description given by Baskerville: ibid., pp. xxx-xxxii.
⁴¹ There are also two printed narrations of Mary's coronation in Saint-Denis on 31 October 1514, see *Inventaire chronologique des éditions parisiennes du XVIᵉ siècle d'apres les manuscrits de Philippe Renouard*, ed. Brigitte Moreau (2 vols., Paris, 1977), ii. 808.
⁴² BNF, ms. fr. 5104, *Discours adressé au nom de l'Université de Paris à Marie d'Angleterre, reine de France, par maître 'May Du Breul', docteur en théologie*.
⁴³ BL, Harley MS 1757, fos. 227-38.
⁴⁴ BNF, RES LB29-52; Gilbert Chauveau dit Montjoie, *Lordre des ioustes faictes a Paris a lentree de la royne . . . Redige et mis par escript par montioye, roy d'armes selon les compaignies & iournees, ainsi comme le tout a este fait* (Paris, 1514).

the account remain in the British and French archives, although none of them are illustrated.[45]

Finally, there are no remaining accounts of Mary's entry into Etaples where she stayed on her way to Montreuil, nor of any entry between Abbeville, which she left on 16 October, and Saint-Denis where she arrived on (or just before) Friday 3 November,[46] although Théodore Godefroy does mention that Mary and Louis 'se partirent dudit Abbeville en tirant vers Paris: en passant par les villes de Picardie, leur furent faites Entrées solennelles. Et delivra ladite Dame, les prisonniers en tous les lieux par où elle passoit par le commandement du Roy'.[47]

All this literary production suggests that there was a market in the early sixteenth century for souvenir books and manuscripts of major political and 'cultural' events. The two imprimatur leave little doubt of the commercial competition that existed between the booksellers-printers of the day. On 25 October 1514, the Prévôt of Paris authorised Guillaume Mart, 'libraire', to publish and sell *Lentree de la royne a Ableville*, and gave him an eight day monopoly.[48] On 10 November, Jehan de Fontaine, Prévôt de l'Hôtel du roi, authorised Guillaume Varin to sell versions 1 and A of Mary's entry into Paris, although without a monopoly.[49] It is impossible to know if the books that do not carry an imprimatur were ever put on the market, although it makes sense to think that if someone had gone to the bother and expense of printing one, it was because he knew he could sell it. The books also give an insight into the printing trade. The fact that some of them share the same illustrations indicates that models of woodcuts were circulating between printers and from town to town, or at least inside some geographical area. It might also signify that Guillaume Mart printed both *Lentree de la royne a Ableville* (BM and BNF) and version B of *Le[n]tree de tres excellente princesse . . .*, although the types are different. It is also possible that when the texts are identical, the different versions of an entry,

---

[45] BNF, ms. fr. 5103, fos. 1-73, *Jouxtes faictes a Paris a lEntree de la Royne dAngleterre en lan 1514*; ms. fr. 23074; n.a.f. 7240, fos. 124-75, *Le magnifique Tournoi faict A Paris a lentree de la Reine Marie dAngl[eter]re femme du Roy Louis XII. 1514*; BL, Add. MS 30543.
[46] For example, they were in Beauvais by 25 October: *LP* i(2). 3387.
[47] Théodore Godefroy, *Le Cérémonial François, contenant les cérémonies observées en France aux Sacres et Couronnements de Roys et Reynes . . .* (2 vols., Paris, 1649), i. 471.
[48] *Lentree de la Royne a Ableville* (BM), p. 17. Rés. 3476.
[49] *Lentree de tresexcellente . . .* (BNF), p. 31.

144 *The English Experience in France*

although they may differ in other aspects (type, etc.), came from the same printer. Brigitte Moreau, on evidence of the woods used, suggests a slightly different possibility: Guillaume Varin might have printed *Lentree de la Royne a Ableville* (BNF) and Guillaume Nyverd *Lentree de tres excellente . . .* (BM) and version B of the Paris entry, these two texts having, as previously noted, the same cuts.[50] But whatever may have been, the Parisien 'libraires-imprimeurs' dominated the printing market: Guilliame Mart, Guilliame Nyverd and Guilliame Varin worked in Paris. Finally, one has little evidence of the readership the books and manuscripts enjoyed. No doubt they were primarily a souvenir for those who had attended the ceremonies. This was certainly the case of the two illuminated manuscripts prepared for Mary. It is likely that the one of the oration was not finished when Mary left France, and so therefore remained in Paris. But its value and interest were not lost to all: some time after Mary's departure, it came into the hands of the Bourbon family. It might have been bought by the duchess Suzanne de Bourbon, wife of Duke Charles, constable of France who also owned, in 1519, a manuscript of the jousts.[51] Similarly, the copy of *Monstreul*, now in the British Library, was certainly brought back by Thomas Wriothesley, garter king-of-arms, who had accompanied Mary to France. As Francis Wormald points out, the manuscript is in a book that formed part of the heraldic collections Wriothesley had made during his lifetime.[52]

II

Because Mary landed in Boulogne, she had to travel to Paris through towns and fields that still carried the stigmas of many Anglo-French wars. The devastation that the English armies and their mercenaries left in their wake were no doubt still vividly etched in the memories of the local inhabitants. In this context, Mary's entries reveal the perception and opinion the French had of Mary and of the English.

Undoubtedly, as the *basoche* inferred, behind all the glamour, the splendour, the noise and the excitement of the wedding, the anti-English

---

[50] Moreau, ii. 825-6.
[51] BNF, ms. fr. 5103, fo. 1: 'ce livre est a madame la duchesse de bourbon connestable de France', (dated 1519).
[52] Wormald, 'Solemn Entry', p. 471.

feeling was still strong throughout the country. One can easily imagine that between Boulogne and Paris, particularly north of Abbeville, the population was rather weary of the English. Maybe some had witnessed Picquigny, when on 29 August 1475, Louis XI and Edward IV had agreed to a truce and the French king had regaled the English soldiers with wine and food in Amiens to the extent that 'D'eau n'estoit nouvelles',[53] or known someone who had.[54] No doubt, many more had experienced the strange and bloodless English campaign of October-November 1492 around Etaples. But certainly all would remember the return of the English armies in the summer of 1513: the battle of the Spurs on 15 August, when the French cavalry was defeated and nobles of high rank taken prisoner,[55] and the surrender of Tournai on 23 September.[56] In 1475, Commynes wrote of the 'hayne . . . de ceux du païs',[57]

---

[53] Philippe de Commynes, *Mémoires* in *Historiens et Chroniqueurs du Moyen Age*, ed. Albert Pauphilet and Edmond Pognon (Paris, 1952), p. 1137. Free and abundant wine and food for the common people played a big part in smoothing bad feelings between French and English. In Montreuil, in Oct. 1514, the municipality opened the town cellars and kept food prices low, despite the great number of people in town, so that 'la prendroit chacun le bon vin et a bon marche': *Monstreul*, p. 478. In 1520, at the Field of Cloth of Gold, fountains ran red and white wine for all at the gates of Henry VIII's 'palace' in Guînes (see Joycelyne G. Russell, *The Field of Cloth of Gold: men and manners in 1520* (London, 1969), and the painting now at Hampton court: 'The Field of Cloth of Gold'). Nicolas Offenstadt also notes the importance of food and wine in the ritual of peace in fifteenth-century France: 'La paix d'Arras, 1414-1415: un paroxysme rituel?' in *Arras et la diplomatie européenne, XVe-XVIe siècles*, ed. Denis Clauzel, Charles Giry-Deloison and Christophe Leduc (Arras, 1999), pp. 73-4. Organised by the city authorities to please the public and to keep order in the streets, these feasts were meant to allow the lower classes to partake symbolically with the powerful in the celebration of peace. Thus, food and wine, although not sheared and of different quality, brought together rich and poor, reaffirming the unity of the kingdom. But such unity was all on the surface and short lived: in Abbeville, on 8 October, a fire broke out in the evening and 'made greater progress than it would have done had it been permitted to ring the bells, but this was forbidden, to avoid disturbing the king at his amusements': *CSP, Venetian 1509-1519*, 511.
[54] See Joseph Calmette and George Périnelle, *Louis XI et l'Angleterre* (Paris, 1930), pp. 199-207.
[55] 'The battle of Therouanne, known as the Battle of the Spurs, because the French used their spurs so much in order to flee the quicker': Francisco Lopez de Gomara, *Annals of the Emperor Charles V*, ed. Roger B. Merriman (Oxford, 1912), p. 37 (and p. 186 for the Spanish text).
[56] See Charles G. Cruickshank, *Henry VIII and the Invasion of France* (Stroud, 1990) and his *The English Occupation of Tournai 1513-1519* (Oxford, 1971). For Tournai, see also Adolphe Hocquet, *Tournai et l'occupation anglaise. Contribution à l'étude du XVIe siècle* (Tournai, 1901).
[57] Commynes, *Mémoires*, p. 1148.

146 *The English Experience in France*

under Burgundian rule, towards the English armies leaving Amiens. On 25 September 1513, the Tournaisiens assembled in the market-place to meet their new sovereign, refused to show 'any amiable countenance' to Henry VIII[58] and, a fortnight later, the *Magistrat* (the municipal authority) was obliged to pass a decree forbidding the inhabitants to 'faire chanchons, ballades ou libelles diffamatoires' against the king and his court.[59] In November 1514 the governor of the city, Sir Edward Poynings, was still complaining that not all the Tournaisiens had taken the oath of allegiance to Henry VIII.[60] Many years later, Brantôme noted that in 1514 the population of Northern France stood in awe of the English: 'car de ce temps quand on parloyt des Angloys entrant en France, il sembloyt que ce fussent tous les diables'.[61] For the French, Anglo-French relations of the previous forty years, not to mention in a more distant past, did no favours to the English.

The relations between the two crowns were also still very tense in the autumn of 1514, Although peace had been signed on 7 August in London and Henry VIII had hosted a lavish reception for the French ambassadors at Greenwich. The Venetian envoy remarked that the women at Henry's court spoke French to Louis XII's ambassadors, which 'delighted them'. Nevertheless, Edward Hall records the suddenly hostile attitude of the Duke of Longueville, who had negotiated the peace whilst prisoner in England, once back in France: 'This Duke was highly enterteyned in England of many noble men and had great chere, but when they came into Fraunce with the quene scace know them' and had been well entertained.[62] The French chroniclers noted that the *Père du Peuple* only married Mary in order to bring peace to the kingdom before his death and to keep out the English: 'qu'il espousa quasy commme par contraincte, se sacrifiant pour son royaume, pour achepter la paix et l'alliance du roy d'Angleterre et qu'il peut mourir paisible roy de France, sans le laisser en trouble, comme certes il fit par le sacrifice de sa mort'.[63] Louis did need peace with England: in

---

[58] Hall, *Chronicle*, p. 566. See also, Cruickshank, *Tournai*, pp. 11-2, 284.
[59] Hocquet, *Tournai*, pp. 113-4.
[60] Ibid., pp. 127-8.
[61] Brantôme, ii. 368 n. 4.
[62] Hall, *Chronicle*, pp. 569-70.
[63] Brantôme, ii. 369. See also, ii. 368 n. 4 and vii. 330; Bellay, *Mémoires*, p. 119. This was the general opinion in Europe. Writing in 1557-58, the priest Francisco Lopez de Gomara reported that 'King Louis of France, at the age of 55 years, in order to gain peace, and recover Therouanne and Tournay, marries Mary, sister of King Henry VIII'. The original text in Spanish reads 'Casa el Rey Luis de Francia, siendo de 55 anos, con Blanca Maria hermana del Rey Enrique IIX' but, according to Merriman 'the "Blanca" of the original text

Mary Tudor's Marriage to Louis XII 147

September 1513 the Swiss were at the gates of Dijon; in June 1514 the French army was defeated at Novarre and lost the Milanese; and in the summer of 1514 Henry VIII and Emperor Maximilian were again planning war in the North of France. In England, few favoured the rapprochement. There was a very strong pro-Spanish faction at court and no celebrations were ordered throughout the country when the peace and marriage treaties were signed in London on 7 August 1514.[64] Nicolo di Favri, a member of the Venetian embassy in London, reported that peace was proclaimed in the city on 11 August by two men on horseback, but that 'Neither trumpet nor any instrument was sounded, and but few persons heard the proclamation; neither were bonfires burnt nor any other demonstration made for this peace'.[65]

On several occasions, French officials and nobles scarcely disguised their feelings (often openly hostile) to the two English embassies sent to France in August-November 1514 and to Princess Mary's retinue. One of the anonymous chroniclers of the Abbeville entry remarked that four or five Englishmen arrived on the 8 October more richly attired than the French nobles were, inferring that the English had little knowledge of good manners (it was contrary to the custom of the country) and that in their desire to impress their hosts, were at risk of causing a diplomatic incident. They dressed down the next day.[66] As we know, Louis dismissed Mary's entourage the day after their wedding. Although the ambassadors' instructions did stipulate that once the marriage was solemnised they were to proceed no further than Abbeville and return to England,[67] Louis XII

---

is of course a mistake'. This is clearly not the case: widowed and childless, Mary was immediately known as the 'reine blanche': *Annals*, p. 39 (and p. 187 for the Spanish text).
[64] *Feodera*, vi(1). 64-8 and 68-70.
[65] *CSP Venetian 1509-1519*, 505.
[66] 'Il y avoit quatre ou cinq hommes q[ue] lon dit ceulx qui gouvernent la fine[n]ce da[n]gleterre q[ui] avoie[n]t plus de drap dor & de orfavrerye a leurs habillemens que ne portent les plus gra[n]s gentilzhommes de par deca. Et pour ce que ce nest pas la coustume on disoit quilz les osteoient des lendemain': *Sensuit lordre . . .*, p. 6. The change of cloths was also noticed by an anonymous contemporary: *CSP Venetian 1509-1519*, 505.
[67] *LP* i(2). 3294. There was even some doubt amongst the English councillors if Worcester and Nicholas West, who had separate instructions, were allowed to go to Paris: *LP* i(2). 3301; Ellis, 2nd series, i. 239-43.

148 *The English Experience in France*

nevertheless made sure that all the 'lords and gentlemen of Englond' who were at the wedding left promptly.[68] They were thanked, praised, given 'good rewardes' and told 'to take no lenger payne'.[69] They departed from Abbeville in two separate groups on 13 and 14 October.[70] Louis XII must have been relieved to see such a large party leave the country.

The ambassadors who did stay on in France (Thomas Grey, marquis of Dorset, Thomas Dowcra, prior of St John of Jerusalem, Charles Somerset, earl of Worcester and Nicholas West, dean of Windsor)[71] were also put through a rather hard time in Paris. Not only did the *basoche* make fun of the marriage, no doubt with the tacit consent of the Parisian municipal authorities, but the university of Paris could scarcely hide its contempt for the English. Master May du Breul, doctor in theology, who delivered the complimentary oration to Mary when she was received en Sorbonne on 26 November, could not resist reminding her that 'Les Rois de France ont une prerogative que jamais nont este tuez ne occis de leur peuple ne par luy chassez ne exillez hors le Royaulme',[72] stopping short of adding that, of

---

[68] There are several lists of the members of Mary's suite, see for example BNF, naf 7240, fos. 175-176v: 'Sensuivent les Princes et seigneurs qui sont venuz dAngleterre pour accompaigner La Royne Marie', and the list published by John Leland, *Joannis Lelandi Antiquarii De Rebu Britannicis Collectanea cum Thomae Hearnii Praesatione Notis et Indice* (6 vols., London, 1770) ii. 701-3.

[69] Hall, *Chronicle*, p. 570. A report, probably from the bishop of Asti, mentions that Louis XII gave silver plate to the amount of 30,000 francs to each of the 'chief English lords and barons' and paid for all their expenses in Abbeville: *CSP Venetian 1509-1519*, 511. See also, *LP* i(2). 3354.

[70] *LP* i(2). 5495; *CSP Venetian 1509-1519*, 511.

[71] They were joined by Suffolk at the end of October: *The Chronicle of Calais in the Reigns of Henry VII and Henry VIII to the Year 1540*, ed. John Gough Nichols, Camden Society, Old Series 35 (London, 1846), p. 16.

[72] BNF, ms fr. 5104, fo. , and BL, Harley MS 1757, fo. 232v. Du Breul was alluding to the numerous bloody incidents that had marred the succession to the throne in England since the murder of Richard II and Henry IV's usurpation in Sept. 1399, and to the fact that Mary's father, Henry VII, had gained the crown of England on the battlefield of Bosworth. The 1399 affair was well known in France through two largely circulated contemporary chronicles: *Histoire du roy d'Angleterre Richard* and the *Chronique de la traison et mort de Richart Deux roy d'Engleterre*. Craig Taylor, 'Sir John Fortescue and the French Polemical Treatises of the Hundred Years War', *EHR*, 114 (1999), 112-29 at 124-5, has shown how the murder of Richard II largely contributed to forge the reputation of regicides the English enjoyed in France. Peter Lewis has drawn attention to the second recension of Noël de Fribois's *Miroir Historial* (BNF, ms. Fr. 4943, c. 1461) which contains, on fo. 41v, a miniature representing 'a pile of six dead kings of England and one defunct and sainted bishop (St. Thomas of Canterbury)' to illustrate Fribois's version of 'the regicidal proclivities of the English': 'Two Pieces of Fifteenth Century Iconography', *Journal of the*

course, the Kings of England could not lay claim to such a privilege. Concluding his lengthy and over-flowery oration, du Breul announced to Mary that 'vostre fille aisnee luniversitte de paris vous p[rese]nte non pas or ne argent mais dons trop plus pretieulx et de meilleur valleur': first, the university's 'tres grande et tres excellente doctrine science et sapience non ayant en ce monde pareille'; second, 'continulles oraisons et prieres privees et particullierement sainctes meditations'; and third, 'processions generalles et universelles et solempnelles de tous ses membres et supostz . . . a tos jours que vous plaira'.[73] Unfortunately, one doesn't know what Mary made of the so-called presents the university so generously offered her and which, clearly, bordered on rudeness. Ironically, it seems that Mary did not even received the illuminated manuscript of the oration!

Furthermore, we are told that during the jousts in Paris 'Thenglyshmen receyved muche honoure and no spott of rebuke, yet they were prively sett at and in many jeopardies'. Indeed, the French cheated in an attempt to stop the English winning. When the fighting on foot at the barriers began on Tuesday 21 November, Francis declared that he was unable to take part, having been slightly wounded in his hand, and asked Dorset and Suffolk to replace him, which they did. Francis then sent in an imposing hooded German, hoping that he would defeat Suffolk. But to Francis's dismay he failed and, according to Edward Hall, 'the Almayne was conveyed by the Daulphin lest he should be knowen'.[74] The English ambassadors reported with delight to Henry VIII and Wolsey the French

---

Warburg and Courtauld Institutes 27 (1964), 319-20. In Dec. 1489, Robert Gaguin, whilst in London waiting for the return of his fellow ambassador Waleran de Sains, bailli de Senlis, composed a long poem, *S'ensuit le passe temps d'oysiveté*, in which he debates with his interlocutor, Thomas Whyting, Chester herald, the advantages of peace over war. Reflecting on the evils of civil wars, Gaguin kindly reminded Whyting that, 'Par vous mesmes le povés veoir;/ Le temps passé vous en fait sage./ Vous aves eu moult beau miroir/ Depuis ving ans sur ce passage;/ Vous avez tins piteux maisnage/ De changer er rechanger roys./ Prince n'est seur en telz destrois', in R. Gaguini, *Epistole et Orationes*, ed. Ludovic Thuasne (2 vols., Paris, 1903), ii. 411. For further examples of the poor opinion the French had of English politics, see David Potter, 'Anglo-French Relations 1500: The Aftermath of the Hundred Years War', *Journal of Franco British Studies*, 28 (1999/2000), 41-66 at 61-62.

[73] BNF, ms fr. 5104, fo.; BL, Harley MS 1757, fo. 237.

[74] Hall, *Chronicle*, p. 572

150   *The English Experience in France*

foul-play and dishonesty and the outcome of the fight.[75] But Montjoie's official account of the jousts tells another story. According to the document there was no meeting on Tuesday 21 November: Monday 20 November was the seventh day of the tournament and Wednesday 23 (a mistake for 22) was the eighth so, of course, no 'Almayne' is mentioned.[76]

Nevertheless, despite all the tension and resentment, the French turned out in great numbers, and peacefully, to see and view Mary along her processional route from Boulogne to Paris. That the population showed no aggressiveness towards the English impressed the anonymous chronicler of the Montreuil entry, who noted that 'tous les seigneurs et dames venuz d'Angleterre . . . allerent sans murmure mais le tout a leur bon plaisir'.[77] In Boulogne as in Montreuil, in Abbeville as in Paris, and no doubt as in all the other towns Mary visited, the inhabitants performed the popular rituals that traditionally accompanied entries and peace celebrations in Northern France, and of which crowd gatherings, noise and thanksgivings were the most important elements. In Montreuil we are told that 'les rues et chauffours [étaient] plaines de peuple tant de ladite ville que des pais d'environ' when Mary entered the city on 5 October. When she left the town on the following Saturday, she was accompanied to the gates of the city by 'Monseigneurs de la ville et de la plus grant partie du peuple' and all those who had come to the market.[78] In Abbeville on the 9 October, the crowds were so thick that the queen could not approach the king's lodgings and had to wait for over half-an-hour whilst the lesser people were being ejected *manu militari*: 'en attendant que la presse du logis du Roy fust gette hors la dicte dame a este arrestee elle & toute sa compaignie deda[n]s ledit jardin environ demy heure'.[79] A similar incident occurred in Paris on 26 November. At the banquet given in Mary's honour at the Hôtel de Ville, the throng was such that the queen was unable to reach the staircase leading to the banqueting hall and had to resort to enter the Hôtel de Ville through the porter's lodge, in fear of being crushed by the crowd. The situation was no better inside and many dishes were never served, the kitchens being blocked by the onlookers:

---

[75] *LP* i(1). 3461.
[76] Montjoie, *Lorde des iustes*, 36th and 39th pages.
[77] *Monstreul*, p. 478.
[78] Ibid., pp. 476-9.
[79] *Sensuit lordre* . . ., pp. 6-7.

Et en effect la compaignie y fut si grosse que tout led[it] Hostel de la Ville, hault et bas, estoit remply de gens en maniere que l'on ne s'y pouvoit tourner. Et ne fut possible aux archers de la garde ne autres savoir fere passaige par la vifz pour monter en hault lad[ite] Dame ne mond[it] Seigneur [Francis]; mais après qu'elle eust été assez longuement attendant à cheval soubz l'allée dud[it] Hostel pour gaigner le piè de lad[ite] vifz, luy convint, pour soy jetter de la foulle, descendre et entrer dedans le logiz du concierge . . . et monterent en hault par une petite vifz bien estroite. . .

Et quant aux autres, fut aucunement interrompu pour ce que la presse y estoit si grande de gentilzhommes et autres, dedans la salle et le long de la vifz, que ceulx qui estoient establiz à porter les viandes ne povoient avoir passage pour les porter . . . une grant partie des viandes du commun demoura es cuysines à bas par faulte de passaige; car chascun vouloit veoir les sollempnitez du service.[80]

Sound also played an important part in Mary's entries: that of the population which was allowed to voice its relief at peace and happiness at the marriage; that ordered by the municipal authorities as part of the festivities. In Montreuil, as elsewhere, at the sight of Mary, all 'hommes, femmes et enffens' shouted 'Noël', the traditional cry that accompanied peace celebrations and royal entries in France, thanking God for having sent her and imploring Him to keep their new queen in good health: 'en louant dieu de sa venue . . . En priant le createur qu'il la vueille garder en benissant le jour de sa nativite'. The clamours of the common people were accompanied by the more orderly and controlled noises of the bells, canons and musicians. On 5 October, the guns of Montreuil, 'tant grosse moienne et deliee', were fired when Mary approached the city walls, making 'le plus terrible et Impetueulx bruyt' that they were heard from Hesdin, fifteen miles away. The anonymous chronicler proudly noted that one of the pieces of ordnance was *La Rose* 'qui avoit esté abatre la Cyte de Ravennes'. Church bells were rung 'tellement que c'estoit merveilleuse chose'[81] and musicians played to the delight of all. What particularly struck the observers was that the English and the French were able to perform together: 'les tro[m]pettes

---

[80], ed., *Histoire générale de Paris. Registre des délibérations du bureau de la ville de Paris*, ed. François Bonnardot, Tome premier: *1499-1526* (Paris, 1883), pp. 218-9.
[81] *Monstreul*, p. 478.

& clarons, haulboys, busines & aultres instrumens tant de france que da[n]gleterre jouoyent, lesquelz il faisoit tres bon ouyr'.[82]

Although marriage to Louis XII was the reason for Mary's presence in France and although she was given the honour of royal entries only because she was soon to be queen of France,[83] all the pageants performed at her entries mainly celebrated the advent of peace between the French and the English. Amidst the conventional biblical and mythological elements and references of the pageants devised for each entry, four main themes were used to celebrate peace between the two countries and, no doubt more importantly for those present, between the people of France and England: passage; youth and beauty; the Garden of Eden; and the Virgin Mary. These themes, or their variants, were not all new: as early as 1431, a ship had been displayed at the Porte Saint-Denis in Paris for the entry of Henry VI of England;[84] the pageantry for Charles VIII's entry into Troyes in 1486 included a garden with flowers and birds;[85] on 19 November 1504, on the occasion of Anne of Brittany's entry into Paris, at the Porte aux Peintres, a play staged the five Annes of the Scriptures and a sixth actress who represented 'Anne noble Royne de France, pour les singulières vertus qui sont en elle et les grands biens qui par son moyen au Royaulme de France sont venus'.[86]

The theme of passage was symbolised by the recurrent presence of a ship in three of the four entries (Boulogne, Abbeville and Paris). The boat, which was one of the emblems of the capital of her new kingdom, represented the only means of transport (and only physical link) between

---

[82] *Lentree de la royne a Ableville* (BM), p. 17.

[83] It was in that respect that she entered the towns under a canopy (a 'poille', a 'ciel or chiel'). In Montreuil it was made of blue satin embroided wirh gold lilies (*Monstreul*, p. 476), in Abbeville of white damask satin embroided with porcupines and roses (*Lentree de la royne a Ableville* (BM), p. 14), and in Paris of cloth of gold embroided with lilies and roses (*Lentree de tres excellente* . . . (BM), p. 26). In Montreuil, the four bearers of the canopy also acted as translators, explaining to Mary the meaning of each of the five pageants performed in her honour. For the French queens' royal entries, see Fanny Cosandey, *La reine de France. Symbole et pouvoir, XVe-XVIIIe siècle* (Paris, 2000) pp. 163-206. Cosandey writes (appendix 1) that Mary's burial-place is unknown. In fact, Mary was buried on 22 Jul. 1533 in the abbey of Bury St Edmunds. In 1784, her coffin was moved to the nearby church of St Mary: Richard, *Mary Tudor*, pp. 262, 266.

[84] Baskerville, *Pageants*, p. xx.

[85] Ibid., p. xxiii.

[86] Delavigne, *Comment la Royne*, p. 294.

France and England and therefore the crossing of the divide between the two countries. It also symbolised the closing of the gap between youth and old age. In Boulogne, a ship painted with lilies and roses, with a young girl (impersonating the Virgin Mary) and two children disguised as angels standing in it, had been placed above the bridge before the gates of the town. By some mechanical device, it was lowered before Mary and the young girl reverently gave her a present from the city: a silver swan of which the neck opened to reveal a gold heart worth 60 *écus d'or*. After Mary's departure, the boat was given to the abbey of Saint-Wulmer, where it had been made and painted.[87] In Abbeville, one of the tableaux consisted of an impressive ship fully equipped with its masts, tops, oars and complete rig.[88] In Paris, at the Porte Saint-Denis, Mary was greeted by an imposing cortege in which the captains of the watch carried 'une navire dargent entrelassee de lettre dor' that represented the fearless city of Paris and, as was customary since the early fifteenth century, the first tableau was 'une grande navire dargent' in which a great number of personages led by Bacchus had taken place.[89] Finally, at the end of the banquet held in the Hôtel de Ville, Mary, now queen of France, gave a similar (the same one?) 'navire dargent' to the heralds and musicians. Although Mary naturally chose a silver boat as present because she was in Paris, nevertheless, the going back and forth of the ship symbolised the renewed amity between France and England.

In Mary, those who devised the pageants had an ideal subject: she was young and all the French observers agreed upon her beauty. In Boulogne she was called 'belle et triumphant pucelle/ Plaine d'honneur, de biauté et de sens; . . . fleur de biaulté'.[90] In Montreuil she was described as the most beautiful flower 'doulce et debonnaire',[91] and in Abbeville as 'tres belle honneste & joyeuse'.[92] In Paris she was told she was 'belle & bonne'[93] and the orator of the university of Paris repeatedly praised her 'beaulte

---

[87] Leest, *Entrée solennelle*, pp. 87-9.
[88] François-César Louandre, *Histoire d'Abbeville et du comté de Ponthieu jusqu'en 1789* (2 vols., Paris et Abbeville, 1844), ii. 16.
[89] *Lentree de tres excellente* . . . , (BNF), pp. 19, 23. See also the splendid miniature of the pageant in BL, Cotton MS Vespasian B II, fo. 4v.
[90] Leest, *Entrée solennelle*, pp. 88-9.
[91] Anonymous song, p. 474.
[92] *Sensuit lordre* . . . , p. 7.
[93] *Lentree de tres excellente* . . . (BNF), p. 24.

excellente . . . eminente'.⁹⁴ But Mary's beauty, as Maître du Breul reminded her, was not only corporal but also spiritual, and reflected the virtues of her soul and her 'beaulte en lame'.⁹⁵ In others words, as War was a 'monstre merveilleux et dommaigeable',⁹⁶ Mary's beauty epitomised Peace. Likewise, all the pageants emphasised and marvelled at Mary's youth which, by her marriage, would rejuvenate Louis and France. In Paris, the tableau before the Church of the Trinity portrayed Louis as the wise King Solomon ('salomon le tressaige') and Mary as the queen of Sheba.⁹⁷ In this pageant, the rich presents of the Bible⁹⁸ were her marriage which was to bring peace ('le beau present de paix en mariage') and, hopefully, the long-awaited heir to the throne (and perhaps an end to Louis's illness). The same theme had been used in Montreuil (although in that instance Mary was not the queen of Sheba but the daughter of Pharaon) and, so that the meaning of the parallel should be lost to none, the anonymous author of the account wrote: 'Laquelle histoire de la bible venoit a proupoz de la Royne et du mariage present'.⁹⁹ In the tableau at the Porte aux Peintres, youth was associated with peace, friendship and confederation and in the one at the Fontaine du Ponceau, with beauty, gaiety and prosperity.¹⁰⁰ All blessings which, thanks to Mary, were returning to France.

Peace was also represented by the allegoric union of the lily of France and the rose of England to which Mary, young, beautiful and of royal blood, was repeatedly compared, thus reinforcing the symbolism of the allegory ('La rose figurant marie').¹⁰¹ As the narrator of the Boulogne entry proclaimed: 'Icy nous véons rozes et fleurs de lys / Tout d'un accord . . .'.¹⁰² and in Abbeville, Mary and Louis indeed met in the garden of the king's lodgings, before mass on their wedding day.¹⁰³ In Montreuil and in Paris, emphasis was put on France being a pleasant garden full of lilies ('ung beau . . . vergier . . . semé de pluseurs beaulz lyz',¹⁰⁴ 'tres beau et tres plaisant

---

⁹⁴ BNF, ms fr. 5104, fos. 1v-2v; BL, Harley MS 1757, fos. 228v, 229v.
⁹⁵ Ibid., fos. 229r-v.
⁹⁶ *Monstreul*, p. 477.
⁹⁷ *Lentree de tres excellente* . . . (BNF), pp. 24-5.
⁹⁸ I Kings 10: 1-13.
⁹⁹ *Monstreul*, p. 477.
¹⁰⁰ *Lentree de tres excellente* . . . (BNF), pp. 24-5.
¹⁰¹ Pierre Gringore, p. 9.
¹⁰² Leest, *Entrée solennelle*, p. 89.
¹⁰³ *Sensuit lordre* . . . , p. 7.
¹⁰⁴ *Lentree de tres excellente* . . . (BNF), pp. 26-7.

Jardin de France'[105]) and where roses could happily flourish: 'Au beau vergier des fleurs de lis/ La Rose a trouvé son repaire'.[106] Only Maître du Breul also compared England to a garden: 'beau preau ou vergier dangleterre'.[107] At the Fontaine du Ponceau, water spouted out of a fountain to nourish a lily and a rosebush thus illustrating, as Pierre Gringore explained, that prosperity stems from turning enemies into friends: 'Car cest souvent lamour la plus durable que des ennemys qui sont faitz amys'. Before the Eglise des Saints-Innocents, one of the tableaux represented the Pope and a Prince (called 'unique vouloir des princes') both standing inside a walled garden and guiding the stem of a rose towards a lily which was descending from the 'vergier de France' where four virtues (mercy, truth, strength and clemency) were devising. At the gate of the garden, Peace was trampling Discord.[108] Thus the union of the lily and the rose brought together the 'parc de france & pays dangleterre',[109] recreating on Earth the Garden of Eden where discord and war were unknown.

That, like the Mother of Jesus, she was a virgin named Mary was no coincidence. It was a gift of God. For the French, this carried a considerable significance as Louis XII had dedicated his kingdom to the Virgin Mary. In Abbeville the second angle exclaimed: 'Loenge à Dieu, le roy de Paradis,/ Ou non duquel, Madame, Je vous dis/ Que vous soyés ycy la bien venue!'[110] And so did those who sung at the Porte Saint-Denis in Paris: 'Louange a dieu du bien quil nous envoye'.[111] All the pageants emphasised the near similarities between Her and the new queen, her 'fillœulle', who shared many of her attributes: 'Comme lassus vous estes adornee/ De biaulx fleurons vertueux et jollis'.[112] The third tableau of the Montreuil entry showed the marriage of the Virgin Mary with the 'Salutacvion Angelique', thus representing the marriage of Louis and Marie. In Paris, the last pageant staged Angel Gabriel and the Virgin Mary, with a lily between them, looking

---

[105] BNF, ms. fr. 5140, fo. ;BL, Harley MS 1757, fo. 228v.
[106] Anonymous song, p. 474.
[107] BNF, ms. fr. 5140, fo. 2v; BL, Harley MS 1757, fo. 228. For the garden as a metaphor for the kingdom of England, see Roy Strong, *The Artist & the Garden* (New Haven and London, 2000), p. 99.
[108] Pierre Gringore, pp. 3-4, 7-10. See also the two miniatures in BL, Cotton MS Vespasian B II, fos. 62, 102.
[109] Ibid., p. 27.
[110] Leest, *Entrée solennelle*, p. 89.
[111] Pierre Gringore, p. 2.
[112] Leest, *Entrée solennelle*, p. 89. 'Lassus' meaning 'in Heaven'.

down on to Louis and Mary in a garden of lilies. The poem that accompanied the tableau made quite clear to the audience the meaning of the pageant:

> Comme la paix entre dieu et les hommes
> Par le moyen de la vierge marie
> Fut jadis faicte ainsy a present sommes
> Bourgoys francoys deschargez de noz sommes
> Car marie avecq nous se marie . . .
> Acquis avons pour nous nul nen varie
> Marie au ciel et marie en la terre.[113]

When Maître du Breul addressed Mary in the University of Paris, he drew a clear parallel between her marrying Louis and the Virgin Mary giving birth to the Son of God:

> et aussy que la glorieuse vierge marie Royne du ciel de laquelle portez le nom a trouvee la grace desiree espouse de dieu Le pere Roy omnipotent et mere de son fils Jh[es]us entant que on pelt co[m]parer les choses mortelles et terriennes aux Immortelles et celestelles vous avez trouve la grace destre espouse du Roy n[ot]re souverain s[eigneur] et mere de tous nous.[114]

Thus Princess Mary was heralded as the alpha and omega of peace. Although she had taken no part in the negotiations, all the entries gave her, not Wolsey, nor Henry, nor Louis, sole credit for the termination of war:[115]

---

[113] Pierre Gringore, p. 15.
[114] BNF, ms. fr. 5104, fo. 1v; BL, Harley MS 1757, fo. 227v.
[115] This must be slightly qualified by the explanation Pierre Gringore gives of the meaning of the three graces who, in Paris, surrounded the fountain at the Fontaine du Ponteau. The first, he says, is called 'gratia preveniens' because one must work at getting the lily and the rose to flower together ('il faut prevenir affin davoir icelle prosperité a assembler lesditz liz et rosier'). The third grace is called 'gratia gratum faciens' because those who decided to nourish the rose and the lily have thus given prosperity to the people ('ceulx qui ont prevenu de faire enrroser de ceste fontaine/ des graces les liz et rosier/ ont donné au peuple prospérité/ liesse et beaulté'). In other words, outside human intervention had been determining. No doubt it was for that reason that before the Eglise des Saints-Innocents, the caption that was attached to the personage representing 'unique vouloir des princes' insisted on the power of princes in making peace: 'La rose figurant marie./ En ce cloz sur toutes provinces./ Soubz le liz la paix apparie./ Par lunique vouloir des princes': Pierre Gringore, pp. 4, 9. Gringore, who had devised the pageants of the entry, knew too well the reality of politics and that complimenting one's patrons would not fall on deaf ears.

'Noble dame bien soyes venue en france./ Par toy vivons en plaisir et en joye./ Francoys angloys vivent a leur plaisance'.[116] Peace was traditionally a female divinity, but the 1514 pageants appear to be the first occasion on which a woman was so deliberately depicted as the main factor of peace and concord between two countries. In Paris, it was proclaimed:

> A Marie qui a mis pour la guerre
> Paix amitie confederation
> Entre les roys de france et dangleterre.[117]

And, a few days later, Maître du Breul told her:

> Et comme la glorieuse Vierge marie a trouve paix entre dieu et nous ainsi et par comparaison que se peult faire en la maniere susd[ite]. Vous avez trouve envers n[ot]re s[eigneur] dieu grace de paix, union et confederation entre les tres hames et tres puissant Roys de France et angleterre.[118]

So had Mary and all those present been told a month before in Boulogne:

> La souveraine et illustre princesse,
> Votre fillœulle apellée Marie,
> Par quy la guerre et discord a prins cesse.
> Comme de paix vous fustes la déesse . . .
> Pareillement, ceste fleur de noblesse
> Est fondement de paix et de léesse.[119]

Maître du Breul also compared her to a star that shined in the sky and brought light to those caught in the darkness of war, and also in the sea (a stella maris) to guide lost ships to the peace and safety of the harbour:

> ceulx qui estoient en lumbre de la mort en danger lung de lautre tuez ont trouve une estoille par laquelle ont este preserves est la tres belle estoille de la mer laquelle vous estes de nom et de co[n]dition . . .

---

[116] Pierre Gringore, p. 2.
[117] Ibid., p. 7.
[118] BNF, ms. fr. 5104, fo. 2; BL, Harley MS 1757, fo. 228.
[119] Leest, *Entrée solennelle*, p. 88. Léesse means joy.

par vostre moyen on a evite pluseurs perilz dangers et Inconveniens et est on venu a port de paix union et confederation.[120]

In May 1515, a few weeks after Louis XII's death and Mary's return to England, Pierre Gringore recalled in a *sotie* (a satirical farce) the general feeling in France:

Mais Marie arriva d'Angleterre,
Qui pour ung temps a fait cesser la guerre
Du Porc apic et des Lieppars passant.[121]

*   *   *

Mary's marriage to Louis in the autumn of 1514 was to prove to be a turning-point in Anglo-French relations. It opened the way to the establishment of reciprocal permanent diplomatic representations on both sides of the Channel[122] and, if it did not deter Henry VIII from attempting to follow in the footsteps of Henry V,[123] it nevertheless showed that peace with France could be a viable foreign policy for England. The marriage of 1514 was also part of the wider humanist movement, exemplified by Robert Gaguin and Erasmus, to bring Christian countries to peace and unity. In that respect, the Treaty of London of August 1514 was the first step in a long process, of which the corner-stone was the normalisation of Anglo-French relations, to restore the peace of God between the European powers. In the bilateral Franco-English context, this was attempted, mainly under the influence of Thomas Wolsey, in the Universal Peace of August 1518, the Field of Cloth of Gold of June 1520 and the Perpetual Peace of 1527 which marked the culminating point of the rapprochement.

The cultural impact of Louis and Mary's marriage was no less important. For the first time in many years, the English nobility (women

---

[120] BNF, ms. fr. 5104, fo. 2; BL, Harley MS 1757, fo. 228.

[121] Pierre Gringore, *Sotye nouvelle des Croniqueurs, Paris, mai 1515* in *Recueil général des sotties*, ed. Emile Picot, (3 vols., Paris, 1902-12), ii. 230.

[122] See Charles Giry-Deloison, 'Les rapports franco-anglais de 1485 au Camp du Drap d'Or', (thèse dactylographiée de IIIe Cycle, Paris, Université de Paris I – Sorbonne, 1986).

[123] See S. J. Gunn, 'The French Wars of Henry VIII', in *The Origins of War in Early Modern Europe*, ed. Jeremy Black (Edinburgh, 1987), pp. 28-51; Gunn, 'The Duke of Suffolk's Mar. on Paris in 1523', *EHR* 101 (1986), 596-634.

included) was able to cross the Channel to rediscover French fashion, to speak French and to learn and experience at first hand the novelties that the French were increasingly bringing back from Italy. When Mary arrived in Abbeville, it was noticed that she was dressed 'à l'anglaise'. Her hair style drew particular attention: 'Labilleme[n]t de la teste a la facon de son pays & tout plai[n] de pierrerye a lentour de ses templettes & grosses bagues pendues au col en facon de carquen'. On the following day she changed 'a la mode de france' which, one of the anonymous chroniclers remarked, 'il faisoit meilleur veoir que a la mode d'angleterre'.[124] More importantly, the lavish pageants held in Paris, which had been designed to surpass those organised for Anne of Brittany's entry in 1504, set a new trend of artistic competition between the two countries. It was on that occasion that the French produced the first illuminated manuscript showing the pageants of a royal entry. No doubt the French knew that the English were impressed by this display of illuminating technique for, in 1527, the skills of the Parisian limners were again called upon, this time to decorate the different treaties between the two countries which were to be signed that August in France. The technical and decorative similarities between these documents and the paintings in the 1514 manuscript are great, not only because of the repetitive use of the allegoric union of the lily and the rose.[125]

So, in many respects Mary's marriage to Louis XII put an end to the Hundred Years War, the origins of which went back to that day of December 1066. But not quite. This was to be accomplished 400 or so years later: the inscription on the frieze of the Bayeux Memorial, erected in honour of the men of the Commonwealth forces who died in the Battle of Normandy in the summer of 1944, proudly recalls: 'Nos a Gulielmo victi victoris patriam liberavimus': 'We, once conquered by William, have now set free the Conqueror's native land'.

---

[124] *Sensuit lordre* . . . , p. 5; *Lentree de la royne a Ableville* (BM), p. 17.
[125] For examples of the illuminations of the 1527 treaties, see *Henry VIII: a European court in England*, ed. David Starkey (London, 1991), esp. pp. 9, 55, 79-82.

8 Sir Nicholas Carew's Journey through France in 1529
ROBERT J. KNECHT

The title of this chapter may suggest a kind of sixteenth century travelogue across France – something along the lines of the journey of Antonio de Beatis, secretary to the Cardinal of Aragon, who visited France in 1517, and whose journal, edited by the late Sir John Hale for the Hakluyt Society in 1979, provides such a vivid description of France in the early part of Francis I's reign.[1] The text to which I mean to draw attention is far more laconic. It is a day-by-day account of a diplomatic mission by two English ambassadors, Sir Nicholas Carew and Dr. Richard Sampson, to the court of Charles V in Bologna in the winter of 1529-30. Yet it is, to my knowledge, almost unique among the literary remains of English diplomacy during the Renaissance, and, for that reason alone, is interesting. The manuscript entitled *Voyage of Sir Nicholas Carewe* was acquired by the British Library in 1945 and is now Egerton MS. 3315. It consists of 35 folios of which 32 contain the text. Each page of text, except the last, contains 23 to 30 lines of writing. In the wider of two margins, alongside each double-spaced entry, Roman numerals, running from lx to cxxvii indicate the number of days elapsed since the start of the voyage. Only 38 days out of 127 were spent in France; the rest in Savoy and Italy. As this paper is only concerned with England's experience of France, it will omit perhaps the liveliest part of the *Voyage*: that is to say, the events in Italy on the eve of the emperor's coronation by Pope Clement VII in Bologna.

---

[1] *The Travel Journal of Antonio de Beatis*, ed. J. R. Hale, Hakluyt Society, 2nd series, 150 (London, 1979).

The Manuscript

Little is known about the provenance of Egerton MS. 3315 before it appeared as 'the Property of a Lady' at Sotheby's on 18 July 1945.[2] It may have belonged originally to Sir Nicholas Carew himself for whom it was almost certainly written. When he was executed in 1539, it presumably passed to his widow, Elizabeth, who died in 1542. It then fell into the hands of William Saunder, a Surrey gentleman, who was Elizabeth Carew's executor and residuary legatee. His family was for long connected with the Carews and his son, Nicholas, married Carew's daughter, Isabel, in 1560.[3] But the manuscript did not stay with Saunder and his family. In the eighteenth century it belonged to Sir Nicholas Carew of Beddington, where it probably remained till the Carew estate was sold in 1859.[4] My own interest in Egerton MS. 3315 was aroused by the late Francis Wormald at whose kind instigation I edited it for the Roxburghe Club in 1959.[5]

The Voyage of Sir Nicholas Carewe was written by Thomas Wall, Windsor herald. The text is so tidy that one can safely assume that it was compiled from notes rather than written day by day in the course of an arduous continental journey. The *Voyage* is an account in the form of a journal of an English embassy to the court of Charles V in Bologna in 1529-30. As such, it belongs to a small group of English diplomatic documents. The nearest parallel is the series of journals by Roger Machado, Richmond herald, describing embassies to Spain, Portugal and Brittany during the reign of Henry VII. Their editor, James Gairdner, concluded from their disorderly appearance and juxtaposition with irrelevant matter in a sort of commonplace book that they were not intended for anyone save the author. Machado wrote 'merely for his own private satisfaction, perhaps to refresh his memory in relating the story of his travels by word of mouth, whenever the king or any one else should call upon him to do so'.[6] Wall's purpose may have been the same, but the fact that his work, unlike Machado's, is tidy and free from adjoining irrelevancies suggests that it was intended for

---

[2] Sotheby's *Catalogue*, Wednesday 18 July 1945, p. 51.
[3] PRO, PROB 11/31, fo. 105v (13 Alen); M. L. Walker, 'The Manor of Batailles and the Family of Saunder in Ewell', *Surrey Archeological Collections* 54 (1955-7), 76-100.
[4] BL, Add. MS. 35838, fo. 23; *V.C.H. Surrey*, iv. 170-1.
[5] *The Voyage of Sir Nicholas Carewe to the Emperor Charles V in the year 1529*, ed. R. J. Knecht (Roxburghe Club, Cambridge, 1959).
[6] *Memorials of King Henry the Seventh*, ed. J. Gairdner (London, 1858), p. xxxviii.

presentation. The hypothesis that it was written for Carew would explain the self-effacing character of the narrative, its ending with the knight's departure from Bologna, the prominence given to him throughout the work, the appearance of his name on the binding and the fact that the work passed into the hands of his family. Sir Nicholas may have required the work, not merely for his own pleasure, but also to assist him in preparing his report for Henry VIII.

A feature common to both Wall and Machado is reticence concerning political business. Gairdner believed that the things which Machado 'thought proper to record were the incidents of his journeys, not their objects', and the same is true of Wall, who was primarily concerned to record the names of places visited, the distances between them, the inns and houses at which the envoys stayed, the persons they encountered and the gifts they received.[7] Vainly does the reader hope for some glimpse of the topics raised by Carew and his colleague Sampson, with their princely hosts. The most painstaking descriptions are those devoted to the Christmas ceremonies in Bologna.[8] Even within his own narrow limits, Wall is tantalisingly reserved. Glimpses of Francis I playing tennis, of a village banquet near Lyons, of an Alpine crossing in 'goodly cleer wedder and depe snawe', of suppers enlivened by trumpeters and minstrels merely whet the appetite. At the same time, a sense of growing monotony is conveyed by such recurrent phrases as 'the chief ambassadour supped at his lodgyng well accompanyed And so they rested that nyght'. Machado's meticulous attention to dress and jewellery is also missing. Wall's limitations seem all the more vexing when his journal is related to other documents. The only surviving letter from the 1529 embassy paints a vivid picture of devastation by French and Imperial armies in north Italy. Yet, in spite of its shortcomings, Egerton MS. 3315 is not without interest.

It needs to be seen as part of a body of travel literature which was growing in importance during the sixteenth century. Sir John Hale in his introduction to De Beatis's journal has indicated some of the main promptings which animated that growth, notably, the passion for compiling lists and the fascination with itineraries. Thus Sanuto in his *Diarii* included a list of all the places where Andrea Gritti had stopped for lunch and dinner on his return in 1513 from a spell of captivity in Blois. A third prompting

---

[7] Ibid., p. xlv.
[8] *Voyage of Sir Nicholas Carewe*, pp. 67-76.

was the need to keep a record for accounting purposes; for travel in the sixteenth century was very expensive and involved much haggling and tiresome currency exchanges. The diary kept by the German artist, Dürer, on a journey from Nüremberg to Antwerp was mainly concerned with his expenses. But, of course, the desire to commemorate was also present. By 1517 the practice of keeping records of prestigious events by heads of family had become commonplace, notably in Italy.[9] So Carew may have wanted an *aide mémoire* to which he might refer when looking back on his career. Modern travellers use their photograph albums or videos in much the same way.

The Author: Thomas Wall

Thomas Wall, the author of our Journal, was the son of a herald.[10] He became Rougecroix pursuivant in 1521 and was soon carrying letters from Wolsey, who was in Calais, to the king and to Worcester's embassy in France.[11] Heralds played a notable part in war. Because of their traditional immunity from molestation, they were ideally suited to act as spokesmen for belligerents. Protests against breaches of the law of war, proposals for exchanging prisoners, safe-conducts to open negotiations were carried from one camp to another.[12] Heralds were also expected to summon beleaguered places to surrender, and it was in this capacity that Wall appeared before Doullens in October 1523 and made a proclamation in French.[13] In 1524 he became Windsor herald.[14] From the fourteenth century onwards, heralds were frequently sent on diplomatic missions, but seldom given ambassadorial status. They lacked the necessary training, experience and social standing. They were expected simply to offer 'a dignified appearance at a public ceremony and firmness in making an unpleasant

---

[9] *Travel Journal of Antonio de Beatis*, 22-8.
[10] Ashmole MS. 1116, fo. 116; J. Anstis, *The Register of the Most Noble Order of the Garter* (2 vols., London, 1724), ii. 374.
[11] Ibid., ii. 374; *LP* iii(1). 1324 (11).
[12] De Maulde-la-Clavière, *Histoire de Louis XII* (Paris, 1893), ii(1). 428-38.
[13] *LP* iii(2). 3422; Ashmole MS. 1116, f. 114a; Anstis, ii. 374. wrongly gives the town as Orleans.
[14] *LP* iv(1). 787 (24), 1939 (p. 869). For the rest of Wall's career see *Voyage of Sir Nicholas Carewe*, pp. 6-14.

164 *The English Experience in France*

announcement'.[15] Wall's duties on the 1529 embassy are not easily deduced from his journal which scarcely mentions his own activities. Only in ceremonial guise during the ceremonies at Bologna does he mention himself.[16] He certainly had no diplomatic authority and his subordinate position is attested by his relatively modest remuneration. Whereas Carew and Sampson received 26s. 8d. per day, he got only 4s.[17] At the close of their mission the envoys were given valuable gold chains by the emperor; Wall had to be content with a hundred Venetian crowns and 'some very goodly word[es]'.[18] Like Machado before him, Wall's duties may have been simply 'to attend and accompany'. But Machado also had to find accommodation for the ambassadors and once rode ahead of them to announce their coming. Wall also probably acted as secretary since the only surviving letter from the 1529 embassy is entirely in his hand.[19]

The Ambassadors: Dr. Richard Sampson and Sir Nicholas Carew

On 26 August 1529 Henry VIII announced his intention of sending two ambassadors to Charles V's court. The king had already made up his mind that Dr. Richard Sampson, dean of the Chapel Royal, would be one of them, but his companion had yet to be chosen.[20] Sampson was a typical 'king's clerk', an ecclesiastic who sought preferment by serving in the royal administration. After graduating in civil law at Cambridge in 1505, he studied in Paris, Sens and Perugia before returning to Cambridge in 1513 to take his doctorate. He then became chaplain to Wolsey, who sent him to Tournai in 1514 as his chancellor and vicar-general. Defending his master's interests against the French claimant to the bishopric caused Sampson much anxiety, but he gained useful experience in dealing with the French and Imperial authorities. It was after Tournai's surrender to the French in 1518 that Sampson became dean of the Chapel Royal. In 1521 war broke out between Francis I and Charles V. After a pretence at mediation between

---

[15] G. Mattingly, *Renaissance Diplomacy* (London, 1955), p. 33.
[16] *Voyage of Sir Nicholas Carewe*, pp. 63, 71, 74.
[17] *LP* v. p. 315.
[18] *Voyage of Sir Nicholas Carewe*, p. 84.
[19] PRO, SP1/56, fo. 120 (*LP* iv(3). 6092), printed as appendix 3 of *Voyage of Sir Nicholas Carewe*, pp. 93-6.
[20] *LP* iv(3). 5911.

them, Henry VIII decided to ally with Charles V. The latter visited England in 1522 and he and Henry agreed to mount a joint invasion of France. It was to assure Charles of England's determination to fulfil her obligations that Sir Thomas Boleyn and Sampson were sent to Spain as ambassadors in September. But relations between the allies cooled as each expected the other to take the initiative. Sampson's time in Spain was also bedevilled by penury and illness. After defeating and capturing Francis I at Pavia in February 1525, Charles V ceased to depend of Henry VIII's friendship. Sampson asked to be recalled and, in 1526, he and Cuthbert Tunstal returned home. Before leaving Spain they called on Francis I in his prison in Madrid. He told them of his gratitude to Henry for not having invaded his kingdom. Back in England, Sampson rejoined the court as king's secretary. In September 1529 he was chosen to go to Bologna where Charles V was about to be crowned Holy Roman Emperor by Pope Clement VII.[21]

After various names had been considered as possible companions for Sampson on his new mission, the king's choice fell on Sir Nicolas Carew. His instructions were drawn up on 21 September and his credentials nine days later. The embassy left on 4 October.[22] The long delay between the first rumour of an embassy to the emperor and its final dispatch is indicative of the care taken by the crown in choosing its representatives. Henry VIII attached a high value to the office of ambassador. 'The discretion or indiscretion of ambassadors', he once said, 'is often the cause of enmities and quarrels of princes as it is also the cause of their friendship and alliances'.[23] According to Etienne Dolet, the perfect ambassador had to be middle-aged, handsome, eloquent, liberal, tidy, obedient, astute, resourceful, cautious and always aware of his country's good.[24] The combination of a churchman with a nobleman was well adapted to the needs of sixteenth century diplomacy. Sir Nicholas Carew, by virtue of his social rank, friendship with the king, handsome physique and sporting renown could most fittingly represent Henry VIII at the fashionable court of France and at ceremonies due to be held at Bologna for Charles V's imperial coronation.

---

[21] *Voyage of Sir Nicholas Carewe*, pp. 21-2.
[22] *CSP Spanish, 1529-30*, pp. 238, 257, 259; *LP* iv(3). 5949; *Voyage of Sir Nicholas Carewe*, p. 46.
[23] *CSP Spanish, 1529-30*, p. 223.
[24] B. Behrens, 'Treatises on the Ambassador written in the Fifteenth and Early Sixteenth Centuries', *EHR* 51 (1936), 616-27 at 624-6; J. E. Neale, 'The Diplomatic Envoy', *History* 13 (1928-9), 204-18 at 208.

166 *The English Experience in France*

For this reason, no doubt, he was made leader of the 1529 embassy. But the intricate political negotiations which were envisaged also required a wily and experienced diplomat, preferably one conversant with Roman law and Imperial affairs. For this task, the duke of Norfolk, who had taken Wolsey's place as chief minister, recommended Dr. Sampson, whom he considered superior to Carew in age, training and experience, but the Imperial ambassador, Chapuys, detected another reason for his appointment. Unlike Carew, who had always been a friend of the French and had received presents from their king, Sampson had Imperialist sympathies. The disappointments which he had experienced in Spain had not eradicated his distaste for France which derived from his earlier career in Tournai.[25] Thus the two ambassadors were complementary and within the bounds set by their allegiance to Henry could be expected to temper each other's partisanship.

Sir Nicholas Carew belonged to a family established at Beddington in Surrey since the reign of Edward III. He was the son of Sir Richard Carew and was probably born around 1490. Nothing is known about him before his appearance as groom of the king's privy chamber in May 1511. Thereafter, he became a squire of the body, cup-bearer, knight of the body and king's carver. The precise date of his knighthood is uncertain. In a list of attendants at the Field of Cloth of Gold in 1520 he figures among the esquires and his wife among the 'Gentilwomen'. But he was certainly a knight by 18 July 1522, when he became master of the horse. Carew's position was equivalent to that of *Grand Écuyer* in France, and foreigners liked to call him 'the great esquire'.[26] As such, he was responsible for managing the royal stables and was also concerned with court pageantry. Numerous are the payments recorded for his costly attire in mummeries and tournaments.[27] It was probably Carew's skill as a jouster which endeared him to Henry VIII who delighted in pitting him against other spirited young men.[28] The best portrait of Sir Nicholas – now in the collection of the Duke of Buccleuch at Drumlanrig in Dumfriesshire – shows him in tilting armour

---

[25] *CSP Spanish, 1529-30*, p. 428; *Voyage of Sir Nicholas Carewe*, p. 21.
[26] R. Doucet, *Les institutions de la France au XVIe siècle* (2 vols., Paris, 1948), i. 126; *CSP Spanish, 1529-30*, pp. 215, 238, 259.
[27] *LP* i(2). 2562; ii(2). pp. 1500-1, 1503-5; 1507, 1510; iii(2). pp. 1551, 1554, 1558; v. 1355, p. 750; Edward Hall, *The Triumphant Reigne of Kyng Henry the VIII*, ed. Charles Whibley (2 vols., London, 1904), i. 171.
[28] *LP* i(1). 144.

holding a broken lance in one hand and a sword in the other.[29] One of his more sensational feats took place on 7 July 1517, when, after a strenuous day of jousting, he appeared as 'the Blue Knight' before a large and distinguished assembly. Clad in blue satin, he rode a tall, blindfolded horse covered of the same material. Three men then heaved on to his lance rest 'the great boordon', a tree trunk nine inches in diameter and twelve feet long, which he proceeded to carry across the lists to everyone's amazement.[30]

Foreign observers regarded Carew as one of Henry VIII's favourites and much of his time was certainly spent in the king's company. The regulations for the royal household required his regular attendance on Henry, and Carew is known to have hunted with him. Sometimes Henry was his guest at Beddington.[31] At Prince Edward's christening, Carew was one of the select few who stood around the font 'in aprons and towels'.[32] The high esteem in which he was held by the king for most of his life is reflected in many grants of offices, pensions and lands. Henry's displeasure was first experienced by Carew in 1519 when he and other minions were expelled from the court and replaced by men of graver disposition.[33] The change was apparently the result of a goodwill visit paid by Sir Nicholas and other English gentlemen to the French court. Their behaviour had not been above reproach, for not only had they ridden with Francis I through the streets of Paris 'throwing Egges, stones and other foolishe trifles at the people', but, on their return home, they had become 'all Frenchmen, in eating, drinking and apparell' and even in 'vices and bragges, so that all the estates of Englande were by them laughed at'.[34] This account, taken from the pages of Hall's Chronicle is a vivid reminder of the degree of familiarity which could exist between English courtiers and the French king but also of the cultural differences between England and France. One area of difference was hunting: Sir Richard Wingfield, writing to Henry VIII in April 1520

---

[29] J. Rowlands, *Holbein* (Oxford, 1985), p. 74, plate 235; O. Bätschmann and P. Griener, *Hans Holbein* (London, 1997), pp. 134, 139. A drawing of Sir Nicholas by Holbein in black and coloured chalks is in the Offentliche Kunstsammlung, Basle. The Drumlanrig painting is now thought to be by a follower of Holbein.

[30] *LP* ii(2). p. 1510; *CSP Venetian, 1509-19*, p. 400.

[31] *CSP Venetian, 1520-26*, pp. 97-8; *LP* ii(1). 2735; iv(1). 1939 (4 &6), 4429; v. 112 308, 927; xii(2). 616; xiii(1). 716-7.

[32] *LP* xii(2). 911.

[33] *LP* iii(1). 246.

[34] Hall, *Kyng Henry the VIII*, i.175.

described a wild boar hunt at the French court. 'sone after thre of the clok the sayde affternone', he writes,' He [Francis] wente to hunte for the wylde bore, and cawsyd me to go with Hym'. The ambassador then describes the baiting of the boar first by a single hound, then by 'twentye cowple of howndes, with thre or fowre brasse of mastyes [mastiffs]'. He clearly felt sympathy for the 'pore bore' as it was brought down and finally dispatched by the king and 'divers others, being a fote, with theyr bore speres'.[35] In 1521 Francis spoke frequently to the English ambassador Fitzwilliam about the French way of hunting deer. He promised to send Henry some wild boar each year and advised him to empark them in the thickest ground possible and allow them to breed.[36] Architecture was another topic which elicited comparative judgements. When Sir John Wallop visited Fontainebleau in 1540, Francis I told him that he had heard that Henry VIII used much gilding in his houses, whereas he himself used little or none, preferring 'tymbre fyndly wrought with dyvers cullers of woode naturall, as ebenye, brasell, and certayne other . . . whiche He rekeneth to be more riche then gilding, and more durable'. He then invited Wallop to see all of this for himself. The ambassador found the king's bedchamber 'very singulier, aswel with antycall borders, as costly seeling, and a chemeney right wel made'.[37]

By way of punishment for Sir Nicholas Carew's misbehaviour at the French court in 1519, he was put in charge of Rysbank Tower near Calais – a task 'sore to hym displeasant' – but his disgrace was short-lived. In June 1520, at the Field of Cloth of Gold, he jousted once more, and soon afterwards attended Henry VIII's meeting with Charles V.[38] The incident which had prompted Carew's temporary banishment from court was consistent with his political outlook. He was ardently francophile, spoke French and often went to the French court on special missions. The purpose of his first mission, in 1521, was to dissuade Francis I from going to Italy, and to ask him to persuade the Scots to send envoys to England. Although Sir Nicholas was only partially successful, he had an enjoyable time and his costs were borne by the French government. In exchange for rubies, which he had brought as gifts for the Dauphin, he carried home scent and smocks

---

[35] *State Papers, Henry VIII*, vi. 57-8.
[36] *LP* iii(1). 1160, 1176.
[37] *State Papers, Henry VIII*, viii. 482-3.
[38] Hall, *Kyng Henry VIII*, i. 178; *LP* iii(1). 247, 259, 261, 265, 906 and pp. 241, 243, 313; Addenda, i(1). 196.

for Princess Mary.³⁹ In 1527 Carew was commissioned to take the insignia of the Garter to Francis I. After a difficult Channel crossing, he and his companions were received at Boulogne by Oudart du Biez. On hearing of their approach, Francis altered his plans in order to welcome them in Paris. The envoys were treated to 'costly cheer and entertainment', which Carew may have recalled as he passed through Paris two years later on his way to Bologna.⁴⁰

The French evidently liked Carew, since in March 1530 Sir Gregorio da Casale told Montmorency of his efforts to obtain the *gran scudiere*'s return to France as ambassador.⁴¹ At the end of the year Carew was among English representatives at the coronation of Francis I's second queen, Eleanor.⁴² In 1532 he again visited the French court, this time to hasten a second meeting between the king and Henry VIII. For once, he left reluctantly, even telling Chapuys that he would prefer to hinder the proposed meeting.⁴³ His attitude may have derived from the sympathy he felt for Catherine of Aragon. Yet Carew continued to be well regarded at the French court. In 1533 Francis I asked Henry to admit him to the Order of the Garter. The request was renewed two years later. Henry explained that the number of knights was limited but promised to remember Carew at the earliest opportunity. Sir Nicholas was, in fact, elected in April 1536, much to the disgust of Anne Boleyn's brother, Viscount Rochford, who interpreted the event as a sign that her influence was waning. The Imperial ambassador, Chapuys, reported that Sir Nicholas would not be to blame if Anne were discarded by Henry.⁴⁴

Carew was no friend of Anne Boleyn. Although he was her cousin and took a prominent part in the joust that followed her coronation, he was in the words of the queen's biographer 'one of Anne's bitterest enemies'.⁴⁵ He was quick to tell Chapuys of any estrangement between her and the king, and reported her 'thousand shameful words' about Francis I and his subjects.⁴⁶ All of this is intriguing, since Anne had spent seven years in the

---

³⁹ *LP* iii(1). 1126, p. 1544; xiv(1). 37; *CSP Venetian, 1520-26*, pp. 97-8.
⁴⁰ *LP* iv(2). 3508, 3554, 3557, 3565, 3567, 3574-5; vi. 589 (5-7).
⁴¹ *LP* iv(3). 6268.
⁴² *CSP Spanish, 1529-30*, p. 854.
⁴³ *CSP Spanish, 1531-33*, pp. 524, 528; *LP* v. 1377, 1429.
⁴⁴ *LP* vi. 555, 707; viii. 174.
⁴⁵ E. W. Ives, *Anne Boleyn* (Oxford, 1986), p. 128.
⁴⁶ *LP*, vii. 1554; *CSP Spanish, 1534-1535*, p. 476.

household of Francis I's first queen, Claude, where she is alleged to have picked up French ways which helped her to ensnare Henry VIII. 'Anne Boleyn', writes Ives, 'had style, and continental style at that'. As de Carles declared at the time: 'no one would ever have taken her to be English by her manners, but a native-born Frenchwoman'.[47] But Carew, perhaps because he knew France too well, was not impressed. Instead, for all his francophilia, he sided resolutely with Catherine of Aragon thereby supporting the Imperial cause at the English court. On the eve of Anne's execution, he entertained Jane Seymour at his house, but his loyalty was, above all, to Princess Mary. In 1536 it was disclosed that he had corresponded with her and believed her fit to be heir apparent should Henry fail to have issue by Jane.[48]

For several years after his embassy to Bologna Sir Nicholas retained Henry VIII's favour. Offices and lands continued to be showered upon him and he appears to have been on friendly terms with Thomas Cromwell. On 31 August 1538 he was still a royal councillor, yet four months later, he was arrested and imprisoned in the Tower of London.[49] His property was confiscated and his offices widely distributed, Sir Anthony Browne becoming master of the horse.[50] On 14 February 1539 Carew was tried at Westminster and sentenced to death. He was beheaded on Tower Hill on 3 March.[51] His fall may be linked to the alleged plot of Lord Montague and the marquis of Exeter to mount a coup d'état in favour of Catherine of Aragon's daughter, Mary, following the birth of Prince Edward.[52] According to the Imperial ambassador, Carew's arrest was part of a systematic campaign to deprive the princess of her friends. But he did not mourn Carew who had always favoured the French even after receiving a handsome present from Charles V at Bologna.[53]

Dr. Sampson's career after the 1529 embassy stood in sharp contrast to that of Carew. He fully supported Henry VIII's remarriage to Anne Boleyn and in his *Oratio*, published in 1534, set out to demolish the theory of papal supremacy. Yet Sampson on his own admission was 'not

---

[47] Ives, *Anne Boleyn*, p. 58.
[48] *LP* vi. 584; vii. 1172, 1554; viii. 826; x. 908, 1134; xiv(1). 37;
[49] *LP* xiii(2). 232.
[50] *LP* xiv(1). 37, 651 (22).
[51] *LP* xiv(1). 466; Hall, *Kyng Henry the VIII*, ii. 284.
[52] *LP* xiii(2). 805, 827, 830: xiv(1). 280; M. H. & R. Dodds, *The Pilgrimage of Grace 1536-7, and the Exeter Conspiracy, 1539* (2 vols., Cambridge, 1915), ii. 319-21.
[53] *LP* xiv(1). 37.

very friendly to novelties' liturgical and dogmatic, which may explain why he had to wait until June 1536 before becoming Bishop of Chichester and also his exclusion from the king's council in 1539. In May 1540 he was charged with treason and sent to the Tower only to be restored to favour after Cromwell's fall. In March 1543 he became Bishop of Coventry and Lichfield and president of the Council of Wales. He died in 1554.[54]

The 1529 Embassy

Although England had set up a number of permanent embassies on the Continent by 1529, she continued to make regular use of special temporary missions. These could be purely ceremonial in character or aimed at carrying out negotiations. If accredited to a single court, they were called 'ordinary'; if required to visit several courts in turn, 'circular'.[55] Carew's embassy combined these aspects: its purpose was to ratify the recently signed treaty of Cambrai, but, at the same time, it was to test the emperor's attitude to Henry VIII's 'great cause of matrimony'.

Many documents which must have arisen from the embassy have vanished. No trace has been found of the original instructions cited by Tuke on 21 September 1529 and only one of several dispatches sent home by the ambassadors has survived. Yet it is possible to deduce their duties from three extant documents: first, a letter written to them by Henry VIII on 5 November; secondly, another missive to them dated 30 November; and thirdly, an abstract of a dispatch they sent from Bologna near the end of their mission.[56] Many interesting passages relating to the mission can be culled from the reports of Eustace Chapuys, the Imperial ambassador in England. From these sources it is clear that the embassy was primarily aimed at confirming the treaty of Cambrai, which released Henry from his alliance with France, which had been unpopular with his subjects and had profited him little. Secondly, it was intended to pave the way for a renewal of friendship with the emperor, whose influence was essential to the accomplishment of Henry's divorce.

---

[54] *Voyage of Sir Nicholas Carewe*, pp. 23-4.
[55] Mattingly, *Renaissance Diplomacy*, pp. 34, 159-61.
[56] BL, Add. MS. 29597, fos. 1-4v; PRO, SP, 1/56, fo. 120 (*LP* iv(3). 6092); SP 1/59, fo. 173 (*LP* iv(3). appendix 253); *LP* iv(3). 5949, 6069; *Voyage of Sir Nicholas Carewe*, pp. 86, 96, 101-103.

The treaty of Cambrai had been signed in August, but could not be regarded as binding until it was ratified by all the parties. As far as possible, it was customary for princes to confirm a treaty at their several courts simultaneously. This explains why Henry was most anxious not to lag behind the French in sending ambassadors to the emperor, but, for some unknown reason, Carew and Sampson did not set out for Italy until long after the departure of their French counterpart, Admiral Chabot. They were forestalled by several weeks and were doubtless so informed by the various diplomats they met on their way. On 29 October they wrote to Henry from Montargis asking whether they should save time by continuing their journey by post. The king agreed, but nothing could alter the fact that the French had already secured the emperor's ratification. Chapuys was later at pains to point out that his master would have preferred to confirm his peace with England first, if only Carew and Sampson had travelled faster. By way of compensation for their sluggishness, Henry confirmed the peace at Greenwich before their arrival at the Imperial court. On being informed that his ambassadors had missed Charles V's arrival in Bologna, the king expressed his regrets. Carew and Sampson only reached Bologna on 2 December.[57]

We are not concerned here with the talks that took place in Bologna, interesting as they were. Suffice it to say that Henry VIII was sufficiently satisfied by the outcome to send a more exalted embassy to the emperor, this time led by Anne Boleyn's father, the Earl of Wiltshire. Carew, meanwhile, left Bologna by post on 8 February and reached England within a fortnight. Sampson left a day sooner, but did not use the post.[58] Having completed his mission, each ambassador was free to act as he wished. Carew's friendship for France, did not, it seems, clash with his loyalty to Catherine. He seems to have been genuinely moved by the emperor's friendly reception, though Chapuys later admitted that his loyalty to France had remained unshaken.

---

[57] *LP* iv(3). 5911, 5931; *CSP Spanish, 1529-30*, pp. 279, 311, 342-4; *Voyage of Sir Nicholas Carewe*, pp. 50-1.
[58] *CSP Spanish, 1529-30*, pp. 470-1; *LP* iv(3). 6205, 6209; *Voyage of Sir Nicholas Carewe*, p. 85.

The Journey

Before leaving on a mission, it was customary for ambassadors to take leave of their prince. He would give them their credentials and instructions, both written and verbal. Carew and Sampson duly observed this practice at Greenwich on 4 October 1529.[59] Next day they called on Brian Tuke, the treasurer of the king's chamber, to collect money for their expenses.[60] Two days later, they passed through Canterbury.[61] At Dover, they shipped their horses across the Channel, and, despite a lack of wind, reached Wissant in the Calais Pale on 12 October. The pace at which ambassadors travelled was in part dictated by the size of their retinue, which was very variable. It might consist of only three or four men or run to nearly one hundred. Wiltshire's embassy of 1530 included between 60 and 80 horses.[62] Not all the company were diplomats, of course. There were heralds, like Wall, scribes and notaries to draw up documents and treaties, messengers to carry letters, grooms to look after the horses, and servants to handle the baggage. However lightly ambassadors liked to travel, they could seldom dispense with a siseable amount of clothes, jewellery, silver plate, food and even pets. We do not know how large Carew's company was, but it seems to have been fairly numerous. Indications in the Journal point to at least a dozen. Many references occur to the chief ambassador and 'all his gentlemen' being invited to meals in Bologna. But some persons may have been placed at the ambassadors' disposal after their arrival there. This would explain why their meals only became 'well accompanied' from this moment onwards. Nevertheless, one may assume that they were accompanied on their journey by a number of servants and a fair amount of baggage. They also had their own horses, which they rode from Wissant to Bologna, except for a river trip between Pavia and Piacenza, while their mounts followed a day behind by a more circuitous route.[63]

A handbook for pilgrims published in 1498 prescribed two routes from the Channel coast to Italy. One was the 'duche' or 'marchandes way' across the Low Countries and Germany; the other was the road across the

---

[59] *Voyage of Sir Nicholas Carewe*, pp. 46, 91.
[60] *LP* v. p. 315.
[61] *LP* iv(3). 5995.
[62] *CSP Spanish 1529-30*, p. 437.
[63] *Voyage of Sir Nicholas Carewe*, p. 57.

heart of France, known to Matthew Paris and probably much earlier.[64] The latter, which was considered shorter and less expensive, was the one chosen by Carew and his company. From Calais, they proceeded southwards through Boulogne, Abbeville, Amiens and Clermont to Paris, which in the eyes of Andrea Navagero, a contemporary Venetian, was the only city worthy of comparison with his own – a city of fine streets, splendid shops, wealthy noblemen and comfortable rather than handsome dwellings.[65] From here, our ambassadors, instead of taking the road through Orléans and Bourges recommended by the pilgrims' handbook, selected the more direct route through Corbeil and Montargis to Gien, whence they followed the right bank of the Loire as far as Nevers. Continuing along the river Allier, they came to Moulins, where they perhaps glanced at the château of the dukes of Bourbon with its gardens, fountains and woods, and its collection of exotic animals and birds.[66] By this time, of course, the château and all the rest of extensive Bourbon estates had been confiscated by the crown following the treason of Charles the third duke in 1523.[67] Carew and Sampson then proceeded across the hills of Beaujolais, noted for their vineyards, to Lyons. Situated as it was at the junction of the rivers Rhône and Saône, it was the most important centre of international trade in France. By 1528 more than half its population was foreign. There was, in particular, a flourishing colony of Italian bankers. Lyons was also the gateway to Italy: troops passed through it, and the French kings used it as an outpost from which to observe political and military happenings south of the Alps.[68] De Beatis describes Lyons as 'not very large, nor yet small. The streets are well laid out, the houses generally of stone. The women of Lyons are some of the most beautiful in France. Merchants of every nation live here, but especially Italians, and because of all the trade the men, the women and the very earth have something of fair Italy about them. And so, such as it is, I judge Lyons to be the fairest town in France'.[69] Of the various mountain passes

---

[64] G. B. Parks, *The English Traveler to Italy* (2 vols., Rome, 1954), i. 495-568.
[65] *Relations des ambassadeurs Vénitiens sur les affaires de France au XVIe siècle*, ed. N.Tommaseo (2 vols., Paris, 1838), i. 30-3.
[66] Ibid., i. 32-5.
[67] R. J. Knecht, *Renaissance Warrior and Patron: the reign of Francis I* (Cambridge, 1994), pp. 200-15.
[68] A.Tilley, *The Dawn of the French Renaissance* (Cambridge, 1918), pp. 166-8; R. Gascon, *Grand commerce et vie urbaine: Lyon et ses marchands* (2 vols., Paris, 1971).
[69] *Travel Journal of Antonio De Beatis*, 139.

accessible from Lyons, the Mont Cenis was generally preferred by English travellers, and was chosen by our ambassadors.[70] After travelling through Pont-de-Beauvoisin they reached Chambéry, the capital of the duchy of Savoy. Even if they had disposed of the time, they probably would not have been able to see its most famous relic: the Holy Shroud that is now in Turin, for it was only displayed on Good Friday and on four days in May. It was housed in a chapel within the ducal castle and, when it was on show, attracted huge crowds of pilgrims.[71] Carew and Sampson then crossed the snowy mountains in clear weather, and came down the steep road to Susa and the Lombard plain, where we must leave them.

France in the autumn of 1529 was fast recovering politically from the chaos that had resulted from King Francis I's defeat at Pavia five years earlier. He had come home in March 1526 and had reorganised his court, filling the places which had been left vacant by the massive slaughter of nobles in that battle. In 1528 Francis announced that he would henceforth spend more time than before residing in or near Paris. In fact, his court remained essentially peripatetic, but he did move the main centre of his building activities to the Paris area.[72] Among the new courtiers none was as important as Anne de Montmorency, who as Grand Master administered the royal household. One of his duties was to introduce foreign ambassadors to the king.[73] The king's mother, Louise of Savoy, who had governed the kingdom as regent during his captivity, remained an important political figure. She had had many dealings with Cardinal Wolsey, who called her 'the mother and nourisher of peace'. Not only had she saved France from an English invasion by signing the treaty of the More in August 1525, she had since negotiated the Peace of Cambrai (3 August 1529) with the emperor's aunt, Margaret of Austria, hence its name 'The Peace of the Ladies'.[74] As a result, France was for once enjoying a spell of peace, though problems remained on the home front. Heavy rains early in the year had virtually wiped out the harvest causing famine among the poor.[75] In Lyon the shortage

---

[70] Parks, i. 506.
[71] *Travel Journal of Antonio De Beatis*, 140-2.
[72] Knecht, *Renaissance Warrior and Patron*, p. 398.
[73] Doucet, i. 122-3.
[74] *Ordonnances des rois de France: règne de François Ier* (9 vols., Paris, 1902-75), iv. 394-5, 398-400, 507; G. Jacqueton, *La politique extérieure de Louise de Savoie* (Paris, 1892), p. 119; Knecht, *Renaissance Warrior and Patron*, pp. 244, 283-5.
[75] *Livre de raison de Me Nicolas Versoris*, ed. G. Fagniez (Paris, 1885), pp. 120-1.

of food had prompted a serious popular riot called the *Grande Rebeyne* in which a mob had attacked the homes of alleged speculators and ransacked municipal and monastic granaries.[76] Religion was another mounting problem as the *Parlement* of Paris and the Sorbonne tried to stamp out the first manifestations of Protestant dissent. Louis de Berquin, a young nobleman with strong evangelical interests, was burnt on the Place de Grève in Paris on 17 April.[77]

Allowing for nine days of rest in different places Sir Nicholas and his party took 42 days to cover the distance of roughly 825 miles between Wissant and Bologna. Their average speed, therefore, was just under twenty miles a day. The longest distance covered was 33 miles between Moulins and Lapalisse, the shortest four miles between an Italian village and Bologna. As one might expect, they travelled faster on flat ground than in the mountains. Whereas their average had been about 21 miles a day in northern France, it fell to about fifteen in the Alps. By modern standards such speeds seem absurdly low, but in the sixteenth century haste was deemed undignified. What is more, the roads were often little better than quagmires. According to Navagero, the road from La Charité to Nevers was extremely muddy all the year round. This would explain why our ambassadors only managed to travel eighteen miles on 1 November.[78] In 1517 the two leagues of road before Aiguebelette were described as 'cursedly bad going, since you are riding the whole way over rocks and stones which are an unspeakable nuisance'. It was customary for travellers on leaving the village to hire cobs, mules and donkeys, local animals used to climbing, in order to get over the Montagne de l'Épine.[79] By 1529 it was possible to go from England to Italy in less than a fortnight by means of a newly established system of posts or relays, which enabled a rider to do an average of 89 miles a day. An itinerary drawn up by Richard Croke in 1530 shows that there were 86 posts nine to thirteen miles apart between Calais and Bologna.[80] The advantages of travelling by post were outweighed by major inconveniences. The post masters often charged exorbitant sums and the horses they provided were not always good. Carew, however, did take

---

[76] Gascon, ii. 768-74.
[77] *Journal d'un bourgeois de Paris sous le règne de François Ier*, ed. V.-L. Bourrilly (Paris, 1910), p. 321.
[78] *Relations des ambassadeurs Vénitiens*, i. 33.
[79] *Travel Journal of Antonio De Beatis*, 140.
[80] *LP* iv(3). 6375; Parks, i. 501-3.

the post with three companions and a guide for his return journey from Bologna.[81]

Wherever the ambassadors passed, they were greeted by local dignitaries. At Boulogne they were received at the town gate by the lieutenant of Oudart du Biez, the governor. He returned after their supper accompanied by 'dyvers gentilmen and other souldiours'.[82] At Breteuil, on 19 October, Jean de Créquy called on them after killing two wolves that day.[83] This may have been the governor of Montreuil-sur-Mer or his son of the same name, who was the Seigneur de Canaples and a gentleman of Francis I's chamber.[84] On reaching Saint-Denis, the ambassadors were met by Sir Francis Bryan, the English ambassador in France, and by two representatives of the French king: Guillaume du Bellay, Seigneur de Langey, and his brother, Jacques du Bellay. Their brother Jean, Bishop of Bayonne, was resident ambassador in England at this time and Guillaume was soon to succeed him. In 1528 Henry VIII had tried to put pressure on the pope to concede his divorce by consulting theologians in various universities, including Paris. The task of canvassing support for the king's cause fell to Guillaume du Bellay, who succeeded in persuading many Paris theologians to support the divorce. On 2 July 1530 the Faculty decided by 53 votes against 47 that Henry VIII's marriage to Catherine of Aragon was null and void. Opponents of the divorce tried to get their own back by pinning a charge of heresy on Guillaume's brother, Jean. He must have been able to clear his name as he was sent back to England as ambassador in October 1531 and appointed Bishop of Paris in 1532. As for Guillaume, he played a major role in negotiations between Francis I and the German Protestant princes about 1534.[85]

The notorious malpractices of inn-keepers did not deter the ambassadors from making regular use of hostelries. In at least 39 of the 43 places where they stopped for the night, they put up at inns. Elsewhere, they accepted private hospitality. Thus in Calais they were accommodated by the council at the 'banner watch out the lantern gate'; in Paris, they stayed at the homes of Lambert Meigret and Germain Vivien in the Grande Rue du Temple. They supped at Sir Francis Bryan's lodging. As *commis à*

---

[81] *Voyage of Sir Nicholas Carewe*, p. 85.
[82] Ibid., p. 46.
[83] Ibid., p. 47.
[84] *CAF*, ix. 723.
[85] Knecht, *Renaissance Warrior and Patron*, passim.

l'Extraordinaire des guerres, Meigret was an important member of Francis I's fiscal administration, popularly known as 'le magnifique Meigret'. It was by no means uncommon for leading financiers to entertain foreign diplomats in their town houses, which were among the finest. Thus in October 1526 Meigret had entertained the papal legate.[86] Like many others of his kind, he was charged with corruption and tried by a special court in the 1530s. He was also accused of being a Lutheran after he had eaten meat in Lent. After a spell of imprisonment, he was banished from the kingdom, all his property being confiscated.[87] As *grenetier* of Paris, Germain Vivien was responsible for the salt tax or gabelle.[88] On 23 October, our two ambassadors were received at the Louvre which was in the early stages of a radical transformation by the king from medieval fortress to Renaissance palace. In 1528 the great central keep had been destroyed to the chagrin of many Parisians in order to open up a central courtyard.[89] The ambassadors spent two hours with Francis I before accompanying him to a tennis court in the rue du Temple. Here they watched two sets of a match played three a side: the king, Jean de Guise, cardinal of Lorraine, and the Great Master, Anne de Montmorency against Henri d'Albret, king of Navarre and two other noblemen. On the 24th the ambassadors returned to the Louvre and spent one hour chatting to the king's mother, Louise of Savoy, in the presence of her daughter, Marguerite, and Charles of Angoulême, the king's third son. The king's sister, Marguerite d'Angoulême, is best remembered for her writings, notably the *Heptaméron* and many religious poems, but she was also politically engaged, often conversing with ambassadors. She had distinctly evangelical views and protected scholars and preachers who were being persecuted as heretics by the *Parlement* of Paris and Sorbonne.[90] Also present were Francis I's two daughters, Madeleine and Marguerite, described by Wall as 'very goodly chyldren', Henri d'Albret's sister and 'other Diuers and many ladyes and gentelwomen and also the great maister

---

[86] Philippe Hamon, *'Messieurs des finances': les grands officiers de finance dans la France de la Renaissance* (Paris, 1999), p. 378.

[87] C. A. Mayer, *La religion de Marot* (Geneva, 1960), pp. 17-8; Philippe Hamon, *L'argent du Roi: les finances sous François Ier* (Paris, 1994), pp. 291-2, 297, 320, 322

[88] In 1522 Vivien was *commis au paiement des archers de la garde du corps*. See Hamon, *L'argent du Roi*, p. 119.

[89] M. Chatenet, 'Le logis de François Ier au Louvre' *Revue de l'Art* 97 (1992), 72-4; *Journal d'un bourgeois de Paris*, p. 274.

[90] P. Jourda, *Marguerite d'Angoulême* (2 vols., Paris, 1930), i. *passim*.

with sondry noble men'.[91] Madeleine and Marguerite were nine and six years old respectively. Madeleine became queen of Scotland in January 1537 after marrying James V but she died soon afterwards while Marguerite became duchess of Savoy in 1559.[92] As for the Great Master, Anne de Montmorency, who became, in effect, Francis I's chief minister, after the king's return from captivity he belonged to one of the oldest and richest aristocratic houses in France. He had been brought up with the king, had shared his captivity, and in 1527 had entered the royal family by marrying Madeleine of Savoy, the half-sister of the king's mother.[93]

Other meetings occurred on the rest of the ambassadors' journey through France. Thus, at Cosne, on 30 October, they were met by Louis de Chandio, *capitaine de la porte du roi* and *grand prévôt de France,* who was accompanied by six or seven gentlemen and many servants. A fine portrait of Chandio, who had served Bayard as aide-de-camp, is among the series of drawings attributed to Jean Clouet. A copy dating from 1526 bears the intriguing inscription: 'Trop petyt pour la cherette, trop grant pour le chaval'.[94] On 7 November they were met on the road two leagues from Lyons by Antoine de La Fayette, who had been captain of Boulogne before 1523 and under Louis XII master of the artillery in the duchy of Milan and in Italy. He 'made theym in a villaige a bancquette of fruiict chese and wyne'.[95]

Almost everywhere our ambassadors preferred to stay at different inns. Thus, in Abbeville, Carew stayed *Au Géant'*, and Sampson *Au Cerf courant*. This may have been for practical reasons. Their suites may have been too large to be comfortably accommodated in a single hostelry. By lodging separately, each could be assured of getting a good room; they could also keep their accounts separate. Even their horses were stabled at different inns. Thus in Paris the horses were stabled in two inns in the rue Saint-Martin. But if Sir Nicholas and the bishop liked sleeping apart, they normally shared their meals. No principle seems to have determined whether they ate at 'the chief ambassadours' or at 'maister deane's'. Two meals a day were the rule: dinner before they set out; supper after they had reached

---

[91] *Voyage of Sir Nicholas Carewe*, pp. 48-9.
[92] R. Peyre, *Une princesse de la renaissance: Marguerite de France* (Paris, 1902), p. 43.
[93] F. Decrue, *Anne de Montmorency, grand maître et connétable de France à la cour aux armées et au conseil du roi Francois Ier* (Paris, 1885), *passim.*
[94] P. Mellen, *Jean Clouet* (London, 1971), pp. 20, 218.
[95] *Voyage of Sir Nicholas Carewe*, pp. 52-3; *CAF*, v. 264, no. 16030.

180 *The English Experience in France*

their destination. On fast days, such as Christmas, dinner was deferred till evening. Occasionally the ambassadors were given food and drink. At Abbeville, they were given two pasties of wild boar by the town's captain, Jean de Haucourt, Seigneur de Huppy, and eight 'stopes of wyne' by the town.[96] On 1 November at Nevers, the countess, Marie d'Albret, who had visited England in 1515, sent them two venison pasties and 'two great siluer pott[es] with wyne'.[97] Carew and Sampson were sometimes invited to other men's tables. Thus, in Paris, they twice dined with Sir Francis Bryan. At Lyons, on 9 November, they dined at the home of Antonio Gondi, the well-known Florentine banker, where 'they were right well entreatyd'.[98]

The road taken by our ambassadors seems to have been very busy at the time. On 26 October between Corbeil and Larchant, they met Cesare Trivulzio, Bishop of Como, who was riding in post from the pope to the French king. Next day, at Montargis, they ran into Paolo da Casale, whom the pope was sending by post to Henry VIII. He dined with Carew at the *Sign of St. Michael*. On 31 October, at La Charité, our ambassadors met Peter Vannes, another envoy sent by the pope to Henry VIII.

*   *   *

Laconic as it is, then, *The Voyage of Sir Nicholas Carewe* is interesting not only as a rather unusual type of English diplomatic record, but also for the light which it sheds on the more mundane aspects of Renaissance diplomacy. It belongs to a broad category of travel books which were becoming popular in Europe under various guises. Some were works with literary pretensions aiming to describe a particular country, its topography, people and customs; others were working documents with severely practical uses. *The Voyage of Sir Nicholas Carewe* was of this kind, but even with its limitations it conveys an impression of closer ties between England and France than one might imagine. The meetings, however brief, which Carew and Sampson had on their journey through France exemplify the informal fraternising which evidently took place outside the context of strictly diplomatic business. The two ambassadors had not been commissioned to treat with Francis I. Their primary purpose was to treat with France's arch-enemy, Charles V, yet that

---

[96] *Voyage of Sir Nicholas Carewe*, p. 47.
[97] *Voyage of Sir Nicholas Carewe*, p. 51; *Dictionnaire de biographie Française*, i. 1320.
[98] *Voyage of Sir Nicholas Carewe*, p. 53.

did not prevent them from being honourably received at several points of their journey through France and even at court. They were given a chance to meet Francis I, his family, ministers and courtiers along with various provincial dignitaries. How many other such exchanges, we may wonder, took place unrecorded in the diplomatic archives of the time, as envoys, merchants, messengers, students and other sorts of travellers passed through France along well-defined paths on their way to more distant places?

9 Courtesy and Conflict: the experience of English diplomatic personnel at the court of Francis I

LUKE MacMAHON

The experiences of Henry VIII's ambassadors and diplomatic staff at the French court differed greatly from those of their predecessors in France and contemporaries at other courts for several reasons. First, the distinctive nature of the French court and the more open and personal style of its prince ensured that many of the ambassadors to France were treated quite differently from those dispatched elsewhere. Furthermore, the historical antipathy that existed between the two countries, exacerbated by the personal rivalry of Francis I and Henry VIII, influenced both the selection of the men chosen to serve, and the nature of the work they were called upon to perform. Finally, the exchange of resident envoys between the Tudor and Valois courts, begun in November 1518, ensured that more ambassadors travelled to France than in any previous reign and remained there far longer than ever before. What follows will assess how these factors influenced the selection, work and treatment of English ambassadors in France and consider how their use and treatment varied during the reigns of Henry and Francis.

So, whom did Henry dispatch to the Valois court? Over a 37 year period 38 men performed 58 embassies to France, more missions than were dispatched to any other court: the emperor received 44 and the Low Countries 23. Furthermore, no less than 22 resident missions were accredited to the Valois court.[1] Although some of these missions were in

---

[1] Luke MacMahon, 'The Ambassadors of Henry VIII: the personnel of English diplomacy, c.1500-1550' (Unpublished University of Kent PhD thesis, 1999), pp. 287-340. Although my own list of envoys and the missions they performed under Henry VIII differs

length indistinguishable from special embassies (those of George Boleyn and Stephen Gardiner in the early 1530s, for example, were only three months each) most lasted for more than a year. There was therefore unrivalled diplomatic contact between the two courts during Henry's reign. However, the number of ambassadors accredited to Francis represented only the tip of the iceberg. If one includes entourages and ambassadorial suites the number of people involved in diplomatic intercourse can be counted in the thousands. The entourage which accompanied Princess Mary to France in 1514 numbered over 400, that led by the Earl of Worcester four years later 600, while Cardinal Wolsey's diplomatic expedition to Amiens in 1527 contained approximately 900 people. Of course the majority of servants and gentlemen included in these huge expeditions remained in France only briefly but not so the suites attached to resident envoys which presumably continued at the host court for the duration of the ambassador's mission and were by no means small in number. A useful insight into the size of an ambassadorial household is provided by Thomas Wriothesley. Writing from the Low Countries in 1538, he observed:

> And a lesse trayne almost we cannot kepe for we occuppie oon man in going to the market an other in recevyng and loking to thorder of the mete at home. A coke we have and his man twoo we have in our buttery that oon may kepe ar plate whilles thother laieth the table. Oon man kepethe continuelly the gate . . . for elles we shuld be faine every daye almost to buye newe vessel. Lesse we cannot have thenne iiij horsses and oon man to oversee them. Every of us must nedes have oon to wayte uppon him in his chamber at the least and a clerk. We occupie oon or twayne every evening to goo before to gete ar lodgyng and stable ready and twoo at the least we be fayne be suretie to ride with ar wagons . . .[2]

At the smallest their suite of servants contained thirteen men. However, it should be borne in mind that the great majority of envoys dispatched to France were of considerably higher rank than Vaughan and Wriothesley and that bishops such as John Clerk, Stephen Gardiner and Edmund Bonner, and courtiers and royal favourites like Richard Wingfield, Francis Bryan and George Boleyn were likely to have had many more staff.

---

considerably from that provided by G. M. Bell, *A Handlist of British Diplomatic Representatives, 1509-1688* (London, 1990), Professor Bell's work nevertheless served as an invaluable guide for my own research.

[2] PRO, SP 1/137, fos. 220-1 (*LP*, xiii(2). 636), Wriothesley to Cromwell, 17 October 1538.

In addition to their servants, it was common practice for an ambassador to include in his suite a number of young gentleman presumably both to complete their training as courtiers, and prepare at least some for future diplomatic service. Germayne Gardiner, writing to Thomas Wriothesley about the behaviour of his uncle's entourage, noted that:

> My lorde hathe here yong gentlemen of xix yeres and under thise: Edwarde Hungerford, James Wingfelde, Robert Gage, Robert Parys & John Broun; a lytel above that age: Thomas Thwaytes, Thomas Hungerforde, Olyver Vachel, John Temple, Robert Preston, Richarde Hampden and Walter Hals.[3]

In all Gardiner's suite contained twelve young gentlemen. Even if we allow that, as Bishop of Winchester, Henry's resident to France in the mid 1530s was likely to have had an unusually large train, it nevertheless seems probable that over the whole period several hundred young men accompanied the king's ambassadors while they resided with Francis.

In terms of the type of envoy dispatched to the French court the great majority were drawn from the gentry and nobility. 47 out of the 58 embassies accredited to Francis, that is 81%, contained a member of the gentry or nobility. Contrast this with their role in Anglo-Imperial diplomacy in which they were involved in only twenty missions out of 44, 45% of the total. A similar difference existed in the number of gentry appointed to resident embassies. Where members of the gentry filled 73% of the resident missions sent to France, only 42% of those dispatched to the Imperial court were similarly endowed. Overall, 27 more embassies sent to France in the period were led or contained an ambassador chosen from the gentry or nobility. Furthermore, the lion's share of missions led by the nobility were also accredited to France. In total sixteen missions to Francis I were led by a peer, twelve more than were dispatched to all the Habsburg courts combined.[4]

The reasons for this sharp contrast in the roles played by the aristocracy in Anglo-French and Anglo-Imperial diplomacy were quite straightforward. The three conflicts between England and France as well as the intermittent periods of cold war were all brought to a close with conspicuous displays of renewed friendship in which members of the nobility played a prominent part. Thus as part of the 1514 embassy

---

[3] PRO, SP 1/129, fos. 95v-6 (*LP*, xiii(1). 327), Germayne Gardiner to Wriothesley, 21 February 1538.
[4] MacMahon, 'Ambassadors', pp. 287-340.

dispatched with the Princess Mary were five of the most senior English peers: the Dukes of Norfolk and Suffolk, the Marquis of Dorset and the Earls of Surrey and Worcester.[5] The central issue unresolved by that short-lived *rapprochement*, England's retention of Tournai, was settled by the treaty of London signed in October 1518, and ratified by the great embassy led to Paris by the Earl of Worcester the following month.[6] In May 1527 Thomas Boleyn, by then Viscount Rochford, was sent to France to ratify the treaty of Westminster, a new pact of eternal friendship. Five months later Arthur Plantagenet, Viscount Lisle, led the mission entrusted with presenting the French king with the Order of the Garter, another mark of the renewed amity enjoyed by Henry and Francis.[7] When in the summer of 1546 the final Anglo-French war was brought to a close, another Viscount Lisle, this time John Dudley, attended both the mission which negotiated the peace and the later embassy dispatched to celebrate its completion.

By contrast Anglo-Imperial relations were notably lacking in such ceremonial displays. The treaties signed between Henry and Charles were of two kinds: first, commercial agreements regulating trade between England and the Low Countries, the province of merchants and civil lawyers; second, the offensive alliances formed against France in 1512, 1521 and 1542. In every case discretion was the key word, and if it was applied in different ways (witness Wolsey's shuttle mission to Bruges in August 1521 in his guise as honest broker) there was nevertheless no part for aristocratic ambassadors in such covert activities.[8]

The reasons for the frequent use of the gentry and nobility in Henry's dealings with Francis were primarily influenced by the special nature of the French court and the behaviour of its prince. While by no means suggesting that the Valois court was lacking in ceremony or that its prince was not entirely aware of his royal dignity, there was undoubtedly an openness in Francis's personal style and at his court that was certainly not present at that of his

---

[5] For details of this embassy see Walter C. Richardson, *Mary Tudor: the White Queen* (London, 1970), pp. 87-97.
[6] Scarisbrick, pp. 67-74; P. Gwyn, *The King's Cardinal* (London, 1990), pp. 92-103.
[7] C. Giry-Deloison, 'A Diplomatic Revolution: Anglo-French relations and the treaties of 1527' in *Henry VIII: a European court in England*, ed. D. R. Starkey (London, 1991), pp. 77-87.
[8] Scarisbrick, pp. 88-94; P. Gwyn, 'Wolsey's Foreign Policy: the conferences of Calais and Bruges reconsidered', *Historical Journal*, 23 (1980) 755-772.

Habsburg rival.[9] In 1526 John Clerk remarked with surprise on the unusual familiarity of Francis's courtiers:

> [Francis] . . . was very merry all dinner time, and had much communication both with the legate, with us and with divers other lords . . . which stood about him; some leaning on his chair, and some upon his table, all much more familiarly than is agreeable to our English manners.[10]

Certainly it would be difficult to imagine a youthful Charles V riding through the streets of Brussels, Augsburg or Valladolid pelting his subjects with 'eggs, stones and other foolish trifles', as Francis did in 1519 accompanied by members of the Earl of Worcester's ambassadorial entourage.[11] On numerous occasions diplomatic dispatches to England recounted how the French king had personally greeted envoys, taking them by the hand and even embracing them. When in February 1519 Thomas Boleyn asked the French king whether in the event of his being elected emperor he would lead a crusade against the Turks, Francis grasped the ambassador's wrist in one hand and placed the other on his heart and swore solemnly that he would.[12] Thomas Cheyne attending his first audience with Francis in April 1526 was met by the French king in the middle of his chamber and taken in a firm embrace.[13] As part of a guided tour of Fontainbleu, Francis showed John Wallop the recently decorated gallery. When the envoy found it difficult to climb up on a bench to examine the material used for the borders the French king gave him his hand and personally hauled him up, afterwards helping him dismount in a similar fashion.[14]

Most importantly of all, however, Francis was prepared to integrate ambassadors into court life and his personal entourage. Richard Wingfield writing in April 1520 assured Henry that 'where [I] hys naturall subgiect, and of hys Pryvye Chambre . . . he cowde no more familierlye use me, then

---

[9] R. J. Knecht, *Renaissance Warrior and Patron: the reign of Francis I* (Cambridge, 1994). For the court of Charles V see W. Paravicini, 'The Court of the Dukes of Burgundy: a model for Europe?' in *Princes, Patronage and the Nobility*, eds. R. G. Asch and A. M. Birke (Oxford, 1991).
[10] *LP*, iv(2). 3173, Clerk to Wolsey, c. June 1526.
[11] Edward Hall, *The Union of the Two Noble and Illustrious Families of Lancaster and York*, ed. H. Ellis (London, 1809), p. 597.
[12] BL, Cotton MS, Caligula D VII, fo. 91 (*LP*, iii(1). 101), Boleyn to Wolsey, 28 February 1519.
[13] BL, Cotton MS, Caligula D IX, fo. 179 (*LP*, iv(1). 2087), Cheyne to Henry, 12 April 1526.
[14] *State Papers, Henry VIII*, viii. 484-5, Wallop to Henry, 17 November 1540.

he doythe contenually; commaundynge me not to forbere to resorte to Hym at my pleasur at all tymes'.[15] In September 1520 Richard Jerningham reported that while other envoys kicked their heels he was invited to attend the king in his privy chamber morning and night.[16] Similarly, William Fitzwilliam found himself invited to lodge in Francis's house, and was apparently treated less like an envoy than one of the king's chamber.[17]

Certainly the opportunities which such open behaviour created were best exploited by members of the gentry. It was they who were most suited to participate in Francis's daily pastimes and talk to the king about those subjects which most interested him. As William Fitzwilliam observed in a letter to Wolsey, 'And if it were not that I can some skill in hunting whereunto he, [Francis] hath a great appetite, and by reason thereof I come n[ear to him], I should know little or nothing'.[18] Francis's seemingly insatiable passion for hunting resulted in invitations to a succession of envoys to join the king in his favourite pastime. While still dauphin Francis was eager to involve ambassadors in his hunting expeditions, including the Duke of Suffolk and the Marquis of Dorset in a particularly successful chase in which both men speared boars.[19] Shortly after his arrival in France Fitzwilliam received a visit from Francis's huntmaster, who gave him some helpful pointers in the French style of the sport.[20] Apparently the French king spoke to the ambassador regularly about hunting, inviting him to take part in nearly every expedition that he organised.[21] Other men urged to join the French king when he took to the field included Richard Wingfield and Anthony Browne, although both were less impressed than Fitzwilliam by the French style of hunting.[22] Francis also often engaged Henry's envoys in conversation about military developments. He boasted to both Wingfield and Fitzwilliam about the new additions to his fleet that included three galleons capable of coming so close into shore that both infantry and cavalry

---

[15] *State Papers, Henry VIII*, vi. 57, Wingfield to Henry, 18 April 1520. Richardson, *Mary Tudor*, pp. 124-9.
[16] PRO, SP 1/21, fos. 53-4 (*LP*, iii(1). 987), Jerningham to Henry, 21 September 1520.
[17] BL, Cotton MS, Caligula D VIII, fo. 23 (*LP*, iii(1). 1212), Fitzwilliam to Henry, 27 February 1521.
[18] *LP*, iii(1). 1278, Fitzwilliam to Wolsey, 14 May 1521.
[19] BL, Cotton MS, Caligula D VI, fo. 188 (*LP*, i(2). 3430), Dorset to Wolsey, 9 November 1514.
[20] PRO, SP 1/21, fo. 204 (*LP*, iii(1). 1160), Fitzwilliam to Wolsey, December 1520.
[21] BL, Cotton MS, Caligula D VIII, fo. 21 (*LP*, iii(1). 1198), Fitzwilliam to Wolsey, March 1521,
[22] *State Papers, Henry VIII*, vi. 57, Wingfield to Henry, 18 April 1520; *State Papers, Henry VIII*, vi. 598, Browne to Henry, 21 August 1527.

could disembark via special bridges built into the ships.²³ On another occasion Wingfield presented Francis with a sword from Henry, and talked for some time with both the king and Admiral Bonnivet about new designs in armour which permitted the use of heavier weapons as well as greater ease of movement.²⁴ Of course it did not follow that simply because Francis was prepared to talk to Henry's envoys about his hobbies he would also divulge a raft of state secrets. Nevertheless, the greater the access an ambassador, particularly a resident one, could have to a prince, the better his chances of finding out up-to-date information of a reliable nature. Furthermore, the opportunity of speaking directly to the king about whatever issues were currently pressing was surely invaluable. Henry and his advisers were no doubt well aware of the potential advantages to be gained from such a situation and through the accreditation of ambassadors primarily drawn from the gentry sought to profit as much as possible from the situation.

For some time now it has been maintained, first and foremost by David Starkey, that of the English gentry dispatched to the French court, Henry's gentlemen of the privy chamber had an especially influential part to play in Tudor-Valois diplomacy.²⁵ One cannot deny that in the few years that linked the treaty of London with Henry's second war against Francis the English king made regular use of his gentlemen of the privy chamber as ambassadors. Furthermore, he did draw particular attention to their status in the letters of credence and instructions with which they were equipped. Thus Richard Wingfield replacing Thomas Boleyn in 1520 explained that although Henry was quite content with Boleyn's service, he nevertheless wished to display his affection to Francis by accrediting one of his 'trusty and near familiars' as resident ambassador.²⁶ Thomas Cheyne, Henry's last resident in France before the outbreak of war in May 1522, was instructed to inform Francis that:

> In consideracion of the parfite love and amytie that is establisched bytwyxt thaym hys grace could not be [fully] satisfied onless he

---

[23] BL, Cotton MS, Caligula D VIII, fo. 21 (*LP*, iii(1). 1198), Fitzwilliam to Wolsey, March 1521.

[24] BL, Cotton MS, Caligula D VIII, fo. 181 (*LP*, iii(1). 685), Wingfield to Henry, 16 March 1520.

[25] D. R. Starkey, 'Intimacy and Innovation: the rise of the privy chamber, 1485-1547' in *The English Court from the Wars of the Roses to the Civil War*, ed. Starkey (London, 1987), pp. 71-119.

[26] *LP*, iii(1). 629, instructions to Sir Richard Wingfield, February 1520.

estsonys visityd hym of now by hym as hys especiall amb[essy?] and famyliar serviturs to hys hyghnesse for parfite knowloge of the same.²⁷

Even after the war some effort was made by Henry to score diplomatic points with Francis by drawing attention to the appointment of his personal attendants as ambassadors. The point was made in Thomas Cheyne's instructions in 1526 and similarly John Wallop, dispatched to France in 1528, was ordered to specify his status to the French king.²⁸

I would argue, however, that this period of chamber diplomacy did not begin in 1519 with the re-organisation of Henry's personal attendants nor did it possess any great diplomatic significance. More than a decade before the dispatch of Sir Richard Wingfield to the court of Francis I Henry VII was already sending his personal attendants and members of his 'secret chamber' on diplomatic missions. The two men who accompanied John Stile on his 1505 mission to Spain – a highly sensitive embassy concerned with evaluating the personal suitability of Joanna of Naples as a possible bride for the king – were Francis Mazrin and Thomas Braybrooke, both members of Henry's secret chamber.²⁹ Mazrin was also active in Anglo-French diplomacy and performed at least five missions to the court of Louis XII in the reign of Henry VII. Another of the king's personal attendants, Matthew Baker, travelled to France in 1502 entrusted with a highly sensitive mission.³⁰

If one looks at the envoys sent to France in the first decade of Henry VIII's reign they differ little in nature, or indeed in some cases in identity from those employed in the 1520s. Charles Somerset, Earl of Worcester, the great chamberlain and head of Henry's household took part in three embassies to France in 1514, 1518 and 1521. Although there is no evidence that he sought to establish a greater degree of diplomatic intimacy with Francis based on his domestic position, he did make just such an overture to the Emperor Maximilian. As he informed Wolsey: 'I . . . spake

---

[27] BL, Cotton MS, Caligula D VIII, fo. 203 (*LP*, iii(2). 1991), instructions for Sir Thomas Cheyne, January 1522.
[28] BL, Cotton MS, Caligula D IX, fo. 164 (*LP*, iv(1). 2039), instructions for Sir Thomas Cheyne, March 1526, *State Papers, Henry VIII*, vii. 57, Wallop to Henry, February 1528.
[29] D. R. Starkey, 'The King's Privy Chamber, 1485-1547' (Unpublished University of Cambridge PhD thesis, 1973), p. 38.
[30] Baker travelled to France to seek Louis XII's support in gaining the extradition of the fugitive earl of Suffolk from Germany. However, in addition to seeking Louis' help he was also instructed to reject an offer of a French marriage for Prince Henry: S. J. Gunn, 'The Courtiers of Henry VII', *EHR*, 108 (1993), 23-49 at 40-41.

190 *The English Experience in France*

to the imperour at my first commyng desiring that I might come unto hym familiarly as one of his servauntes at all tyme'.[31] In the event Maximilian declined, no doubt reluctant to have the regular attendance of an experienced English ambassador when so much of his effort was currently devoted to emptying Henry's treasury. Other close companions of the king dispatched to France included Richard Wingfield in 1515 and Thomas Boleyn in 1518. That more were not sent was largely due to the Anglo-French cold war that prevailed between 1515 and 1518 and the absence of any agreement to exchange permanent envoys prior to the treaty of London.

It is also worth noting that even when the practice of accrediting gentlemen of the privy chamber was at its height in the early 1520s, one of the most popular residents was William Fitzwilliam, a childhood companion of the king and certainly a royal favourite, but not one of Henry's personal attendants. Despite this Fitzwilliam was accorded the same treatment by Francis as Wingfield, Jerningham and Cheyne and invited to attend upon the king as though he were one of Francis's own gentlemen. Conscious of his position, Fitzwilliam did not initially exploit the offer to the full and in so doing caused considerable surprise at the French court.[32] Francis knew full well that the ambassador was not one of Henry's personal attendants and clearly did not care. Fitzwilliam was a gentleman of high social rank and interested in the same things as the king. As Richard Jerningham assured Wolsey:

> the said Mr Fitzwilliam hath ordred hym self soo here that he hath the frenshe kinges favour my ladyes and the admyralles and is in as good credence aswell with theym and with all the counsaill as any man of his degre that hath been here of a grete space.[33]

From 1525 the role of the privy chamber, certainly in the king's resident diplomacy, diminished rapidly. A few of Henry's personal attendants were posted to permanent embassies, notably Francis Bryan, George Boleyn and William Howard, though the missions these men performed were relatively brief and in the case of the latter two their selection probably had as much to do with their relationship to Henry's

---

[31] BL, Cotton MS, Galba B V, fo. 101 (*LP*, ii(2) 2940), Worcester and Tunstall to Wolsey, 18 February 1517.
[32] BL, Cotton MS, Caligula D VIII, fo. 15 (*LP*, iii(1). 1176), Fitzwilliam to Wolsey, 22 March 1521.
[33] PRO, SP 1/22, fo. 191 (*LP*, iii(2). 1337), Jerningham to Wolsey, 9 June 1521.

wives as the king himself. By the 1530s the status of the king's personal attendants became increasingly less relevant. Anthony Browne sent to France as a special envoy in September 1538 found himself housed three miles from Francis, refused interviews with the king and snubbed by his advisers and courtiers.[34] Yet Browne had been a gentleman of the privy chamber for nearly twenty years and had previously been popular at the French court. On this occasion his status was quite unimportant. What determined his treatment was the current state of Franco-Imperial relations, at that time on the road to recovery, thus leading to a cooling of Francis's friendship for Henry.

Another aspect of the French court that made Henry's courtiers, whether of the privy chamber or not, particularly suitable envoys was the role played by a small number of women in the conduct of diplomatic affairs. Of course Charles V relied heavily on the female members of his family to assist him in the government of the Low Countries, just as Francis I depended upon his mother to govern France in his absence. What was different about the interaction of Louise of Savoy, Marguerite d'Angoulême and perhaps the Duchess d'Etampes with Henry's ambassadors was that it took place on a personal level where the women involved made use of both their familial relationship to Francis and their gender to advance diplomatic overtures and place ambassadors at a disadvantage.

During an audience with the king's sister in 1521 William Fitzwilliam politely listened as Marguerite accused his master of both duplicity and disloyalty. News of the investment and burning of a frontier town, Ardres, had reached the French court the previous day. The king's sister complained that despite Henry's professions of friendship to Francis and supposed neutrality in the current war he bore much of the blame for the town's fall since it was only at his request that Francis had forborne from fortifying Ardres. Furthermore, English soldiers had been seen amongst the Imperial

---

[34] *LP*, xiii(2). 641, Browne to Cromwell, 17 October 1538. Unfortunately although the original manuscript has faded to the point where much of it is now illegible, we can nevertheless gain a clear impression of how Browne and Bonner were treated from Henry's reaction to their report: 'And wheras We perceve, not only by your letters and of your collegge allsoo, but by sundry other most credeable reaportes and relations made unto Us, that ye have had very slendre recuel at your arryvaile, and worse entreteignement sythens the same, as well in appointement of lodging as other your necessaries to be hadd ther, and much under that hiegh and moost honorable estate you beare, being our Ambassadour ther, and representing in maner our Personne, to our no litle mervaile that in a cuntrey called of so muche civilitie, and amonges personnes taken of so gentle and curtoyse entreteignment, ye find so litle gentylnes and curtoyse; being veray displeasaunt of such proceding with you by them, whom We have somuche estemed and loved': *State Papers, Henry VIII*, viii. 73, Henry to Browne, October 1538.

troops involved in the sack of the town. How could any honourable prince support such actions? Fitzwilliam assured her that Henry had been ignorant of any plan to attack Ardres and that any Englishmen involved in the action could only have been rebels living in the Low Countries. In this case Francis used his sister to make clear to the English ambassador that he was well aware of Henry's friendship with Charles. Yet where such accusations coming from the lips of the king or one of his advisers could well have precipitated a serious diplomatic incident at a time when English neutrality, no matter how hollow, still served France's best interests, the immunity afforded Marguerite by her gender allowed her to make such remarks. Fitzwilliam himself admitted that upon hearing her comments his anger was such that had she not been a woman he would have been unable to restrain himself from replying in decidedly undiplomatic terms.[35]

Francis was also prepared to allow certain highly sensitive matters to be broached first by the women in his trust. When in 1527 negotiations were under way between England and France for the marriage of the Princess Mary to the French king, it was Francis's mother who discussed the somewhat touchy subject of marital consummation. Louise explained to John Clerk, Henry's resident envoy in Paris, that although she understood Mary to be quite young she thought it would be a good idea, once all the conditions had been agreed if the betrothal took place as speedily as possible, and the union be consummated straight afterwards.[36] Clerk pointed out to Louise that Mary was in fact eleven, and surely far too young to consummate the marriage. The Queen mother brushed aside his concerns reminding him that the princess would be nearer twelve than eleven by the time of the wedding, and that she herself had been that age when she first came to her marriage bed. The real issue here for Francis and his mother was to tie Henry into an alliance as quickly and bindingly as possible. While verbal and written marriage agreements were frequently reneged upon a consummated union would provide a far stronger link between the houses of Tudor and Valois.

In the 1530s and early 1540s English envoys to the French court approached Marguerite D'Angoulême on a number of occasions as an alternative means of raising sensitive diplomatic overtures. John Wallop, performing his second residency in France in 1540 spoke privately with Marguerite a number of times, on one occasion coming to her bedside after she had feigned illness in order that they might talk more secretly. Wallop

---

[35] BL, Cotton MS, Caligula E I, fo. 98 (*LP*, iii(2). 1581), Fitzwilliam to Wolsey, 15 September 1521.
[36] BL, Cotton MS, Caligula D X fo. 39 (*LP*, iv(2). 2981), Clerk to Wolsey, March 1527.

urged her to use her influence with Francis to dissuade him from friendship with the emperor, passing on information provided by Cromwell that supposedly demonstrated that Charles was deceiving the French king. Interestingly, one of the firmest pieces of advice Marguerite gave the ambassador was that he must cultivate the friendship of the king's mistress, the Duchess d'Etampes, if he wished to persuade Francis to reject his friendship with the emperor in favour of closest amity with Henry.[37] One is left in little doubt of the importance of d'Etampes's role in the formulation of French foreign policy at this time. Of course ambassadors did not have to be members of the gentry or nobility in order to cultivate relationships with the king's sister or his mistress, yet it is undeniable that those of Henry's courtiers dispatched to France appeared to make a better job of it than their clerical colleagues. Thus the Duke of Norfolk travelling to Marseilles in 1533 stopped in Paris for several days and enjoyed a number of meetings with Marguerite d'Angoulême each lasting in excess of five hours. Amidst the various discussions of diplomatic affairs which no doubt took place, the king's sister found time to recount Francis's current marital difficulties, caused by the excessively amorous nature of the emperor's sister, which apparently she found highly amusing.[38] Norfolk left Paris with what appears to be genuine affection for Marguerite. By comparison John Clerk in 1528 managed to thoroughly annoy Louise of Savoy by suggesting that if the emperor refused to return her grandchildren she should, being a woman, go down on her knees to him and beg for their release.[39] Undoubtedly it was Henry's courtier ambassadors who got on best with the ladies of the French court.

Yet, despite the many gestures of friendship and moments of apparent intimacy shared between Francis, his inner circle and Henry's ambassadors, England and France remained perennial rivals and rarely ceased to perceive each other as a threat. Although not frequently mentioned in the dispatches of Henry's envoys, one does occasionally come across evidence highlighting the antagonism which existed between English diplomatic staff and French courtiers. The context of Germayne

---

[37] *State Papers, Henry VIII*, viii. 318, Wallop to Henry, 18 April 1540. For a detailed account of Wallop's dealings with Marguerite d'Angoulême and the importance of the Duchess d'Etampes in the formation of French foreign policy in the 1540s see D. L. Potter, 'Diplomacy in the Mid-Sixteenth Century: England and France, 1536-1550' (Unpublished University of Cambridge PhD thesis, 1973), pp. 43-81.
[38] PRO, SP 1/77, fos. 82-5 (*LP*, vi. 692), Norfolk to Henry, June 1533.
[39] PRO, SP 1/48, fos. 25-6 (*LP*, iv(2). 4270), Clerk to Tuke, 16 May 1528.

Gardiner's letter in which he listed the young gentlemen in his uncle's suite, was to defend their behaviour at the French court. Reports had reached Cromwell that Hungerford, Wingfield, Gage and the rest had been deliberately provoking their French hosts and insulting them with bad language. In their defence Gardiner observed that in nearly every case the young men's French was so poor that it would be another seven years before they could ask for their meals without the aid of an interpreter. Yet even if Gardiner's claims were true, it seems unlikely that the reports made to Cromwell were entirely fabricated, and that the young men in the Bishop of Winchester's entourage, no doubt with too much time on their hands, took advantage of their diplomatic immunity to taunt their French hosts.

Certainly in the aftermath of Henry's final war with Francis the government was taking no chances. Thomas Cheyne travelling to France to attend the christening of the dauphin's daughter was instructed by the council:

> You are in the king's name to declare to such gentlemen as accompany you into France that they behave among the Frenchmen . . . so as to give no occasion of displeasure by reference to feats of the war past. They should either say nothing unless provoked, or call the things that happened *fortune de la guerre* without comparison of events on either side, but turn the conversation to peace.[40]

It was a facet of this often apparent tension that existed between England and France that provides the remainder of the explanation for the dominant role of Henry's gentry in his dealings with Francis. Many of the gentry and nobility later accredited to the French court had first served as officers in either the Calais Pale or Tournai. Richard Wingfield had served both as deputy and high marshal of Calais before his appointment as resident to France in 1520. John Wallop, who would spend much of the 1530s in France, was high marshal from 1524 to 1530 and lieutenant of Calais castle from 1529 until his appointment to the French residency in 1532. William Fitzwilliam, already vice-admiral of the English fleet at the time of his first embassy to France in 1521, was respectively Lieutenant of Guînes and Calais castles from 1523 to 1526 and 1526 to 1529.[41] Another English resident at the French court, Richard Jerningham, had been prominent in

---

[40] *LP*, xxi(1), 1094.
[41] For a complete list of officers in Calais between 1485 and 1547 see David Grummitt, 'Calais, 1485-1547: a study in early Tudor politics and government' (Unpublished University of London PhD thesis, 1997), pp. 219-28.

the government of Tournai during its brief period of occupation by the English, serving first as treasurer before being appointed governor of the city in January 1517.[42]

The use of garrison officers on diplomatic missions had definite advantages, most notably the range of contacts such men were able to make use of while abroad. As governors of Calais or Tournai men such as Wingfield and Jerningham were expected to maintain networks of informants to give the government early warning of any possible encroachments planned by the French. Frequent letters from Wingfield to Wolsey during those periods he was actually resident at Calais deal with the payment and disposition of spies.[43] On other occasions the cardinal issued Jerningham with specific instructions for the deployment of his informers, primarily with regard to gaining information about the movements of Richard de la Pole.[44]

Of still greater value to the government was the personal experience and knowledge of military affairs that many of the ambassadors drawn from the gentry were able to make use of while on diplomatic service. Particularly useful was the technical information they could supply to Henry and his advisers. During his first embassy to the French court, William Fitzwilliam sent a stream of military intelligence back to Wolsey. This included warnings of increased naval preparations at both Brest and New Haven which the ambassador believed were being made in anticipation of war with England, and reports on the strength of French fortifications and troop dispositions. This latter information passed to Wolsey during his embassy to Calais and Bruges between August and November 1521 would no doubt have been especially welcome. In late

---

[42] C. G. Cruickshank, *The English Occupation of Tournai* (Oxford, 1973), pp. 44, 46, 54, 96-7, 100.

[43] PRO, SP 1/11, fos. 12, 97-8; BL, Cotton MS, Caligula E I, fo. 103 (*LP*, ii(1).665, 953; ii(2). 2761), Wingfield to Wolsey, 6 July, 27 September 1516 and 9 January 1517. See also Wingfield's accounts for the payment of spies, from 1 July 1515 to 1 August 1518: PRO, SP 1/17, fos. 46-9 (*LP*, ii(2). 4406).

[44] 'Master Jernyngham . . . it is the kinges pleasure that ye with al diligence do sende some discrete, wise and sure felowe being a burgonyon unto Meyse in Lorayn to understonde and bring you perfite report of Richard de la Pole; where he is and what he dothe with all other thinges concernyng hym and his affaires . . . And in likewise that ye sende an other in to the corte of Fraunce by whom ye may be ascertayned of what preparacions or other occurrantes be there; taking such ordre that ye may be daily advertised aswel from these places as from al other parties about you where any good knowlege may be had . . '.: PRO, SP 1/14, fo. 223 (*LP*, ii(2). 2846), Wolsey to Jerningham, 29 January 1517. See also SP 1/15, fo. 11 (*LP*, ii(2). 2967), Jerningham to Henry, 14 February 1517.

August Fitzwilliam wrote to the cardinal detailing the numbers of French troops Francis had told him he would be committing to his invasion of Hainault. The Duke of Bourbon was bringing 12,000 foot and 2,000 horse, the Duke of Vendôme would soon be arriving with a further 10,000 infantry and 400 'spears', and Francis had also hired 6,000 landsknechts as well as some thousands of Swiss mercenaries. Although Fitzwilliam could not be certain as to the real number of soldiers available to Francis he was extremely doubtful with regard to the French king's claims. He had only counted 3,000 soldiers in Troyes, yet the French king was boasting that in less than two weeks he would march with more than ten times that number. One thing the ambassador did assure Wolsey was that Francis's efforts to gather an army for the relief of Picardy and invasion of Hainault were denuding the country of troops. Whatever the French king's battlefield strength, he ran the very real risk of over-extending himself, and was certainly in a far more vulnerable position than he would have the king and cardinal believe.[45]

When Fitzwilliam finally accompanied Francis on his campaign to relieve Mézières and Tournai at least some of his doubts were confirmed. By October Francis was claiming he had 12,000 Swiss under his command, far more than the ambassador had been able to count. Furthermore, the French king had informed Fitzwilliam that his artillery train would include sixteen great canons, twelve culverins and twelve demi-culverins, yet his own survey of the French ordinance had revealed only four great canon, six culverins and ten smaller guns of assorted calibre.[46] For Wolsey, still seeking to arbitrate between the French and Imperial commissioners at Calais, such information would have been most useful. Given the repeated claims made by both parties with regard to the respective strengths of their armies, even a partially accurate report from a trusted source which indicated that the French were at least exaggerating would have served to reassure the cardinal. Not only did such knowledge put him in a stronger position when negotiating with Duprat and his colleagues, it would also have been comforting to know of French military limitations given the increasing likelihood that England would be at war with her the following year.[47]

---

[45] BL, Cotton MS, Caligula D VIII, fos. 89-91 (*LP*, iii(2). 1521), Fitzwilliam to Wolsey, 30 August 1521. The number of Swiss soldiers is illegible.
[46] BL, Cotton MS, Caligula D VIII of.102 (*LP*, iii(2). 1643), Fitzwilliam to Wolsey, 7 October 1521.
[47] See Pace's letter to Wolsey, 'Hys grace sayth he percevyth by the sayde extracte off Sir Wyllum Fytzwilliams letters, that there is boith fere and scarcytie of moneye in Fraunce,

Even when the prospect of war with France appeared distant, however, the government was quite prepared to use ambassadors with military experience to obtain better intelligence about French troop numbers and fortifications. Thus in 1536, as Francis and Charles returned to war, Henry instructed Sir John Wallop, joint resident ambassador in France to:

> devise to reasort to the Frenche kinges campe and such principal fortresses as ye may have recourse unto without daunger and diligently to vieu and peruse the force and strength of the same conceyving suche lightlywoodes therupon as ye wold gather if ye shuld be an actor in the playe yourself.[48]

Given the ostensibly cordial state of Anglo-French relations at this time one might fairly question the ethics of Henry's instructions, yet the opportunism that lay behind them is understandable. In the only war between the houses of Habsburg and Valois which did not include the Tudors, one of Henry's most experienced officers had access, albeit limited, to the defences which might one day be used to repulse England's own armies. In such circumstances the most important aspect of Wallop's diplomatic status was the slight freedom it gave him to practise his trade as a soldier.

The final ten or fifteen years of Henry's reign saw a definite change in the style of diplomacy practiced by English ambassadors at the French court. The decreasing use of the gentlemen of the privy chamber has already been mentioned. Yet although the gentry as a whole continued to play an important part among English envoys dispatched to France, one receives the impression that even when relations between the two countries were good the earlier intimacy which had been present at Francis's court had largely gone. Part of the explanation can be found in the age of the protagonists. In 1535 Francis was 40 years old: he had endured the indignity of defeat and capture, seen large portions of his country pillaged, been betrayed by the Duke of Bourbon and handed his sons into captivity. Under the circumstances it is hardly surprising that his approach to diplomacy took on a somewhat more serious aspect. Furthermore, the ambassadors travelling to France were older. Francis Bryan and Anthony Browne had first come to the Valois court in their mid twenties, at the time of their final embassies in 1538 both men were 46. Thomas Cheyne, a favourite at the French court in the 1520s, completed his final mission to

---

whyche 2 thyngis makyth muche for hys intendydde purpose': *State Papers, Henry VIII*, i. 45, Pace to Wolsey, 29 August 1521.

[48] BL, Add MS, 25,114, fos. 203v-4 (*LP*, xi. 445), Henry to Wallop, 12 September 1536.

France for Henry in 1546 at the age of 64, while the Duke of Norfolk performed his last mission in 1540 aged 67. One can safely assume that egg throwing binges or participation in protracted wild boar hunts no longer offered these sextegenarions the satisfaction they had once done.

Equally significant was the growing part played in Anglo-French diplomacy by the clergy. Their expertise in civil and canon law and knowledge of Latin had always ensured their presence in special embassies concerned with treaty negotiations, but from the mid 1520s they were ever more frequently accredited to resident postings. Thus the first resident appointed to France after the treaty of the More in 1525 was Dr. John Taylor who was followed by John Clerk, Bishop of Bath and Wells. Even when Henry chose to appoint members of the gentry and nobility as residents he tended to twin them with clerics. George Boleyn, accredited resident ambassador to France in October 1529, was accompanied by John Stokesley, future Bishop of London. John Wallop, appointed alone in March 1532, performed the final two and a half years of his mission in company with Stephen Gardiner, while Francis Bryan's final residency in France was shared with Thomas Thirlby, shortly afterwards elected Bishop of Westminster. Already having less in common with Francis than Henry's courtier ambassadors, a number of the clerics who served in France further widened the gap between themselves and the French king by behaving in a fashion designed to antagonise him. Stephen Gardiner earned Francis's everlasting opprobrium by his tactless behaviour at Marseilles in 1533. Involved in sensitive negotiations with the pope at least partially concerned with finding a compromise for Henry's marital situation, Francis claimed that all his work was ruined when Gardiner, and that other subtle diplomatist Edmund Bonner, forced an audience with Clement and demanded that he meet all Henry's demands or suffer the consequences.[49] Francis never forgave the Bishop of Winchester his behaviour at Marseilles, and was still bitterly complaining about it nine years later to another resident envoy, William Paget.[50]

It was, however, Edmund Bonner that provoked the most trouble. With his tactless behaviour and blind determination to defend the interests of his master, the Bishop of London succeeded in antagonising much of the French court and most importantly the king himself. The final straw came when upon discovering that his efforts to gain the repatriation of one Robert Brancestor had been thwarted Bonner accused Francis of acting,

---

[49] Scarisbrick, pp. 319-20.
[50] PRO, SP 1/180, fo. 73 (*LP*, xviii(1). 902). Paget to Henry, 4 February 1543.

'totallement contre Dieu, raison, et devoir chose infâme, injuste et contre les traictes qui estoient entre son dict maistre et ce Roi de France'.[51] Probably as much annoyed by the tone of Bonner's rebuke as by its contents, Francis demanded the bishop's immediate recall. The Duke of Norfolk sent on a damage limitation mission was informed by Louis Perreu, seigneur de Castillon, an old resident envoy to England, that, 'my Lorde of London had doon more good to thEmperours affayres here, then himself and all his agentes here'. Norfolk's opinion was unequivocal, 'he [is] meverlously hated here, and shall never be able in this plase to [do] You gode service'. The duke's further observation that, 'busshops be no mete men for Imbassitours here', may well have struck Henry as being a trifle gratuitous.[52]

Rather wisely Bonner was the last prelate accredited to the French court as a resident ambassador. He was not, however, the last cleric. In the aftermath of Henry's final war with Francis Nicholas Wotton, Dean of York and Canterbury, was appointed permanent envoy in France. In proposing him for the office, William Paget, Henry's secretary of state, observed that:

> Mr Wotton were meet at the beginning . . . both because he is a personage of peace and for that also, being a sober discreet man, beaten now in these matters and not over hasty in practices, the Frenchmen, who no doubt will straight be in hand with new devices, may with his demureness and temperance be put off the better.[53]

Paget was not far wrong in his assessment. Wotton represented an excellent choice. England, all but bankrupted by Henry's last war, certainly did not need an aggressive ambassador in France inflaming relations between the two countries. Nor was there much point in dispatching some young courtier who might insinuate himself into the French king's favour. By 1546 Francis was a very tired prince indeed, the youthful pastimes in which Henry's gentlemen ambassadors had been able to share were long behind him. For a brief time at least the keynotes of Anglo-French diplomacy were neither courtesy nor conflict but rather restraint and circumspection, policies which Wotton, Henry's final ambassador to France, and perhaps one of England's first professional diplomats, was well qualified to put into practice.

---

[51] G. M. V. Alexander, 'The Life and Career of Edmund Bonner until his Deprivation in 1549' (Unpublished University of London PhD thesis, 1960), pp. 232-7.
[52] *State Papers, Henry VIII*, viii. 255, 260, Norfolk to Henry, 17 February 1540.
[53] *LP*, xxi(1). 906, Paget to Petre, 24 May 1546.

10 The Private Face of Anglo-French Relations in the Sixteenth Century: the Lisles and their French friends

DAVID POTTER

In November 1533, a few months after the arrival of Lord Lisle as deputy at Calais in June, his twelve-year-old step-daughter Anne Basset travelled south to go to live at the castle of Pont-Rémy on the Somme with Jeanne de Saveuse, Madame de Riou (staying until the summer of 1536). M. de Riou invited Honor Lady Lisle to visit Pont-Rémy while on a pilgrimage to Amiens in May 1534 and it was probably then that the arrangements were made for the younger daughter Mary (then eleven or twelve) to go to Bours to be looked after by Riou's sister Anne, Madame de Bours in August 1534 (staying with their household until 1538).[1] The acquaintances and friendships to which these arrangements gave rise, viewed through the correspondence they generated, are the subject of this paper. We have in Lisle's papers a precious and rather unusual testimony to the existence of friendship between families which crossed national and in some ways cultural frontiers. Such documents in one sense are not unique. There is plenty of evidence, for instance, of the existence of familial and friendly ties between the nobilities of France and the southern Low Countries in the sixteenth century (if only because they had formed part of the same interrelated social group for many

---

[1] M. St. Clare Byrne, *The Lisle Letters* (6 vols., Chicago and London, 1981) i. 135, 175, no. 570. Thibault Rouault to Lisle, 11 May 1534, *LL*, iii. no. 572 (French text). St. Clare Byrne argues that the arrangements for Mary Basset were probably made on this occasion: *LL*, iii. 145; Anne Rouault to Lady Lisle, 3 & 8 Mar., [1538] *LP* xiii(2). 411, 457, on her return.

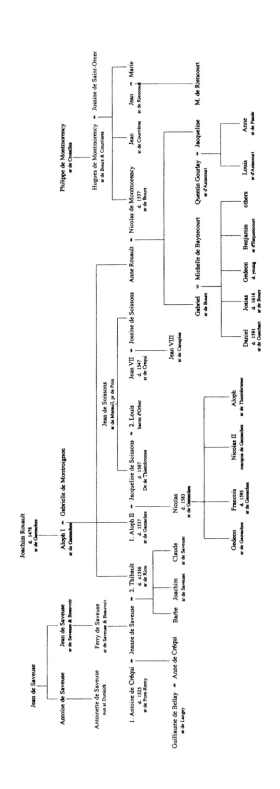

Figure 10.1: The French friends of Lord Lisle

centuries).² The friendships revealed by the Lisle papers are different in that they constitute perhaps some of the earliest evidence in Anglo-French history of purely personal friendship (as opposed to the interests involved in the cross-channel relations of the English and French nobilities stemming from the tenurial problems of the Hundred Years Wars period).

It can hardly be claimed of course that the papers are newly discovered.³ Their content has been partly available since Mrs Wood published some in the nineteenth century and the editors of the *Letters and Papers of Henry VIII* calendared them⁴ (it must be said with very uneven accuracy, particularly in dating) and more recently in the six volume work by Muriel St. Clare Byrne. This is not the place for a detailed critique of the latter, especially in view of the great contribution of the editor in bringing the letters to a wider readership.⁵ However, St. Clare Byrne's approach in translating most of the French documents she printed, selecting them and rearranging them in groups is not particularly conducive to the study of the French correspondents of the Lisle family,⁶ while her dating, although given some thought,⁷ is often no less a matter of guesswork than that of *Letters and Papers*. We cannot get a clear overall impression, then, of the texture of the friendships without recourse to the original texts and viewing them as a whole.⁸

The Lisle archive is of course skewed by the fact that it consists mainly of letters received.⁹ There are occasional draft replies on the reverse but we know that, although Lisle himself could speak French, Lady Lisle could neither speak nor read it (though her children wrote to her in French) and it is clear that her letters were written by secretaries, while verbal messages were taken by the Lisle

---

[2] For example, the letter-books of the Boffles family of Artois, see R. Muchembled, 'Famille, Amour et Mariage: mentalités et comportements des nobles artésiens à l'époque de Philippe II', *Revue d'histoire moderne et contemporaine* 22 (1975), 233-61.
[3] They are preserved primarily in four volumes, PRO, SP 3/15-18 [hereafter simply SP 3], the French texts of the Lisle correspondence.
[4] M. E. A. Wood, *Letters of Royal and Illustrious Ladies* (3 vols., London, 1846).
[5] For St. Clare Byrne's rationale in presentation of the texts, see *LL*, i. 104-13.
[6] St. Clare Byrne as a result even repeated one letter, that of Antoinette de Saveuse, 27 July [1537] (*LL*, iii. no. 603 and v. no. 1499) translating it differently.
[7] *LL*, iii. 140
[8] For this reason, substantial passages from the original texts will be considered in the notes below. Most have not hitherto been published in original form.
[9] A point made by St. Clare Byrne in *LL*, i. 102.

servant John Smith.[10] The French texts fall into a number of categories. The most formal are the letters received by Lisle himself from French military commanders who were neighbours of the Calais Pale, most notably Oudart du Biez but also his deputies and the governors of Ardres. These are as one might expect couched largely in terms of the necessary exchanges between frontier commanders and deal with questions of border raids, frontier disputes, extraditions and diplomacy. They also involve a constant exchange of compliments and presents, especially in the earlier years when Anglo-French relations were relatively close. St. Clare Byrne was largely uninterested in this correspondence.[11] Lisle, of course, was also in charge of information gathering in France of an espionage kind, although I am not concerned with that aspect here.[12] Clearly, much of this is correspondence of a business kind although none the less interesting for its exchanges of compliments.

St. Clare Byrne was more interested in the female correspondents of the Lisles, mostly writing to Lady Lisle (they seldom addressed more than compliments to her husband, while M. de Riou, husband of one of those correspondents almost always wrote to Lisle rather than his wife).[13] Of the 44 letters of Antoinette de Saveuse she published 28 in translation, of the 37 from Anne Rouault she published 28, of the twelve from Jeanne de Saveuse she published ten. This gives the reader more to go on but the picture we get of the identity of these correspondents is fragmentary. There is, of course, a scattering other female correspondents, some of whom, such as Jeanne Quierot, wife of Jean de Calonne, sr de Landretun near Ardres were related to most of the thickly-strewn *gentilhommerie* of Guînes and Boulonnais and on very friendly terms with the Lisles.[14]

---

[10] *LL*, i. 32. See in particular *LP* xv. 750. The secretaries appear to have been Peter Beckwith and Richard Wyndebank.

[11] There are 58 letters from du Biez, only seven of which were translated in the *LL*, and many of which were misdated or misunderstood by the *LP* editors. In addition there are 24 letters from du Biez's son-in-law Vervins, eight from his cousin Bécourt (both of whom stood in for him at different times) one from his wife Jeanne de Senlis and another from his daughter Isabeau (none of these in the *Lisle Letters*).

[12] See, for instance, the report transmitted by Lisle to Cromwell on 27 May 1539 that Francis I was unlikely to launch a war. His informant 'lyethe myghtelye when hee is ther in Kannaples chamber and have promised to shewe me more': PRO, SP 1/151, fo. 244 (*LP* xiv(1). 1032).

[13] It is noticeable that only three of Riou's twelve letters were adressed to Lady Lisle while Guillaume du Bellay also wrote only to Lisle.

[14] Mme de Landretun wrote several letters, *LL*, iii. nos. 801, 801a, iv. no. 950b, v. no. 1221. For her, see L.-E. de La Gorgue-Rosny, *Recherches généalogiques sur les comtés de Ponthieu, de Boulogne, de Guînes et Pays Circonvoisins* (4 vols., Boulogne, 1874-7) iii. 1208. There were

The boarding out of young boys and girls in France to learn the language – the case of the Boleyn sisters is an obvious example – was not uncommon in this period and was likened by St. Clare Byrne to a sort of finishing school and debutante season.[15] On a lesser level, the undermarshal of Calais had his daughter brought up by a French gentleman, the sieur de 'Bewloze' in the Somme area.[16] In 1537, we learn that an English boy had been left to be brought up at Amiens on the promise of payment to the host if he were brought up well. No one had come to claim him and the host was out of pocket.[17] Of the two Basset girls' brothers, George went to Saint-Omer in November 1536 to study and learn French with a priest-schoolmaster, Jean des Gardins, and James, the youngest and most precocious, went to Paris aged seven to study first at the Collège de Calvi in August 1535, and then, after a summer break at Saint-Omer in

---

also Lamberde du Flos, whose family held a fief at Tardinghen in Boulonnais (ibid, ii. 580) and Jeanne de Bours, Mme d'Ignaucourt (confused by St. Clare Byrne with Jacqueline de Montmorency-Bours, wife of Azincourt), was also an acquaintance of Mary Basset and was probably related to the sr de Gennes, an important member of the Bourbon-Vendôme household (*LP* xiii(2), 549; Rosny, i. 244).

[15] *LL*, i. 135.

[16] Lisle to Cromwell, nd, Nov. 1538 – Jan. 1539, BL, Cotton MS. Caligula II, fo. 249 (not in Lisle letters): 'the undermarshall sent a [servan]t to fetche his doughter whiche he had put ffurth [to] [learn]e frenche, to oon monsr de Bewloze who dwells vi le[gis from] Abeville and iij legis from Pounte Dormy, wher he w[ent ove]r the water of Some, with whom I sent a servaunt of my[ne to] here newis'.

[17] Antoinette de Saveuse to Lady Lisle, ? Aug. 1537 SP 3/18, fo. 20 (*LP* xii(2). 615; *LL*, iii. no. 604): 'Madame, vou plesse de savoer que il y a eu aucun personnaiges de Angleterre quy ont mené ung jeune filz demeurer en Franse en la ville de Amiens à l'ottel du bon gentil homme nommé monsieur de Ghouwy & luy fut promis que arroet bon salere moiennant que il se acquita bien au dit enfant, che que le bon sieur a foet & le tient encores & depuy che tanps ny personne quy soet venu au logis dudit sieur pour rien paier v pour savoer comment choet enfant se conduit. Sur che, Madame, ledit sr m'a baliet ches copies signifient comment il a eut cherge de prendre en sa messon ledit enfant. Madame, je vou suplie de ferre visiter ches deux copies pour savoer sy n'y a personne qui congnoet les personnaiges à quy chette aferre touche'. See same to same, 13 Aug. [1537] SP 3/16, fo. 113 (*LP* xiii(2), 32, misdated 1538): 'Madame vou plese de savoir que en fesant ces presentes j'ey rechut lecttres de Amiens lesqueles me a envoié monsr de Gouwy & prie fort humblement de savoir response sy j'ey foet diligense par dever vous Madame de ce que je vous envoyet thouchant de son petit filz de Angleterre. Sur che je vou suplie madame par cheus quy poroient congnoitre les parens du dit enfant vous enquerre à savoer'. The reference is almost certainly to the family of Gouy which produced several archers and *gens d'armes* in the Picard companies in this period: Rosny, ii. 682-3. In 1529, Jean, Antoine and Ferry de Gouy had contributed the ransom of Francis I in the bailliage of Amiens: E. de Rosny, 'Liste de personnes tenant fiefs nobles . . '. in *Mémoires de la société des antiquaires de Picardie*, vi. 434-49.

1536, he returned to Paris via Bours in December to stay with the Paris merchant Guillaume Le Gras and then the Collège de Navarre.[18] The cultivation of French for the English nobility and gentry had become a more pressing matter as those groups ceased to be bilingual and as French began to emerge as a key international vernacular in the sixteenth century. The explains the rather rich publishing history of French phrasebooks and grammars from the late fifteenth century onwards, culminating in Palsgrave's monumental *Esclaircissement de la Langue Françoyse* in 1530. It will never be possible to assess accurately the extent of knowledge of French in England but by the middle of the sixteenth century, according to Jacques Peletier du Mans, 'En Angleterre, amoins entre les Princes et en leurs cours, iz parlent François en tous leurs propos'.[19] Educating the Basset sons in French was thus almost a matter of course, although the French education of the girls is an interesting and important testimony to their parents' ambitions for them.

Why did the Lisles chose these families, who were they and what can we learn from their letters? The origins of the Lisle connection with their French friends remains obscure. There is no evidence that Lisle ever set foot in France until the campaign of Thérouanne and Tournai in 1513,[20] when it seems entirely likely that he made the acquaintance of local French nobles such as Pont-Remy and du Biez, the defenders of Thérouanne. He certainly met du Biez at Boulogne at the start of his Garter embassy to France in 1527, when he was received also at Montreuil, Abbeville and Amiens. Both Lisle and his wife accompanied the king and Anne Boleyn to Boulogne for the meeting with Francis I in October 1532[21] and Riou and his wife would almost certainly have been present on those occasions. The acquaintance was quickly renewed on Lisle's appointment as deputy of Calais in 1533. The exact relationships of the Lisles' French friends raise problems that are not solved by the fact that the main genealogical collections in the Bibliothèque Nationale and consequently the works of du

---

[18] For James Basset and his contacts, with whom this paper is not directly concerned, see *LL*, iii. 106-135; iv. 468-525. He gave Mme de Bours the news of Lady Lisle's pregnancy in Dec. 1536: *LL*, iii. 554. He was at the Collège de Navarre from Nov. 1537 to Oct. 1538, when he entered the household of Stephen Gardiner on his return to England. The correspondence concerning him is from Le Gras and various scholars such as John Bekinshaw, mainly concerning his practical needs. On Le Gras's later problems, see *Calendar of State Papers, Foreign Series, Mary*, ed. William B. Turnbull (London, 1861), pp. 144, 161.
[19] Jacques Peletier du Mans, *Dialogues d'Ortografe* (1550), p. 60.
[20] *LL*, i. 160.
[21] *LL*, i. 171, 199-202, 247-52.

Chesne, Père Anselme and later the local antiquarian Darsy are seriously confused at this point on the identity of Mme de Bours and her relations with the other correspondents.[22] From the Lisle papers themselves it is much clearer who they were[23] although those documents are also sometimes ambiguous and can only be understood in the context of the histories of the families concerned. Briefly, Jeanne de Saveuse was sister-in-law to Madame de Bours, having married her brother Thibault Rouault sr de Riou. Antoinette de Saveuse, a nun of the Carmelite order at Dunkirk, was Jeanne's cousin, depending on her and Lady Lisle for family support and friendship in a place where she had no living relatives of her own.[24]

---

[22] Père Anselme, *Histoire généalogique et chronologique de la maison royale de France* (3rd edn., 9 vols., Paris, 1726-33), vii. 97-100, the genealogy of the Rouault omits Anne Rouault in the genealogy and makes the wife of Nicolas de Montmorency to be Barbe, the daughter of Aloph II and Jacqueline de Soissons; in the genealogy of the Montmorency-Bours, ibid., iii. 614 he correctly makes Anne to be the wife of Nicolas but the daughter of Aloph I and Jacqueline de Soissons. The date of Anne Rouault's marriage, 1512, follows du A. du Chesne, *Histoire de la maison de Montmorency* (Paris, 1624) p. 494, *preuves* pp. 329-30, followed by Darsy, 'Gamaches et ses seigneurs' *Mémoires de la société des antiquaires de Picardie*, xii. 99-189, xiv. 393-529. Darsy, xiv. 410-25, places Anne and Nicolas de Bours in an earlier generation than is possible; while Belleval, who points out the inconsistencies in Anselme and du Chesne correctly states that Anne was the wife of Nicolas but makes her mother Jacqueline de Soisson: R. de Belleval, *Lettres sur le Ponthieu* (1868), pp. 24-9. The misapprehension certainly goes back to the seventeenth century printed genealogy in BNF, pièces originales 2555 no. 264 which gives 'Barbe Rouault' the daughter of Aloph II as the wife of Nicolas. Anne Rouault, who married in 1512, cannot have been the daughter of Jacqueline de Soissons, who died in 1567. The genealogy of the Soissons places Jacqueline (whose father died in 1509) in the same generation as Anne: Anselme, vi. 719-20. The correct picture seems to be that Jacqueline de Soissons was the wife of Aloph II, sister-in-law of Thibault and Anne. Thus the lawsuit brought against the baron d'Orbec by Anne in 1544 (mentioned du Chesne, *preuves* p. 329), was as the second husband of Jacqueline, by Anne as her sister-in-law. St. Clare Byrne simply accepts the identity of Jacqueline de Soissons as Anne Rouault's sister-in-law: *LL*, iii. 137.

[23] One interesting revelation for instance is that Anne Rouault had a brother 'feu monsr de Gamaches mon frere' whose death she reported to Lady Lisle in 1537: SP 3/16 fo. 11 (*LP* xii(1). 284). Aloph I had died in 1530 and Aloph II who is sometimes held to have died in 1562 (eg. Darsy, 'Les seigneurs de Gamaches'), certainly died in 1537. Another brother seems to have died in 1538, see Anne Rouault to Lady Lisle, SP 3/18, fo. 33 (*LP* xiii(2). 603; *LL*, v. no. 1250): 'J'é esté tousiours la plus part depuis ce temps là hors de ceans pour l'amour de l'un de mes freres qui a esté malade et qu'il a pleu à Dieu prendre de sa part depuis quinze jours'.

[24] Made clear by Jeanne de Saveuse to Lady Lisle, 27 July [1537] SP 3/17, fo. 145 (*LP* xiii(1). 1480, wrongly dated 1538; *LL*, iii. no. 603, dated 1537; v. no. 1499, dated 1539). St. Clare Byrne, who relied heavily on La Chesnaye-Dubois, *Dictionnaire de la noblesse*, knew of no Saveuse genealogy: *LL*, iii. 176-7. It can in fact be reconstructed from Rosny, iii. 1368-70. This genealogy, though, does not mention Antoinette. She may have been a daughter of Antoine de Saveuse, Jeanne de Saveuse's uncle, or a sister of the cadet branch of Imbert de Saveuse. At any

Anne Rouault, we can be fairly sure, was the daughter of Aloph Ier sr de Gamaches (an important fief of Vimeu on the borders of Normandy) and grand-daughter of a figure of the first rank, Joachim Rouault sr de Gamaches, who had begun his career in the 1430s as *premier écuyer* of the dauphin Louis and was appointed marshal of France by Louis XI on his accession in 1461. Rouault was a prominent figure in the *Guerre du Bien Public* and was at one time governor of Paris and the marches against Burgundian land. The Rouault, possibly of English origin, had acquired Gamaches in the thirteenth century, but Joachim had been *sénéchal* of Poitou before making his mark in the reconquest of Bordeaux and Normandy in 1449-53. He seems to have depended on Louis XI's favour both as dauphin and king[25] and his semi-disgrace in 1476 (he died in 1478) reduced the role of his descendants, although both his son Aloph I and grandsons held royal household posts.[26] Anne's brothers Aloph II[27] and Thibault were both military men, Thibault playing a major role as military commander in the 1540s and 1550s. Aloph II had married the younger daughter of Jean II de Soissons-Moreuil, prince de Poix (d.1509), Jacqueline de Soissons heiress of Thiembronne

---

rate, she wrote that all her close relatives were dead and that she thus treated Mme. de Riou like a sister or mother: letter to Lady Lisle, 3 Oct. [?1535], SP 3/15, fo. 105 (*LP* xiii(2). 531, wongly dated; *LL*, iii. no. 579a, dated 1535): 'touchant de madame de Riou j'entens par le porteir de chette que que elle ne et pas encorre en couche. Dieu luy veulie par sa benigne ottroie ung grasieux traveil & à l'anfant nom & bapthesme. Madame il a pleut à Dieu moy otter tout mes parrens. Je n'ey à present que laquele j'eime comme sy ettoie sa seur & vou suplie madame sy vous envoies par de là que j'en puis avoer nouvelles'. Same to same, 20 Aug. [1536] SP 3/15, fo. 41 (*LP* xi. 336): 'vous ettes chelle laquele j'ey au plus pres de mon cuer vous & madame de Riou de tout cheux que j'eime vivans sur la terre & sy me veul obliger tant que je vivrey de vou tenir en tele recommandasion dever nre bon Dieu comme de long thanps j'ey accoutumé de y avoer maditte madame du Pont de Remy laquelle je tiens pour ma bonne mere'. Same to same, 12 Jan. [1537] SP 3/18, fo. 117 (*LP* xii(1). 76; *LL*, iii. no. 600): she could not have accomplished what she had begun in honour of the holy sacrament without the Lisle 'car je n'ey pres de moy nulz parrens'. Same to same, 19 May [1537] SP 3/17, fo. 131 (*LP* xii(1). 1248; *LL*, iii. no. 621): 'de tout mes amis, car y demeurent tous en Franse mes en che peys de Flandres toute ma parentee et trespassee'.

[25] Anselme, vii. 95; Darsy, 'Gamaches et ses seigneurs', 410.

[26] Aloph II Rouault, écuyer paid his relief for Gamaches 30 Apr. 1509. This gives us the date for Aloph I's death: Rosny, iv. 76. In June 1531, the king remitted the dues of the *quint et requint* on a transaction which involved the repurchase for 4000 lt. of an annual rent on Gamaches which had been conceded by the 'late' Aloph Rouault to Anne Rouault: *CAF*, ii. 4378. It was therefore Aloph II who was receiving a pension of 1000 lt. in 1520 (see BNF, pièces originales 2555 no. 34). He remained on the lists for 1523 and 1525 then disappears.

[27] Died 1562 according to Darsy but there is some doubt about this.

etc. (her elder half-sister Jossine had married a favourite of Francis I, Jean VII sr de Créqui and Canaples, d.1547). In the course of the 1530s a number of Anne's brothers (otherwise unknown) died and in January 1537, Anne's eldest brother M. de Gamaches also died.[28]

The family into which Anne Rouault married was that of a cadet branch of the house of Montmorency, the srs de Bours. This branch had prospered in Flanders in the fifteenth century in the service of the dukes of Burgundy and in the person of Jean sr de Courrières continued to serve their Habsburg successors. In the early sixteenth century Courrières' father Hugues de Montmorency, sr de Bours in Artois settled at Abbeville (d.1512) and his elder son Nicolas established himself as a landowner in Ponthieu by his marriage to Anne Rouault in 1512 and took up residence at Guéchard (near Crécy, Somme). Her eldest son was Gabriel de Montmorency and the younger Christophe; in 1534 or 1535 her daughter Jacqueline was married to Quentin Gourlay sr d'Azincourt in Artois (bailliage of Hesdin). The Montmorency-Bours were classic examples of a lineage which straddled the artificial divide between France and the Low Countries in the sixteenth century, their castle at Bours[29] in Artois (like that of Azincourt in the bailliage of Hesdin) was confiscated during wartime and was to be burned by French troops in 1543.[30] They were committed to royal service in France:

---

[28] Anne Rouault to Lady Lisle, 29 Jan. [1537] SP 3/16 fo. 11 (*LP* xii(1). 284; *LL*, iii. no. 610): 'depuis x ou xij jours j'esté fort ennuiés de la mort de feu monsr de Gamaches mon frere. Il n'a esté que deux jours malade'. Aloph II Rouault is sometimes noted as living until 1562 (eg. Darsy, 'Gamaches et ses Seigneurs', 425) but this plainly cannot have been the case. Then in 1538 another brother died: Anne to Lady Lisle, 13 Oct. [1538] SP 3/18, fo. 33 (*LL*, v. no. 1250). She also mentions her brother 'de Beaumont', otherwise unknown: Anne to Lady Lisle, 27 Jan. [1538] SP 3/16, fo. 159 (*LL*, iii. no. 623). See also note 23.

[29] 'La terre et chastel de Bours' was in 1472-3 a fief of the county of Saint-Pol and held by Nicolas de Mailly sr de Ravensberghe until his death, s.p., in 1476. It then passed to his brother Jean III de Mailly but the latter was a supporter of Louis XI against Burgundy: A. Ledru, *La maison de Mailly* (2 vols., Paris, 1893) i. 156-9; ii. 226, 237. However, a title to Bours in Artois was inherited by Philippe de Montmorency-Croisilles (d. 1474) by marriage to the daughter of Guillaume sr de Bours (killed at Azincourt): Rosny, i. 244.

[30] See the register for war damage for the Emperor's lands in Artois, AN, J 1017, fo. 310v. In the bailliage de Pernes, Bours was 'scitué à demie lieue prez de la ville de Pernes distant du bailliage de Hesdin de lieue et demye'. It suffered damage especially in 1543 'lors que l'armee du Roy de France bruslit ladicte ville de Pernes une compaignie de ladicte armee passa à travers dudict villaige le pillant de besteaulx et utensilz de maisnage y estans, en boutant le feu au chasteau en la bassecourt et quatre des maisons dud. villaige'. Bours was held in confiscation during that period and we know that, in the war of 1536-7, when the king's camp was at Pernes on 30 Apr. 1537 the king made a gift to him of confiscated revenues of Regnauville, Quesnoy etc. in compensation: *CAF*, iii. 310, 8947.

Gabriel de Montmorency was a military figure in the region[31] and also frequently in attendance at court in the late 1530s.[32] However, their most important kinsman was one of Charles V's must trusted advisers. Similarly, although M. d'Azincourt held most of his property in Artois[33] his family stemmed from Vimeu and he was governor of Abbeville from 1537 to 1542.[34]

Anne Rouault was closest to her brother Thibault. The latter had inherited the seigneurie of Riou from a cadet line and also properties mainly situated in Artois,[35] but was relatively poor as a younger son, even though he had briefly served at court as an *enfant d'honneur* in 1518-19.[36] There is no doubt that his fortune was made by his acquisition of the hand of Jeanne de Saveuse, only daughter of the Ferry sr de Saveuse (cousin to a leading royal administrator in Picardy, Imbert de Saveuse) and widow of the outstanding military commander of the 1520s in Picardy, Antoine de Créqui sr de Pont-Remy (killed at Hesdin in early 1525). Jeanne had borne a daughter to Pont-Rémy, Anne de Créqui, whose marriage became the object of considerable pressure in 1527-8 involving the *grand maître* Anne

---

[31] For instance, Anne Rouaud to Lady Lisle, 14 Oct. [1539] SP 3/15, fo. 71 (*LP* xiv(2). 332; *LL*, iii. no. 1567): 'Montmorency se attendoit bien de y aller quand on feist les monstres à Boullongne. Il vint icy une bonne compagnye de gentilz hommes lesquelz le empescherent'. Same to same, 12 June [1539] SP 3/18, fo. 168 (*LP* xiv(1). 1106; *LL*, v. no. 1450: 'ne pouvons encores faire nostre voiage de Boulongne. Monsr de Ryou mon bon frere s'en va à l'entree de monsr de Therouenne et Montmorency avecq luy et sy je attendz monsr de La Rochepot qui doibt venir'. On the arrival of François de Créqui, Anne's kinsman, as bishop of Thérouanne, see Lisle to Cromwell, 22 May 1539: *LP* xiv(1). 1032.

[32] E.g. Anne Rouault to Lady Lisle 13 Oct. [1538] SP 3/18, fo. 33 (*LP* xiii(2). 603; *LL*, iii. no. 1250): 'Il y a six sepmaines que Montmorency est allé à la court'.; 18 Feb. [1540]: SP 3/16., fo. 20 (*LP* xii(1). 460, misdated 1537; *LL*, iii. no. 1352, misdated 1539): 'il ne bouge plus de la court ou l'atend bien tost le Roy Abbeville'. He had long since been at court: *LP* xv. 29.

[33] See register of war damage in Artois, 1545, AN J 1017, fo. 267. Azincourt and the neighbouring hamlet of Maisoncelles were half in the bailliage of Hesdin and half in that of Pernes. They were ruined in 1543 and 1544-5 and paid no rent to the lords who held them during wartime confiscation.

[34] He became captain on the resignation of Huppy in Oct. 1537 although Huppy remained as his lieutenant at the castle: Bibliothèque Municipale, Abbeville MS 347, fos. 32, 39, delib.14, 15 Oct. 1537. He was still captain in 1542: *LP* xvii. 199. The Gourlays were seigneurs of Pandé-lès-Saint-Valéry and acquired Azincourt by marriage of François de Gourlay to its heiress Françoise d'Azincourt c. 1510-20: Rosny, ii. 677; iv. 350.

[35] BNF, pièces originales 2555, no. 261: the srs de Riou were descendus from marshal Joachim's brother Jacques, bailli de Caux. That Riou's seigneuries were partly in Artois is confirmed by the letters of Henri II of 31 Mar. 1553, taking his villages of Messières, Penyn, Savyer, Ouvyn, Marteloy and others into his protection during the war: Archives Départementales, Pas-de-Calais 9B 1, fo. 226v-227.

[36] BNF fr.21450, fo. 27. His name disappears from the list after that.

de Montmorency amongst others, but she also retained the castle of Pont-Remy in usufruct and her rapid remarriage in 1525 to Thibault Rouault may not have been to the liking of her Créqui relatives. Yet by 1527 Thibault was 'haut et puissant monseigneur' and 'chevalier'.[37] His patrons included Montmorency, since he was the ensign of his gendarmerie company by the 1530s and in 1538 defraying money for the king's secret services.[38] He was also a frequent messenger to and from court and in 1534 was trusted with the half year's pay of the garrison in Picardy.[39]

In 1527 Montmorency was pressing for Anne de Créqui's marriage to his nephew Jean de Mailly sr de Conti and it seems that Jeanne was quite agreeable to this. The marriage contract was in fact drawn up at Amiens in August 1527 in the presence of Anne, François and Louise de Montmorency, Thibault Rouault and Jeanne de Saveuse, Jean and Guillaume d'Humières (close to the Montmorency) as well as Jean and Georges de Créqui, the bride's paternal uncles.[40] We get from this a fair sample of the families' circle. Conti, though, died in the siege of Naples in 1528 and the alliance was abandoned. New suitors emerged and there was some competition until Guillaume du Bellay sr de Langey, a first rank diplomat and brother of cardinal du Bellay, whose case was pressed by Charles duc de Vendôme, won the day in 1531.[41] The Rouaults were already distantly related to the du Bellays[42] and connections of the Rouaults extended, then, as far as the king's closest advisers and a prince of the blood and this gave them something of a entrée into the world of the court. Their own territory extended from Gamaches on the borders of Normandy, through Vimeu to Pont-Remy (the residence of Mme. de Riou) through Ponthieu and Hesdin

---

[37] Ledru, ii. 275.
[38] *CAF*, viii. 212, 31223, repayment of 90 lt. he had advanced on the king's service for secret purposes in Dec. 1538 (he was then ensign of Montmorency's company).
[39] *CAF*, ii. 687, 7100; viii. 145, 30600.
[40] Amiens, 13 Aug. 1527: Ledru, ii.275-6.
[41] Louise de Savoie had pressed the case for M. de Busset. See Vendome to Montmorency: 27 Dec. [1528] BNF fr.3095, fo. 16. Marriage contract Pont-Remy, 12 Sept. 1531 in presence of Thibault Rouault, Créqui. Canaples, Imbert de Saveuse, Rambures, Sarcus, Jacques Blondel sénéchal of Ponthieu and Oudart du Biez sénéchal of Boulogne for the bride's family: V.-L. Bourrilly, *Guillaume du Bellay seigneur de Langey, 1491-1543* (Paris, 1905) pp. 110-11, based on Trincant's 'Histoire généalogique', Bibliothétheque Sainte-Geneviève, Paris, MS 537.
[42] Marshal Joachim's father Jean, sr de Boismenart, had married Jeanne du Bellay, dame de Langey, daughter of Hugues du Bellay (killed at Azincourt) 'compagnon fidèle' of Louis I d'Anjou. The seigneurie of Langey passed via Catherine du Bellay to Guillaume du Bellay's father Louis: Anselme, vii. 99-100; Bourrilly, *Guillaume du Bellay*, pp. 4-5.

with the castles at Bours and Guéchart where Anne Rouault lived. Abbeville was their main urban centre. In their own right, though, the Rouault and Montmorency-Bours were modest landowners. We know from the 1557 survey of fiefs that the seigneurie of Gamaches, then still held by Jacqueline de Soissons in usufruct, was worth 1500 lt. pa. although this was only part of the revenues, which included 600 lt. for other fiefs.[43]

This was in some ways a difficult and unusual time to board children abroad. In April 1537, the priest des Gardins had planned to get George Basset back to Calais via Flanders if the French had attacked Saint-Omer.[44] The middle years of the girls' stay in France were thus extremely dangerous. Jeanne de Saveuse found it impossible even to stay at Pont-Remy (relatively secure from the frontier) and suffered severe losses in the war.[45] Anne Rouault's castle of Bours was in Imperial territory and Guéchard near the borders. When war between France and the emperor broke out in June 1536 it was obviously impossible to remain there. In fact, Anne had previously brought the household, along with her husband, who seems already to have been ailing, to Abbeville and stayed there for most of the time until the truce of Bomy in 1537.[46] 'Je desiroie bien que nous puissions avoir une bonne paix adfin d'avoir le moien de vous aller voir', she wrote in January 1537, indicating how difficult travel was even from French to English territory.[47] French infantry operating in the vicinity of Abbeville kept her there in February 1537[48] and in March she was seriously

---

[43] In 1577 Nicolas Rouault de Gamaches received 500 lt. for the fief of Hellicourt alone and in 1584 the sr de Gamaches was estimated by an English observer, Richard Cook, as worth 6000 lt. a year, which would have put him in the middle ranks of the provincial nobility (see David Potter, *Two English Treatises on the State of France, 1580-84*, forthcoming).
[44] *LL*, iii. no. 548, 101.
[45] Antoinette de Saveuse to Lady Lisle, 5 Nov. [1536], SP 3/18, fo. 158 (*LP* xi. 991; *LL*, iii. no. 599): 'je ne estime point que ele se tient au Pont de Remy à quause de la gherrre. ... Elle a grand cherge de petis enfans & sy a ung mal que par fortune de gherre elle a perdu bien xv mile'.
[46] Anne Rouault had already moved in Mar. 1536, cf. letter to Lady Lisle, 13 Mar., SP 3/15, fo. 98 (*LP* x. 465; *LL*, iii. no. 586): 'il y a x ou xij jours quy m'a falleu amener monsr de Bours et toute nostre mainage en cheste ville pour crainte du mauvais tans comme vous dira plus au long ce porteur. Y me viendroit bien mal à pourpos sy falloit que j'eussions guerre je perderons tout nostre bien. J'avons bon besoin que nostre seigneur nous fayt en aide'.
[47] Anne Rouault to Lady Lisle, Abbeville, 17 Jan. [1537], SP 3/16, fo. 147 (*LP* xii(1). 117).
[48] Anne Rouault to Lady Lisle, Abbeville, 22 Feb. [1537] SP 3/17, fo. 95 (*LP* xii(1). 487; *LL*, iii. no. 612): Mlle de Gamaches did not bring Mary Basset back from Amiens 'ce qu'elle n'a peu faire pour l'amour qu'il y a beaucoupt de aventuriet par les champs comme vous dira plus à plain mon homme'.

alarmed by the situation.[49] With the royal army operating a few miles away in Artois the court briefly stopped at Abbeville, allowing Mary Basset to be presented to Queen Eleonore. Still there in April, Mme de Bours reported the death of her husband.[50] Even after the Franco-Imperial truce of July 1537, Mme de Bours still felt unable to travel far. In June 1538, a little before the ten-year Truce of Nice, she wrote that she was not going to travel without news of a peace.[51]

I

The main themes that emerge from the letters to the Lisles concern of course at first the welfare of Mary and Anne Basset and the exchange of routine graciousness; gradually an extensive exchange of benefits in kind is established, including hunting-birds, dogs, weapons, fabrics and household equipment. Naturally, the hosts kept the parents routinely informed of their charges' health and seem to have taken trouble to present them socially. In Spring 1536 Jeanne de Saveuse took Anne Basset on a long journey to Vendôme 'laquelle j'ay fait voir touplain de pays et de bonnes compaignies'[52] and her sister Mary was at court in 1537. It seems that very rapidly an attachment of some kind formed between Mary Basset and Mme. de Bours' son Gabriel de Montmorency (referred to by her always as 'Montmorency' but formally M. de Bours after his father's death in 1537). Lady Lisle observed late in 1535(?) that Gabriel

---

[49] Anne Rouault to Lady Lisle, Abbeville, 17 Mar. [1537] SP 3/15, fo. 63 (*LP* xii(1). 672; *LL*, no. 614): 'vous promeptz que je suis bien à grande peine de voir le danger en quoy s'en vont toutz mes bons amis. J'avons bien besoing de l'aide de nostre seigneur'.

[50] Anne Rouault to Lady Lisle, Abbeville, 16 Apr. [1537] SP 3/15, fo. 134 (*LP* xii(1). 955; *LL*, no. 618): 'estes advertie la grande fortune qu'il a pleu à Dieu de m'envoier. Ce m'est ung ennuist fort à passer. Il ne m'eust seu plus mal venir ... la rayne a este en cheste ville. Elle a veu mademoiselle vostre fille et l'a trouvé fort à son gré'.

[51] Anne Rouault to Lady Lisle, Bours, 8 Mar. [1538] SP 3/16, fo. 53 (*LP* xiii(1). 57; *LL*, iii. no. 626): 'J'é bien esperanche si je n'avons la guerre pardecha que je vous yré bien tost veoir aprez pasques'. Same to same, 1 Apr. [1538] SP 3/16, fo. 112 (*LP* xiii(1). 655; *LL*, iii. no. 627): 'je crains que je ne puisse avoir ce bien de vous aller veoir aprez ces pasques comme j'en avois bonne intention. Je ne voy point qu'il y ait apparance d'avoir encoires la paix'. Same to same, Gamaches, 13 June [1538], SP 3/15, fo. 121 (*LP* xiii(1). 181; *LL*, iii. no. 1179): 'je me attendoys que nous deussions avoir la paix que je vous iroye veoir comme je vous avoye promys et mademoiselle vostre fille'.

[52] Jeanne de Saveuse to Lady Lisle, Pont-Remy, 12 Mar. [1536], SP 3/15 fo. 77 (*LP* x. 455; *LL*, iii. no. 585).

was making much of Mary and M. de Riou remarked in 1537 on Mary's increasing charms.⁵³ This all came to a head dramatically in 1540 as part of the legal attack on her step-father Lord Lisle which sought to read sinister implications into the receipt of letters from France.⁵⁴ In October 1538 there had been some talk of Gabriel's marriage and Antoinette de Saveuse reported that 'ma etté dit qu'il se marie. Je ne sey sy les noches sont tenues' and in March 1539 that Gabriel had visited Calais.⁵⁵ Mary testified in 1540 that the attachment had formed around 1536 and that after her return to Calais in 1538 Gabriel continued to shower her with gifts.⁵⁶ Around mid Lent 1540 he actually came to Calais with letters of recommendation from his kinsman the Constable de Montmorency to ask for her hand and this was followed by a message brought for M. de Riou and his sister Mme. de Bours by M. de Millencourt.⁵⁷ Mary admitted to a secret betrothal to Bours on Palm Sunday but said she had thrown all the letters in the jakes (though the dossier did contain one 'love letter found in the jakes'). Lady Lisle claimed to have known nothing about the betrothal although she was aware of the messages from the Montmorency family and spoke to Gabriel through an interpreter. The Basset daughters were detained and marriage was thwarted. Gabriel's marriage to Michelle de Bayencourt-Bouchavannes took place some time after this.

One of the most engrossing aspects of the letters concerns the gossip retailed by sister Antoinette in letters written from Dunkirk about her relatives in France and most notably about her cousin Jeanne de Saveuse's marriage to Thibault Rouault.⁵⁸ Antoinette obviously found it difficult to stay in touch with her relatives. In October 1538, not having seen her cousin for over a year, she reported: 'je avoe ichy de Abbevyle

---

⁵³ Lady Lisle to Anne Rouault Nov. [1535] *LP* ix. 768(2); Riou to Lisle, Pont-Remy 16 Aug. [1537] *LP* xii(2). 528.

⁵⁴ St Clare Byrne's argument is that part of the implicit attack on Lisle, put forward by Cromwell to distract Henry VIII from accusations by Norfolk, involved the suggestion that the deputy was in contact with the French court, with a view to selling out Calais, as well as with Pole: *LL*, vi. pp. 236 *et seq*. The examination of all contacts with French individuals therefore becomes comprehensible.

⁵⁵ Antoinette to Lady Lisle, 17 Oct. [1538] SP 3/16, fo. 1 (*LP* xiv(2). 365, misdated; *LL*, iii. no. 1570, misdated). Same to same, 24 Mar. [1539] (*LP* xii(1). 719, misdated; *LL*, iii. no. 602, misdated.): Lady Lisle's secretary had informed her that 'Monsieur de Bours ettoet venu à Calles par devers vous'.

⁵⁶ *LP* xv. 750; *LL*, vi. pp. 142-47.

⁵⁷ Probably Jean d'Aigneville sr de Millencourt in Ponthieu, m. to Antoinette Le Ver: Rosny, i. 12; ii. 991.

⁵⁸ See in detail *LL*, iii. 176-80.

ung marchant à quy je priey de les faire tenir à nostre ditte dame, che que il me promit. Depuis je n'ey veu l'omme touseign mes madame de Riou m'en envoiet ungne femme laquelle me a raporté ungne lettre'.[59] Another problem was war. The Franco-Imperial war that broke out in June 1536 and was not concluded in the north until the truce of Bomy (in July 1537) was a natural impediment to travel and information. Antoinette already hinted at problems for her cousin in November 1536 but had heard little more early in the following year when she asked for her help in putting on entertainments for Twelfth Night in her convent.[60] In September 1537 Antoinette replied to enquiries about the well-being of Mme de Riou that she had gone to visit her cousin once the truce had been concluded. It seems that Lady Lisle had got the idea that Jeanne de Saveuse had financial troubles but sister Antoinette replied that she had meant rather 'aucugne necessité espirituelle'. The story she tells is a vivid one. Jeanne had inherited 15,000 lt. *per annum* revenue and had been persuaded by 'pervers consul' to marry Thibault by those (including Anne Rouault) who 'ne ont serchiet en elle que d'en avoer la jouwissance de son bien'. Anne had persuaded her to the marriage even though she could have had two other men worth 20,000 and 30,000 respectively. The marriage had brought her only grief (though she had borne twelve children) since Thibault was a spendthrift who would not stop at breaking open her family coffers and wagering the contents at dice.[61] Lady Lisle would have thus received from

---

[59] Antoinette to Lady Lisle, 'la veile de St Luc' [17 Oct. 1538]: *LP* xiv(2). 365, misdated; *LL,* v. no. 1570, misdated).

[60] Antoinette de Saveuse to Lady Lisle, 5 Nov. [1536], SP 3/18, fo. 158, letter already cited above, note 45 concerning her financial problems in the war and burden of children: 'La bonne dame a bien à soufrir & et environnee de biaucoup de manieres de tribulasion esqueles Dieu luy permet à venir en chette valee de misere dont je suplie Dieu luy asister en tout son aferre. ... la plus grande ennuy quy exede biaucoup plus que chette sy je ne les voudroie pas recrire mes il me depplet fort ma bonne dame que dever Dieu je ne feis optenir la grase pour elle tele comme mon povre cuer le desire pour sa consolasion'. Same to same, 20 Jan. [1537], SP 3/15, fo. 46 (*LP* xii(1). 180; *LL,* iii. no. 601): 'et vous prie madame sy vous seves aucoingne nouvelles de madame de Riou quy vous plesse de moy en recrire aucungne petite porsion. Je creins fort que que elle ne soet partie du Pont de Remy car j'ey à present ung petit aferre de son eide à cause que j'avoie bonne envie de ferre ugne recreasion à toutte nou religieuses de nre monastere à cause que j'ey au jour des rois etté leur reiingne'.

[61] Antoinette to Lady Lisle, Dunkirk, 10 Sept. [1537] SP 3/18, fos. 65r-v (*LP* xii(2). 675; *LL,* iii. no. 605): 'Je vous decleire secretement que madame de Riou porte autant de doleur au cueur que dame du reyaume de Franse. La bonne dame, laquelle et du grand sang et de sa grosse messon, elle ettant riche de xv M de rente, par l'enhort de pluseurs lesquelz monstrent fondement apres avoer leur pervers conseil mis en execusion comment il ne ont serchiet en elle que d'en avoer la jouwisanse de son bien. Car monsieur de Riou ettoit ung bien povre gentil homme de bonne

this letter a much grimmer picture of Anne Rouault's machinations than she would have been aware of when she sent her daughter to stay with her, although how genuine the picture was it is difficult to say. Certainly, Mme. de Bours' role in pressing her son's marriage with Mary Basset – practically every letter in 1538-9 contained recommendations from him – confirms that she was a determined matchmaker.

As for Jeanne de Saveuse, she had been married to Thibault for twelve years by this time and so would have been pregnant every year. The letters refer to several pregnancies in the period.[62] At least seven children survived to adulthood although none of the sons had children. Two daughters entered religion as carthusians at Gosnay near Béthune. Sister Antoinette shortly after this mentions that she has asked Lady Lisle to arrange for Riou to be corrected by 'la creignte humaigne'.[63] Honor responded by promising to bring the case to the personal attention of Francis I although Sister Antoinette begged her

---

grose messon et madame de Bours la seur dudit sieur de Riou laquele, des le vivent de fu monsr de Pontderemy hyentat fort la messon car madame luy avoet levé ung enffant à maditte dame de Bours. Apres le trespas de le desu nommé monr du Pont de Remy fort cauteleusement, Madame de Bours labouret de persuader la bonne vefve de voloer prendre à mariage son frere de Riou, elle ettant jeune et veuliant et de son plessir le print au deplessir de tout ses propre parens, car elle poet avoer allianse à deux grand mettres dont l'ugne avoet à deppendre xxM de rente et l'autre xxx mille. Madame je ne vous serroie exprimer l'ennuy que je y portey l'eppase de troies semaignes que je me suy tenu empres d'elle car elle me a dit tant de feys de ses doleurs que je ne les euse peut auwer sans en repprendre grand habondanse de larmes aveuc elle. Et sy me donne grand mervelie comment elle a eu de che second mariage jusque au nombre de douze enfans ettant en la douleur tele que elle me a dit. Car elle m'en verifyet que ung jour quy pasa monsieur enfondra à ung grand coffre lequel avoet apartenu à monsieur de Saveuse le pere de madame, lequel ettoet tout plein de belle vaiselle, la fit sur ugne table jouoet à deix pour quattorze mille valisant en ung apres disner sans tout autres folies et grand dons que il foet à ses parrens prochains come s'il volloet totalement destruire . . '. (Dated by a reference to recent destruction of Saint-Pol and publication of the Franco-Burgundian truce).

[62] Anne Rouault to Lady Lisle, 2 Sept. [1535] SP 3/15, fo. 14 (*LP* ix. 257; *LL*, iii. no. 579): 'je suis ceans avec madame de Ryou quy est fort malade. Elle n'est pour encoires acouchee et la craint on pour l'amour de cela'.; Sister Antoinette, 3 Oct. [?1538] *LP* xiii(2). 531; same to same, 12 Apr. [?1539] *LP* xiv(1). 751.

[63] Antoinette to Lady Lisle, no date [Autumn 1537] SP 3/17, fo. 72 (*LP* xiv(1). 25, wrongly dated; *LL*, iii. no. 607): 'La bonne dame a pluseur foes recommandé son petit cas en mes petite oorrojons dont passé long thamps je y continue & prins eide de pluseurs bonne religieuses mes j'ey matiere de moy humilier creignant que je ne suy pas digne d'ettre exausiet, mes congnoesant que nre signeur dit "eidies vous et je vous eidrey", pour chette cauze, madame, par ychy devant je me suys retournoié par devers vous pour en vreie & loialle confidense de vre bon conseil & cuide reisgarder plus outre sy par voie de la creignte humaigne son maris ne sse voedroet corrigier. Au moien de che je vous suplie tres humblement madame de savoier comment vous en aves besoegnet & quant à vre bonne prosperité & que vous ettes venu au desi. de vre afferre ..'.

to be discreet.[64] It seems that Lady Lisle had promised to act through the English ambassador. Whether she did so is not clear but by May of 1538 Sister Antoinette was being told by Jeanne that her husband was behaving very differently, trying to be a good manager of his affairs and showing his love for his children, 'en somme . . . et autant changiet comme du nuit au jour'. Antoinette feared this news may have been sent only to still her anxiety and hoped that God had worked his will since her visit the year before.[65] Lady Lisle was still anxious for news in October, when she was told by Antoinette that she had finally heard that Thibault had been away at court for three months.[66] He had promised on his return to visit Guillaume du Bellay (recently returned from Turin) in order to collect his

---

[64] Antoinette to Lady Lisle, 27 Oct. [1537] SP 3/16, fo. 155 (*LP* xiv(2). 403 wrongly dated; *LL*, iii. no. 606): thanks for her letter of 26th 'par le contenu dechelles j'entens que de vre grase aves intension de ferre dever le Roy de Franse pour remedier au cas de madame de Riou. Je prie Dieu vou voloer ottroyer la vertu de sy tres bien moienner à chette aferre que la peix & union laquelle se doet meigntenir en vrey marriage en soet augmentee à l'ongneur de Dieu & salvasion de leurs ames. Mes surtout tres humblement, Madame, je vou suplie autant que vou desires de ferre plesir à maditte dame de Riou que sy tres discretement chette aferre soet decleriet que james ne soet pourpos dont il prochede, car je creins sy monsieur de Riou s'enperchevoet que la reprehension du Roy ne luy pourfitroet pas tant comme elle fera, en la sorte comme en vous, Madame, j'ey la confidense que biaucoup mieux en ferres ferre que je le vou serroie exprimer'.
[65] Antoinette to Lady Lisle, 6 May [1538] SP 3/15, fo. 141 (*LP* xiv(1). 931, misdated; *LL*, iii. no. 608): 'Madame je vou suplie de savoer sy vous aves feet diligense de avertir l'enbasadeur d'Engleterre comme par ychy devant de vre grase le me aviois promis de souvenir par bon moien ung petit à la desolasion de madame de Riou. La cauze que j'ey desirré avoer la congnoessance et Madame que sy vous avies feet tiele diligense, comme je avoye en vous la bonne confidense, je croie matiere de vous en remerchier mes souvereignement à la bonté divigne, congnoesant que par sa benigne grase il touche le cuer au viif, don pour devoier je ne vou puy cheler les bonne nouvelles que lundy dernier je rechus de par ugne femme laquelle se tient au chatiau du Pont de Remy & ve[n]u veor sa filie laquele et mariee à troes lieue pres de Dunkerke & ne me aporta nule lectres mes elle me dit que madame luy avoet requis de soy enquerre quant viendroet au logis de sa filie combyen il y avoet de là à Dunkerke & sy elle trouvoet que il y avoet peu longs laditte femme luy froet de moy aller voer grand plesir pour luy en raporter cherteine nouvelles dont la bonne femme sa de....é vi grose lieuwes & sy me a dit les joieuse nouvelles comment monsieur de Riou se fachonne à chet eure tout autrement que il ne soloet ferre & que il feet grand paschens à Madame & regharde dorenavant de ferre de bon meignagier & montrer en tout pleign d'amour à ses petis enfans & en somme la ditte femme me a dit que le dit sieur et autant changiet comme du nuit au jour. Madame je ne vou serroie exprimer combien j'en suy resiouwy moienant ches nouvelle soient vreies mes je creins que maditte dame de Riou ne luy eye fert einsy parler pour moy donner à entendre à chell.. que oubliache tant mieux le regres & fascheries dont elle se pleindoet à moy alors cant elle me requit de moy trouver par dever elle che que il n'y a pas encore ung an ..'.
[66] Riou had been an *enfant d'honneur* at court, 1518-19 (BNF fr.21450, fo. 27r) but was not to become a gentleman of the chamber until 1551.

step-daughter Anne de Créqui 'laquele a etté par l'espase de scet angs separé de sa mere'. Antoinette remained sceptical[67] but we know that Guillaume du Bellay and his wife were at Pont-Remy in the following spring.[68]

The letters reveal incidentally a great deal about the other preoccupations of the women, particularly private anguish of one kind or another, expressed essentially in concise terms familiar from the diction of the sieur de Gouberville. Anne Rouault reports the death of her brother Gamaches in 1537: 'il n'a esté que deux jours malade. Je ne suis jamais sans avoir de nouveaux ennuis. Je ne voy aultres moien quy fault que je me contente de ce qui plaist à Dieu'.[69] Then came the death of her husband shortly afterwards and in 1538 that of a brother (possibly de Beaumont) 'qui a esté malade et qu'il pleut à Dieu prendre de sa part depuis quinze jours; incontinant que j'é esté de retour ceans je me suys trouvé malade et me trouve encores fort'.[70] Early 1539 saw a serious illness of her little three year old Azincourt grandson. At first reluctant to give him medicine, she received some from Lady Lisle but found the boy too 'fin'('sly' or 'fussy') to take it.[71] In 1540 she reports herself as 'bien souvent malade mays pour

---

[67] Antoinette to Lady Lisle, 17 Oct. [1538] SP 3/16, fo. 1 (*LP* xiv(2). 365, misdated; *LL*, iii. no. 1570 wrongly dated 1539). Antoinette sent the letter of 22 Nov. she received from Jeanne telling of the joy she felt at the coming of her daughter, see SP 3/16, fo. 2 (*LP* xiv(2). 571; *LL*, v. no. 1617a, wrongly dated 1539). The date is confirmed by the return of M. and Mme. de Langey from Turin in Nov. 1538 (they stayed in France for health reasons until Sept. 1539). See Bourrilly, *Guillaume du Bellay*, pp. 278-84. The journey of Mme de Riou and Anne Basset, possibly in Spring 1536, to the relic of the *sainte larme* at Vendôme is suggested by St. Clare Byrne to have been in the course of a visit to Mme de Langey, but this presumably could not have been the case if mother and daughter had not seen each other for seven years in 1538: *LL*, iii. 158-9.

[68] Antoinette to Lady Lisle, Dunkirk, 24 May [1539] SP 3/15, fo. 51 (*LP* xii(1). 719, misdated; *LL*, iii. no. 602 misdated): 'j'ey bonne envie de savoer sy Monsr de Langier & madame sa femme sont party du Pont de Remy car la plus grand part des lectres que j'envois adresient à sa personne et serroie mary de pas en avoer repponse. Jé foet que en Madame de Riou j'ey bonne confidense que elle en fera son devoer quant vre secreterre serra du retour..'. Bourrilly does not mention Langey's visit to Picardy. Langey wrote to Lisle in Sept. 1539 from Compiègne, just before his return to Piedmont, offering to supply him with wine in return for lead for his building operations, 28 Sept. 1539, SP 3/15, fo. 58v (*LP* xiv(2). 233; *LL*, v. no. 1552).

[69] Anne Rouault to Lady Lisle, Abbeville 29 Jan. SP 3/16, fo. 11 (*LP* xii(1). 284); same to same, 8 Feb. [1537], SP 3/15, fo. 53 (*LL*, iii. no. 611), on the wearing of mourning.

[70] Anne Rouault to Lady Lisle, 13 Oct. [1538], SP 3/18, fo. 33 (*LP* xiii(2). 603; *LL*, no. 1250).

[71] Anne Rouault to Lady Lisle, 23 Feb. [1539] SP 3/17, fo. 15 (*LP* xiv(1). 351; *LL*, v. no. 1353): 'j'esté long tans malade. Incontinent que j'é esté guerie le fievre a prins à mon petit filz d'Azincourt qu'il les a tous les jours. Je ne scay que faire. Il n'a que trois ans. Il n'est point pour luy bailler medechemens. Il me survient tousjours quelque ennuistz et empeschemens que je ne

ceste heure je ne trouve que bien et seroys encore myeulx que si je pouvoys estre aupres de vous'.[72] Early 1540 saw Mlle. d'Azincourt give birth to a very premature yet living child[73] and Mme de Riou ill for six or seven weeks.[74]

II

To put all this in perspective, we need to know something of the aftermath. The extent to which Thibault Rouault reformed his character after the 1530s remains obscure. Introduced to the military life in the Italian wars and under Montmorency he went on to acquire a considerable military reputation in the 1540s as lieutenant of Heilly, Mme. d'Etampes's brother and then in 1546 of du Biez's company,[75] colonel of 10 Picard infantry companies[76] and governor of Oultreau under marshal du Biez. In the mid 1540s and again in 1549-50 as governor of Oultreau, his main dealings with the English was as an enemy in war, involved in the campaigns to wrest Boulogne back from them.[77] There also is some possibility that he joined the expedition of Termes to Scotland in the summer of 1549.[78] By the late 1540s he was regularly soliciting favours from the duc de Guise.[79] Governor of Corbie and *gentilhomme de la chambre*

---

puis laisser la maison'. Same to same 15 Mar., SP 3/15, fo. 116 (*LP* xiv(1). 527): 'Mon petit filz d'Agincourt avoit perdu sa fiebvre quant le laquet de Memorensi retournit. Il l'a pris depuis trois ou quatre iours et lui vauldroie bien faire user de che que m'aves envoié. Il est si fin qu'il ne veult boire que de che qu'il a en fantasie'. Lady lisle to her, *LP* xiv(1). 352; *LL*, v. no. 1354.

[72] Jeanne to Lady Lisle, Pont-Remy, 18 Feb. [1540] SP 3/16, fo. 20 (*LP* xii(1). 460, wrongly dated 1537).

[73] Anne Rouault to Mary Basset, 5 Jan. [1540], SP 3/17, fo. 122 (*LP* xv. 29; *LL*, vi. no. 1635): 'ma fille d'Agincourt est allee à Jumelle là où elle est acouchee, et sy n'estoit point à my terme. Toutesfois l'enfant est en vie'.

[74] Anne Rouault to Lady Lisle, 12 Feb. [1540], SP 3/16, fo. 42 (*LP* xv. 914; *LL*, vi. no. 1647).

[75] Du Bellay, iv. 310; BNF nafr.8621, no. 8, muster at Clermont-en-Beauvaisis, 11 Apr. 1546

[76] BNF fr.25792, no. 520-21, musters of Mar. 1545 in bailliage of Hesdin and fr.25793 Feb. 1546 at Oultreau under Thaix as colonel-general.

[77] Thibault Rouault, sr de Riou, to Aumale, Oultreau, 30 Jan. 1549, BNF fr.20553, fo. 156 (concerning an enterprise planned against the English at Boulogne); same to same, Oultreau, 27 June 1549, BNF fr. 20534, fo. 51; Cobham to Riou, 30 June 1549, BL, Harleian 288, fo. 110.

[78] See Rouault to Aumale, Dunbar, 26 Sept. 1549: A. Teulet, *Relations politiques de la France et de l'Espagne avec l'Ecosse au XVI*e *siècle* (5 vols., Paris, 1862), i. 195-6

[79] T. Rouault to Aumale, Hesdin, 5 June 1549, BNF fr.20549, fo. 84; same to same, Saint Leu, 5 May 1550, BNF fr.20543, fo. 123; same to same, 25 Feb. 1553, BL, Add. MS. 38032, fo. 153-4, asking for a command of light horse.

du roi in 1551,[80] he was appointed governor of the castle of Hesdin in December 1552 and remained until its fall on 19 July 1553, captured there with his son Claude sr de Saveuse. By that time he had acquired a reputation for cruelty in the region. In 1543 he has carried out extortion raids in Artois and a bourgeois of Arras noted in 1553 he had 'avoit durant toute ceste guerre fort travaillé par diverses exactions et compositions ce pays d'Arthois'. His nephew Gamaches had also been taken prisoner, in his case at the capture of Therouanne on 20 June.[81] Riou was released from prison in January 1554 and was dead by 1557 when Jeanne de Saveuse was noted as a widow in the roll of the feudal levy of Vimeu. Two of her children, Anne and Marie, became nuns in the Carmelite house at Gosnay near Hesdigneul, south-west of Béthune with which sister Antoinette had had some connection.[82] Of her sons Claude and Joachim, both srs de Saveuse, we know that neither married and that they died young some time after the fighting of 1553. The succession thus passed to the eldest daughter Barbe, wife of Adrien Tiercelin sr de Brosses, of an important family that, originating in Touraine, had acquired interests in both Normandy and Picardy. Brosses was later lieutenant-general of Champagne and had close connection with the Guises. Curiously, although the castle of Pont-Remy itself, presumably under the influence of Jeanne de Saveuse, was to become a place of refuge for the Huguenots of Ponthieu in the difficult days of the early civil wars, the suburbs of the village were the only authorised place for public worship under the terms of the peace of 1563.[83]

Anne Rouault disappears from view except for a lawsuit which she launched against the Baron d'Orbec, second husband of Jacqueline de Soissons,

---

[80] BNF Picardie 31, fo. 277: sums paid out (Oct. 1551-Jan. 1552) on the orders of 'Messire Thibault de Rouault chevalier, seigneur de Riou, gentilhmme ordinaire de la chambre du Roy, capitaine et gouverneur de la ville de Corbye'; BNF fr.3132, roll of the royal household for 1551, the year in which he was appointed.

[81] AN J 1017, fo. 195; X. de Gorguette d'Argoeuves (ed.), 'Un livre de Raison en Artois (XVIe Siècle)' (Jean Thieulaine), *Mémoires de la société académique de la Morinie* 21 (1888), 151. He had been with the duc de Vendôme at the camp of Dampierre in June 1553: Vendôme to Guise, 29 May 1553, BNF Clair.346, fo. 1127.

[82] Antoinette to Lady Lisle, 31 July [1539] *LP* xiv(1). 1341; same to same 10 Oct. [1539], SP 3/17 fo. 44 (*LP* xiv(2). 313; *LL*, v. no. 1566).

[83] 'Rolle des Villes, aux Faulxbourgs desquelles l'Exercice de la Nouvelle Religion a esté Ordonné' in D. Secousse (ed.), *Mémoires de Condé ou recueil pour servir a l'histoire de France* (6 vols., The Hague, 1743), iv. 536.

widow of M. de Gamaches, in 1544.[84] Orbec is in the pays d'Auge and the barons claimed descent from the dukes of Normandy in the direct line but Louis was involved in interminable litigation about his titles by the 1540s. His marriage to a rich widow was an obvious recourse.[85] Of Anne Rouault's children, Gabriel sr de Bours is mentioned in this suit and married Michelle de Bayencourt daughter of Bouchavannes, the governor of Doullens. When he died in 1547 his widow remarried François d'Aumale sr du Quesnoy. Another son, Christophe, may have died at Rome without heirs. Jacqueline, 'Madame d'Azincourt' went on to have several children by her husband, Quentin Gourlay.[86]

As the link with Bouchavannes and the role of Pont-Remy hints, many of these individuals were gravitating towards Protestantism by the 1550s and joined the Huguenot camp early in the civil wars. This is certainly the case with Louis baron d'Orbec and Bouchavannes (one of the chiefs of the Huguenot cause until his murder in 1572). Orbec joined several other local lords in sacking the cathedral of Lisieux in August 1562 and died in 1565, two years before Jacqueline de Soissons.[87] Anne Rouault's grandson Jean succeeded to the titles when he was a child and entered the service of the emperor under the patronage of his childless great uncle Courrières. When it became clear that he was sympathetic to the Reform, Courrières cut

---

[84] Du Chesne, *Histoire de la maison de Montmorency*, preuves, p. 329; also mentioned Anselme iii. 614. The cause of this is almost certainly the assignation that had been made to Anne by her father of a rente of 200 lt. on the seigneurie of Gamaches some time before 1531: *CAF*, ii. 4378.

[85] Vte. L. Rioult de Neuville, 'Les barons d'Orbec', *Mémoires de la société des antiquaires de Normandie* 3rd series, 10 (1880), 712-69 at 756-9. Jacqueline and Louis did hommage for Thiembronne, inherited by Jacqueline from her maternal uncle Louis Bournel, in June 1550 on the restoration of French rule in Boulogne and in Aug. 1553 declared the value *per annum*. for the feudal levy as 800 lt.: Rosny, iv. 107, 189. The seigneurie of Lambessart was seised in 1550 for non-payment of *chambellage*, although Jacqueline and Louis claimed in 1566 to have paid this to the then French governor, Rasse: Rosny, iv. 355.

[86] Gourlay may have been dead by 1545 when he was replaced as captain of Abbeville. His children included Louis sr d'Azincourt, vicomte de Domart (three years old in 1539, *LP* xiv(1). 351,527), and Anne (probably born 1540, *LP* xv. 29) sr de Pandé-lès-Saint-Valéry, *échanson du roi* (Rosny, iv. 1676). Louis declared three small fiefs worth 72 lt. in the bailliage of Amiens in 1557 and Anne's fief in Vimeu was worth 200 lt.: V. de Beauvillé, *Recueil de documents inédits pour servir à l'histoire de la Picardie* (4 vols., Paris, 1865-90).

[87] Rioult de Neuville, 'Les barons d'Orbec', 756-9. Jacqueline made her will on 18 July 1567. She had had no children by Louis d'Orbec, who was succeeded as Baron d'Orbec by his brother Jean sr du Plessis, a strong Calvinist who married Catherine de L'Hospital-Choisy in 1571 and died in 1579.

him off.[88] The names of his sons: Daniel, Josias, Gédéon, Benjamin are clear enough testimony to his religous loyalties.[89]

Nicolas de Rouault-Gamaches got into trouble after the Conspiracy of Amboise and in January 1561 wrote to Secretary Bourdin promising to come to court to plead his case over an infraction of the recent legislation on firearms. He assured Bourdin that 'moy et mes gens n'avons porté autre armes allant querir madame d'Orbec ma mere que l'espee et la dague'.[90] Nicolas was definitely a Protestant as well a *gentilhomme ordinaire de la chambre*. He was described in the 1580s as 'fort de la religion et la presche se tient encores en sa maison'. His son Gédeon, then 33 'homme bien aymé par tout' was among the following of Henry of Navarre.[91] The prevalence of Protestantism among these families may be a coincidence but there is a distinct possibility that the influence of the strong personality of Anne Rouault was a major factor in common.

* * *

The French correspondence of the Lisles emerges from an era in Anglo-French relations shaped by the great treaties of 1525 and 1527 which established an unusually lengthy peace between the two realms. Despite clouds on the horizon in the late 1530s, the authorities at Calais and in France were, to use their own phrase 'bons voisins' throughout the decade. The correspondence is vastly more extensive than the documents I have discussed here and throws important light on the use of the Picard dialect among the nobility in the sixteenth century, but what these letters from Jeanne, Anne and Antoinette reveal is a degree of familiarity and warmth which seems to ignore any national boundaries. With the notable exception of Antoinette de Saveuse, the language they employ is fairly formal and yet they manage to convey a genuine affection and concern.

The social profiles of the correspondents were curiously parallel; on both sides in some senses they were members of the provincial gentry of middle rank yet both had connections with the highest in the land and at court. This perhaps ultimately explains the capacity for reciprocity between them, in the form of an exchange between equals unhampered by problems

---

[88] Du Chesne, *Histoire de la maison de Montmorency*, p. 329; Belleval, *Lettres sur le Ponthieu*, pp. 24-9
[89] Anselme, iii. 614.
[90] Rouault to Bourdin 21 Jan. 1561 BNF impr F220, fo. 80.
[91] Potter, *Two Treatises*, forthcoming.

of language and distance. The first substantial body of evidence for Anglo-French relations in the early modern period outside the realm of diplomacy and war provides a rich resource both for the history of manners and of women, and of a fascinating and otherwise largely unknown segment of the northern French nobility.

Index

Abbeville, 68-70, 128, 134, 138-41, 143, 145, 147, 148, 150, 152-4, 159, 174, 179, 180, 205, 208-9, 211-2
Alençon, John II, Duke of, 10
Allington, William, 28
Ambassadors, 64, 72, 182-99
Amicable Grant (1525), 9, 13
Angoulême, Charles of, 179
Angoulême, Marguerite of, 178, 191-3
Angoulême, Mary of, 12
Anne, Duchess of Brittany, 12, 109, 111, 113, 119, 134, 137, 159
Armies, size of, 7-8, 120, 122, 126-8, 195-6
Arthur, Prince of Wales, 12

Baker, Matthew, 189
Basset, Anne, 200, 204, 212-4
Basset, George, 204-6, 211
Basset, James, 204-6
Basset, Mary, 200, 204, 212, 213-5
Battles, Agincourt (1415), 1, 8, 54; Barnet (1471), 84; Chastillon (1453), 2, 24; Bosworth (1485), 104-5; Nancy (1477), 3, 10; Novarre (1514), 146; Pavia (1525), 13, 175; The Spurs (1513), 5, 136, 145
Beatis, Antonio, 160, 162, 174
Beauchamp, Richard, Bishop of Salisbury, 76
Beaufort, John, Duke of Somerset, 35-42
Beaujeau, Anne of, 11, 86, 92

Bedford, John, Duke of, 49
Bellay, Guillaume du, 177, 210, 217
Bellay, Jean du, 177
Berquin, Louis de, 176
Biez, Oudart du, 169, 177, 203, 205, 218
Blount, Sir Walter, Lord Mountjoy, 75
Boleyn, Anne, Queen of England, 18, 21, 169-70, 172, 204, 205
Boleyn, George, Viscount Rochford, 169, 183, 190, 198
Boleyn, Mary, 204
Boleyn, Thomas, Earl of Wiltshire, 165, 172, 185, 186, 188-90
Bonner, Edmund, 184, 198-9
Bonnivet, Admiral, 188
Boorde, Andrew, 21
Boulogne, 5, 137-8, 152, 156, 169, 174, 177, 179, 219
Bourbon, Charles, Duke of, 174, 196
Bourchier, John, Lord Fitzwarin, 101-3
Brandon, Charles, Duke of Suffolk, 134-6, 149, 185, 187,
Browne, Sir Anthony, 19, 20, 170, 187, 191-3, 197
Bryan, Sir Francis, 177, 180, 184, 190, 198
Buckingham's Rebellion (1483), 86, 90, 91, 95
Byrne, Muriel St Clare, editor of *The Lisle Letters*, 202-4

Calais Act (1536), 57-61

Calais, 3, 5, 8, 10, 14, 15, 16, 20, 21, 24, 27, 45, 97, 107, 109, 119, 121, 123, 125, 126, 128, 163, 168, 173, 176, 177; English administration of, 46-62; and diplomacy, 63-84, 194-5
Cambrai, League of (1508), 12
Carew, Sir Nicholas, 160-81,
Catherine of Aragon, Queen of England, 14, 169-70, 177
Chabot, Admiral, 172
Chandée, Philibert de, Earl of Bath, 105
Channel Islands, constitutional status of, 52, 55, 58
Chapuys, Eustace, 166, 169, 171-3
Charles the Bold, Duke of Burgundy, 4, 6, 10, 72, 74, 79, 82, 83
Charles V, Holy Roman Emperor, 5, 7, 13-6, 137, 160-1, 165, 170, 172, 180, 186, 191, 209
Charles VI, King of France, 2, 14
Charles VII, King of France, 2, 10, 25, 30, 32, 34, 35, 42
Charles VIII, King of France, 4, 11; support for Henry Tudor, 85-105; and war with England, 106-31
Chauveau, Gilbert, Montjoie King of arms, 142, 150
Cheyne, Sir Thomas, 186, 188-90, 194, 197
Claude, Queen of France, 170
Clement VII, Pope, 14, 165
Clerk, John, Bishop of Bath and Wells, 183, 186, 192-4, 198
Colt, Thomas, 74, 76
Courtenay, Henry, Marquis of Exeter, 170
Créqui, Antoine de, Seigneur de Pont-Remy, 205, 210, 211, 217, 221
Créquy, Jean de, 177
Cromwell, Thomas, 8, 57-60, 170-1, 193-4

d'Albret, Henry, King of Navarre, 178
Daubeney, Sir Giles, Lord Daubeney, 123-4, 129
De Vere, John, Earl of Oxford, 96-7
Dorset, Marquis of, *see* Grey
Dowcra, Thomas, Prior of St. John of Jerusalem, 148
Dudley, Sir John, Duke of Northumberland, 15, 185
Dunkirk, 3, 206, 213, 214
Duras, Gaillard, Marshall of Calais, 56

Edward III, King of England, 4, 47-9, 51
Edward IV, King of England, 6, 91, 94, 97, 145; French policy of, 3-4, 10-1, 63-84
Edward VI, King of England, 167; French policy of, 15-7
Eleanore, Queen of France, 169, 220
Elizabeth I, Queen of England, 63
Elizabeth of York, Queen of England, 90, 91, 96, 102
English possessions in France, legal status of, 52,
Esquerdes, Philippe de Crèvecoeur, Lord 98, 103, 104-5, 123-4, 129
Everingham, Sir Thomas, 3
Evil May Day (1517), 18
Exeter, Marquis of, *see* Courtenay

Fayette, Antoine de la, 179
Ferdinand, King of Aragon, 6, 12, 99, 105, 108
Field of the Cloth of Gold (1520), 6, 13, 19, 54, 158, 166-8
Fitzalan, Henry, Lord Maltravers, 59
Fitzwilliam, Sir William, 20, 58-9, 168, 187-8, 190-92, 194-6

Fowler, Robert, 59
Fox, Richard, Bishop of Winchester, 123
Francis I, King of France, 5-6, 7, 12-5, 54, 160, 162, 164-5, 167-9, 175, 177, 178, 180, 182, 184, 186, 189, 191, 205, 216; as Duke of Vendôme, 134, 136 145
Francis II, Duke of Brittany, 4, 10, 11, 74, 82, 92-4
Frederick III, Holy Roman Emperor, 112
Fynderne, Sir Thomas, 53

Gal, Sir Raoul de, 40
Gardiner, Germayne, 184, 194
Gardiner, Stephen, Bishop of Winchester, 183-4, 198
Gardins, Jean des, 204, 211
Garter, Order of, 4, 16, 19, 102, 168
Gaugin, Robert, 86, 149,
Gloucester, Humphrey, Duke of, 49
Golafre, John, 28
Gondi, Antonio, 180
Gresham, John, 24
Grey de Wilton, Lord William, 7-8
Grey, Thomas, first Marquis of Dorset, 101-3
Grey, Thomas, second Marquis of Dorset, 148, 149, 185, 187
Gringore, Pierre, 141-2, 155, 158
Guînes, 7, 13, 47, 48, 50, 51, 56, 59, 60, 68, 69, 123, 194, 203
Guise, Jean de, Cardinal of Lorraine, 178

Hall, Edward, 18
Hammes, 3, 50
Harfleur, 1, 27
Hastings, Sir William, Lord Hastings, 50, 51
Hatclyff, William, 76

Haucourt, Jean de, Seigneur de Huppy, 180
Henry II, King of France, 15-6, 22
Henry V, King of England, 1-2, 4, 6, 13, 25, 27, 112, 158
Henry VI, King of England, 2, 24, 27, 51, 65, 93, 95-7, 153; French policy of, 2-3
Henry VII, King of England, 4, 5, 7, 25, 58, 189; French policy of, 9-12, 106-31; attitude towards aliens in Calais, 56; exile in Brittany and France, 85-105
Henry VIII, King of England, 17, 19-21, 23, 147, 150, 158, 164-6, 169-70, 171, 172, 177, 179, 205; French policy of, 4-8, 12-5, 54-5; attitude towards aliens in Calais, 55-7
Heralds, use of in diplomacy, 66-8, 71-3, 76, 78, 80-1, 161-3
Hoo, Thomas, 33
Howard, Henry, Earl of Surrey, 21
Howard, Lord William, 190
Howard, Thomas, third Duke of Norfolk, 185, 193, 198
Hundred Years War, The, 1-3, 8, 159, 202; English administration during final phase of, 24-45

Isabella, Queen of Castille, 94, 99, 105, 108

James V, King of Scotland, 179
Jerningham, Sir Richard 187, 190, 194, 195

Kent, Thomas, 74-6
Kyriell, Sir Thomas, 43

Landais, Pierre, 11, 86, 89, 101
Le Gras, Guilliame, 205

Leland, John, 21
Leo X, Pope, 13
Lisle, Lady Honor, 200-22
Lisle, Viscount, *see* Dudley, Sir John and Plantagenet, Sir Arthur
Longueville, Louis d'Orleans, Duke of, 146
Louis XI, King of France, 5, 11, 51, 63-84, 86, 90-2, 104, 127, 129, 144, 207
Louis XII, King of France, 13, 18, 180, 189; and marriage to Mary Tudor, 132-59
Lyon, 174

Machado, Roger, Richmond Herald, 161-3
Madeleine, Queen of Scotland, 178, 179
Mailly, Jean de, Seigneur de Conti, 210
Marguerite of Anjou, Queen of England, 83
Margaret of Austria, 175
Margaret of York, Duchess of Burgundy, 75-8, 81-2
Marguerite, daughter of Maximilian I, 113-4
Mary I, Queen of England, French policy of, 9-10, 15-6; as Princess Mary, 13, 17, 170, 192
Mary Tudor, Queen of France, 12, 132-59, 183
Maximilian I, Holy Roman Emperor, 7, 11, 98, 137, 147, 189; and cooperation with Henry VII, 106-31
Mazrin, Francis, 189
Montague, Lord, *see* Pole
Montmorency, Anne de, 169, 175, 178, 179, 214, 219
Montmorency, Gabriel de, Seigneur de Bours, 208-9, 212-4, 220

Montmorency, Nicolas de, Seigneur de Bours, 213
Montreuil, 6, 151,
Monypenny, William, 63, 78, 80
Morison, Richard, 9
Morton, John, 102
Mundford, Osbern, 30, 42

Nassau, Engelbert, Count of, 113, 114, 115, 123, 127
Neville, Richard, Earl of Warwick, 63-84
Norbury, Sir Henry, 35
Norfolk, Duke of, *see* Howard

Paget, William, 199
Palsgrave, John, 21, 205
Paris, 140-1, 152, 156, 158, 204, 207
Parliament, representatives of French possessions in, 60
Paston, John, 24
Pennec, Pierre le, 117
Perreu, Louis, Seigneur de Castillon, 199
Philip II, King of Spain, 9, 16
Philip of Cleves, 113, 123
Philip the Good, Duke of Burgundy, 10, 67, 71, 72, 78
Plantagenet, Cecily, second daughter of Edward IV, 102
Plantagenet, Sir Arthur, Viscount Lisle, 58, 185, 200-22
Pole, Henry, Lord Montague, 170
Pon, François de, 115
Poynings, Sir Edward, 146
Privy Chamber, use of in diplomacy, 187, 188
Prophesy, 110-11
Pynson, Richard, 18, 110

Quierot, Jean, 203

Richard II, King of England, 52
Richard III, King of England, 85-93, 95-8, 101-2, 105; French policy of, 11; as Duke of Gloucester, 8
Rouault, Aloph I, Seigneur de Gamaches, 207
Rouault, Aloph II, Seigneur de Gamaches, 207
Rouault, Anne, Mme de Bours, 200, 203, 206-8, 211-5, 218, 220-2
Rouault, Thibault, Seigneur de Riou, 206, 207, 209-10, 214, 216-8, 219
Rysbank Tower, Calais, 50, 168
Rysley, Sir John, 107

Sampson, Dr. Richard, 160-81,
Sandes, Sir William, Lord Sandes, 59
Saveuse, Antoinette de, 203, 206, 213-7, 221, 222
Saveuse, Imbert de, 204
Saveuse, Jeanne de, Mme de Riou, 200, 206, 209, 210-3, 214-6, 218, 220
Savoy, Louise of, Duchess of Angouleme, 175, 178, 191-3
Saxony, Albrecht, Duke of, 113, 123
Scales, Lord Thomas, 45
Schaumberg, Wilwolt de, 107, 128
Schmalkaldic, League, 6
Scrope, Ralph of Upsall, 102
Seymour, Edward, Duke of Somerset, 15
Smith, John, 203
Somerset, Charles, Earl of Worcester, 54, 148, 183, 185, 186, 189
Somerset, Duke of, *see* Seymour
Sorbonne, The, 141, 149, 153, 155, 176, 178
St. Michael, Order of, 19, 139

Stafford, Thomas, 16
Staple, merchants of, at Calais, 49, 60
Stile, John, 189
Stokesley, John, 198
Suffolk, Duke of, *see* Brandon
Surrey, Earl of, *see* Howard

Talbot, John, Earl of Shrewsbury, 2, 18-9, 37, 38-8, 44
Taylor, Dr. John, 198
Therouanne, 5, 219
Thirlby, Thomas, 198
Tiptoft, Sir John, 28
Tournai, 5, 55, 145, 184, 196
Treaties and Truces, Ancenis (1468), 82; Anglo-Burgundian (1467), 79; Arras (1482), 11, 113; Boulogne (1550), 15; Brétigny (1360), 47, 51; Cambrai (1529), 14, 171, 175; Campe (1546), 14, 185; Cateau-Cambrésis (1559), 16; Crépy (1544), 6; Etaples (1492), 11, 107; Hampton Court (1526), 13, 14; London (1514), 146, 157; London (1518), 12, 157-8; Medina del Campo (1489), 108; Mutual Aid (1543), 14; Nice (1538), 14, 212; Péronne (1468), 82; Perpetual Peace (1527), 13, 158-9; Picquigny (1475), 4, 8, 144; Rome (1496), 12; Senlis (1493), 11; The More (1525), 13, 175; Tours (1444), 2; Troyes (1420), 1-2, 14, 25, 29; Vaucelles (1556), 16; Woking (1490), 108, 111, 130
Trollope, Andrew, 42-3
Tuke, Brian, 173
Tyrell, Sir James, 123, 129

Urswick, Sir Christopher, 107

Vannes, Peter, 180
Vaughan, Stephen, 183
Vaughan, Thomas, 76
Vendôme, Charles, Duke of, 196, 210
Venice, Holy League of (1495), 12
Vivien, Germain, 177, 178

Wall, Thomas, Windsor Herald, 161-81
Wallop, Sir John, 7, 186, 189, 193-4, 196-8
Warbeck, Perkin, 4, 90, 103, 120
Warwick, Edward, Earl of, (d. 1499), 120
Wenlock, Sir John, Lord Wenlock, 7, 65, 71-3, 76-7, 78
West, Nicholas, dean of Windsor, 148

Weston, Sir Richard, 20
Whetehill, Richard, 68-9, 73, 76
Whytston, James, 18
Willoughby, Sir Robert, Lord Willoughby de Broke, 118
Wiltshire, Earl of, *see* Boleyn
Wingfield, Sir Richard, 167, 183, 186, 187, 188-90
Wolsey, Cardinal Thomas, 9, 157, 183, 185, 189, 195, 196
Worcester, Earl of, *see* Somerset
Wotton, Nicholas, 199
Wriothelsey, Thomas, 144, 184

York, Richard, Duke of (d. 1460), 10, 24, 45, 94
York, Richard, Duke of (d. 1483), 120

Printed in Great Britain
by Amazon